Lecture Notes in Computer Science 5668

Commenced Publication in 1973
Founding and Former Series Editors:
Gerhard Goos, Juris Hartmanis, and Jan van Leeuwen

Catherine Dubois (Ed.)

Tests and Proofs

Third International Conference, TAP 2009
Zurich, Switzerland, July 2-3, 2009
Proceedings

 Springer

Volume Editor

Catherine Dubois
ENSIIE-CÉDRIC
1 square de la résistance, 91025 Évry Cedex, France
E-mail: dubois@ensiie.fr

Library of Congress Control Number: 2009929546

CR Subject Classification (1998): D.2.4-5, F.3, D.4, C.4, K.4.4, C.2

LNCS Sublibrary: SL 2 – Programming and Software Engineering

ISSN 0302-9743

ISBN 978-3-642-02948-6 Springer Berlin Heidelberg New York

springer.com

© Springer-Verlag Berlin Heidelberg 2009

Typesetting: Camera-ready by author, data conversion by Scientific Publishing Services, Chennai, India
Printed on acid-free paper   SPIN: 12717774   06/3180   5 4 3 2 1 0

Preface

This volume[1] contains the research papers and invited papers presented at the Third International Conference on Tests and Proofs (TAP 2009) held at ETH Zurich, Switzerland, during July 2–3, 2009.

The TAP conference is devoted to the convergence of proofs and tests. It combines ideas from both sides for the advancement of software quality. To prove the correctness of a program is to demonstrate, through impeccable mathematical techniques, that it has no bugs; to test a program is to run it with the expectation of discovering bugs. The two techniques seem contradictory: if you have proved your program, it is fruitless to comb it for bugs; and if you are testing it, that is surely a sign that you have given up on any hope of proving its correctness. Accordingly, proofs and tests have, since the onset of software engineering research, been pursued by distinct communities using rather different techniques and tools. And yet the development of both approaches leads to the discovery of common issues and to the realization that each may need the other. The emergence of model checking has been one of the first signs that contradiction may yield to complementarity, but in the past few years an increasing number of research efforts have encountered the need for combining proofs and tests, dropping earlier dogmatic views of incompatibility and taking instead the best of what each of these software engineering domains has to offer.

The first TAP conference (held at ETH Zurich in February 2007) was an attempt to provide a forum for the cross-fertilization of ideas and approaches from the testing and proving communities. The 2008 edition took place in the Monash University Prato Centre near Florence. For the third TAP conference we came back to ETH Zurich. This third edition was co-located with other software conferences, in particular TOOLS Europe.

We wish to sincerely thank all the authors who submitted their work for consideration. We would also like to thank the Program Committee members as well as the additional referees for their great effort and work of high quality in the review and selection process. Their names are listed on the following pages.

There were 20 submissions. Each submission was reviewed by at least three persons. The Committee decided to accept ten research papers. The program also included two keynote talks. We are grateful to Sriram Rajamani (Microsoft Research, India) and Boutheina Chetali (Gemalto, France) for accepting the invitation to address the conference.

The conference also included some short presentations that were reviewed by at least one Program Committee member. They are not included in this proceedings volume but are part of a technical ETH report entitled *TAP 2009: short papers*.

---

[1] This volume was prepared with EasyChair. Many thanks to its developer.

The success of the conference resulted from a team effort. We are grateful to the Conference Chair and the Steering Committee members for their support at every stage in the conference preparation. We also thank all the members of the Organizing Committee, in particular Yi Wei and Stephan van Staden, ETH Zurich. Finally, we gratefully acknowledge the material and financial support provided by the Chair of Software Engineering, ETH Zurich.

May 2009   Catherine Dubois

Conference Organization

Conference Chair

Bertrand Meyer   ETH Zurich, Switzerland

Program Chair

Catherine Dubois   ENSIIE, France

Program Committee

Bernhard Aichernig	TU Graz, Austria
Bernhard Beckert	University of Koblenz, Germany
Patrice Chalin	Concordia University, Canada
Yoonsik Cheon	University of Texas at El Paso, USA
Koen Claessen	Chalmers University of Technology, Sweden
Gilles Dowek	École Polytechnique, France
Angelo Gargantini	University of Bergamo, Italy
Arnaud Gotlieb	IRISA, France
Yuri Gurevich	Microsoft Research, USA
Bart Jacobs	Katholieke Universiteit Leuven, Belgium
Reiner Hähnle	Chalmers University of Technology, Sweden
Ewen Maclean	Heriot-Watt University, UK
Karl Meinke	KTH Royal Institute of Technology, Sweden
Sam Owre	SRI International, USA
Wolfram Schulte	Microsoft Research, USA
Mark Utting	Waikato University, New Zealand

Additional Reviewers

Bernard Botella	Richard Bubel	Andrea Calvagna
Bruno Dutertre	Frédéric Gervais	Christoph Gladisch
K. Rustan M. Leino	Patricia Mouy	Ulf Norell
David Pichardie	Vlad Rusu	Natarajan Shankar
David Streader	Ashish Tiwari	Margus Veanes
Burkhart Wolff		

Steering Committee

Yuri Gurevich	Microsoft Research, USA
Bertrand Meyer	ETH Zurich, Switzerland

Local Organization

Yi Wei	ETH Zurich, Switzerland
Stephan van Staden	ETH Zurich, Switzerland
Claudia Günthart	ETH Zurich, Switzerland

Sponsoring Institutions

Chair of Software Engineering, ETH Zurich, Switzerland
ENSIIE, Évry, France

Table of Contents

Security Testing and Formal Methods for High Levels Certification of Smart Cards

Boutheina Chetali

Gemalto, Security Labs,
6 rue de la Verrerie, 92197 Meudon Cedex, France
boutheina.chetali@gemalto.com

Abstract. We will discuss security testing and formal methods in the framework of the Common Criteria certification of smart cards. The discussion will introduce the requirements of the standard on the test activity and on the description of the design and will identify their impact on the methods and tools to use. Emphasis will be placed on the high levels of certification in which formal methods are required to demonstrate the correct design of the security. We will discuss the advantage of a mixed approach of formal model-based testing, that will allow to reach, in a pragmatic way, high levels of certification.

1 Smart Cards and Security Certification

Smart cards provide a high level of security in a large variety of domains such as banking, mobile communication, public transport and e-citizen. Due to their bounded resources (in terms of memory and CPU) and to strict requirements in term of correctness (and robustness), they have been considered as a good candidate for formal methods based techniques [4] and advanced methods for security software testing. Moreover the need of security certification of this kind of IT products advocates for a concrete use of those techniques to reach high levels of Common Criteria (**CC** [5]) certification.

Common Criteria (ISO 15408) is the standard used to evaluate the security of IT products. From a practical point of view, the main goal is to protect the assets of the product against risks and threats. The CC define seven levels of security from EAL1 to EAL7[1] and this assurance scale is used to evaluate the effectiveness of the security mechanisms ensuring this protection. The high levels (5 to 7) allow the user to protect high value assets against significant risks using security engineering techniques and a rigorous development environment. These security engineering techniques include formal methods, to demonstrate the correct design of the security mechanisms, but also tests[2] to demonstrate that the product (its security mechanisms) behaves as described.

---

[1] EAL stands for Evaluation Assurance Level.

[2] This discussion does not address penetration testing performed to identify vulnerabilities.

C. Dubois (Ed.): TAP 2009, LNCS 5668, pp. 1–5, 2009.

In the smart cards industry, the level EAL4 is the common level of security, which provides assurance that the product is methodically designed, tested and reviewed. The level 5 (semi formally designed), 6 (semi formally verified design and tested) and 7 (formally verified design and tested) increase the level of rigor required in the several activities of the product development[2].

2   Common Criteria Requirements on the Development

Roughly, evaluating a system in the CC context consists in rating the mechanisms that it uses to maintain security w.r.t. the identified threats. If we consider the target (product under evaluation) as a set of security mechanisms, it must ensure two main properties: *Correctness*, the target works correctly with respect to its specification, and *robustness*, the target cannot be used in a way such that its security mechanisms can be corrupted or bypassed. For the correctness, the CC require, using a traditional waterfall model, a functional specification, a description of the design, a representation of the implementation, and provide a set of requirements on each element. The functional specification describes *what* are the security services to be provided in term of calls and responses, the design description details *how* the target accomplishes those services, and the implementation representation describes *where* the source code implements those services. The knowledge obtained from these elements is used by the evaluator, as the basis for conducting vulnerability analysis and testing.

For the high levels, the CC require semi-formal and formal methods to build the different descriptions of the product. The correspondence between the different refinement levels could be informal, semi formal or formal, depending on the level of description used for the adjacent elements.

3   Common Criteria Requirements on Testing

The purpose of the testing activity in the context of the Common Criteria is to demonstrate to the evaluator that the product behaves as described in the functional specification and in the different descriptions of the design. The developer provides three main assurances about its testing activity : the *functional tests* describe the tests performed by the developer (developer test documentation includes test plans and test procedures), the *coverage* describes the rigor of testing the functional specification and the *depth* describes to which extent the design has been tested.

The requirements on the *functional tests* are to demonstrate that the tests described in the test documentation are performed correctly. Filling those requirements is supposed to provide assurance that the risk of undiscovered flaws is relatively low. The objective of the *coverage* requirements is to demonstrate that the developer performed exhaustive tests of all interfaces described into the functional specification. The objective of the depth is, from the CC perspective *to counter the risk of missing an error in the development of the target*, because the tests of intermediate descriptions of the target force to test the internal functionalities. This demonstrates not only that the target has the desired security behavior but also that this behavior is the result of correct operations of the internal functionalities.

4   Discussion

The new release of the CC seems to be less demanding in term of formal design. Indeed, the previous release (V2.3) requires a complete formal chain, from the security functional specification down to the source code. The chain of refinement includes the security policy model, the functional specification, the high level design and the low level design. First this has been difficult to fill, due for example to the lack of tools for code generation to achieve the last correspondence. On the other hand, formal methods still suffer from a scalability problem. Moreover it seems also that in the Information Technology context, there is not many products where the assets to be protected are human being. For systems and products with this kind of assets, other certification schemes are more appropriate and effective in practice.

But for smart cards, the level of CC certificate is an important differential factor: for the clients, a high-level CC certificate is a measurable assurance on the security of the product. For smart cards, the short time to market, the volume and the impact of errors, leads to a race to increase the level of the certification and to the use of techniques to speed up the process of certification, and in particular the production of documents and all the elements necessary for the evaluation. Not to mention also the Identity markets, that include e-passports, that have strong constraints in terms of security properties such as privacy.

For formal methods for the design description, a set of language and tools have been used to achieve the CC requirements but always on a subset of the target. Experiments [2] that have been done show that even for constrained resources system, the use of such techniques, for evaluation purpose, is prohibitive in terms of cost and are difficult to justify.

For testing, conventional testing methods for smart cards uses low-level commands and writing use cases and test scripts is complex and costly. A way to improve the testing phase is to use an automated tool for test scripts generation which can also improve the test coverage. But those testing tools must support various constraints such as being integrated into an existing industrial test environment. Moreover, taking into account the test expertise of the validation teams is also a heavy constraint.

For high levels certification in which the intermediate descriptions are formal models, the testing seems to be redundant with the formal proofs that demonstrate that the most detailed description (the source code) verifies the less detailed one, that is its abstract specification. But for the reasons given above, the development of complete formal models describing all the security functionalities of the target is not realistic. The current version of the CC (V3.1) has alleviated the requirements on the formal modeling, allowing the establishment of mixed approaches that are more pragmatic to reach high levels of certification. The approach consists of first using formal specification but only in addition to the semi-formal descriptions of the design, for proving the security properties on a formal model (of the security policy) of the target. Then an automated test tool is used to meet the requirements on the three activities for the tests : writing scenarios and producing test plans, that contribute to satisfy the requirements on *functional testing*, providing processes that allow the refinement of the scenarios into operations and functions, for the *depth* requirements and finally allowing negative testing and bounds testing for the *coverage* requirements.

This combined approach allows to gain confidence in the security of the target at a reasonable cost. The formal verification is used to prove that the system under test ensures some critical properties, derived from the security objectives claimed in the security specification. The testing is then used not only to demonstrate the correct operation of the system but also to generate test scripts from scenarios, that formalize the validation engineer's expertise.

More precisely, for high levels, it is required to test the interfaces described in the functional specification with a coverage requirements specifying that **all** the parameters of **all** the interfaces must be exercised. For the depth of test, the requirements is that the target is tested against its most detailed description that is the modules design (level 6) or the implementation representation (level 7). For smart cards software, it is a heavy requirement knowing that testing the functional specification is a kind of blackbox test, where the tests are made of a set of commands APDU sent to the card and the expected responses. Testing at the modules level is then a graybox test and testing the implementation is whitebox test.

On the other hand, at high levels, the deliverables are a formal security policy, a semi-formal functional specification, a formal description of the target in term of subsystems, and a semi-formal description of the design in term of modules. Another strong requirement is to trace the security mechanisms, claimed in the security specification, to the functional specification, to the the tests and to the design documents. For example, for a given security mechanism one must show how it is tested, to which extent, and where it described in the target description, etc. This traceability is generally described by tables giving the mapping between the security mechanisms and a name corresponding to the set of tests performed for each security mechanism. The main issue is obviously the consistency in case of modification in the implementation and/or in the documentation.

A mixed approach supported by an automated tool, is then a good candidate that could allow to meet the above requirements on the design and on the test. This tool (or a tool environment) must provide (1) a formal language to describe the security policy and the high level description of the design, (2) a semi-formal language to express the tests scenarios, the functional specification and the detailed design description, (3) automatic generation of test scripts from these models. Some existing tools already fullfil parts of this specification [1] [3]. They need to be extended and confronted to industrial constraints, mainly for scalability issue.

References

1. Chetali, B., Nguyen, Q.-H.: An Automated Testing Experiment for Layered Embedded C Code. The International Journal on "Software Tools for Technology Transfer" (STTT-IEEEIsola2005) (2008) (special edition)
2. Chetali, B., Nguyen, Q.-H.: Industrial Use of Formal Methods for a High-level Security Evaluation. In: Cuellar, J., Maibaum, T., Sere, K. (eds.) FM 2008. LNCS, vol. 5014, pp. 198–213. Springer, Heidelberg (2008)
3. Masson, P.-A., Julliand, J., Plessis, J.-C., Jaffuel, E., Debois, G.: Automatic Generation of Model Based Tests for a Class of Security Properties. In: A-MOST 2007, 3rd Workshop on Advances in Model Based Testing, London, UK (July 2007)
4. Lanet, J.L.: The use of Formal Methods in the Smart Card Industry. In: International Workshop on Formal Method and Security, Nanjing, China (May 2004)
5. Common Criteria, http://www.commoncriteria.org/

Verification, Testing and Statistics

Aditya Nori and Sriram K. Rajamani

Microsoft Research India
{adityan,sriram}@microsoft.com

Abstract. Though formal verification has been the holy grail of software validation, practical applications of verification run into two major challenges. The first challenge is in writing detailed specifications, and the second challenge is in scaling verification algorithms to large software. In this short paper, we present possible approaches for these problems. We propose using statistical techniques to raise the level of abstraction, and automate the tedium in writing detailed specifications. We propose combining testing with verification to help scalability.

Software validation is the task of determining if the software meets the expectations of its users. For the most part, industrial practice of software engineering uses *testing* to validate software. That is, we execute the software using test inputs that mimic how the user is expected to interact with the software, and declare success if the outcomes of the executions satisfy our expectations. There are various granularities in which testing is performed, ranging from unit testing that tests small portions of the system, to system-wide tests.

Testing is incomplete in the sense that it validates the software only for the test inputs that we execute. The software might exhibit undesired behavior with test inputs we do not have. The holy grail of software validation is *verification*. Here, the goal is to formally prove that the software meets its expectations for all possible test inputs, and for all possible executions.

In practice, verification efforts run into two major difficulties. First, it is very hard to formally specify expectations as *specifications* in a formal language that can be input to a verification tool. Complete specifications of complex software (like an operating system) could be as complex as the software itself, and it is very hard to get programmers and system designers to write specifications. Next, even if specifications were to somehow exist, the scale and complexity of large software (which can run into tens of millions of lines of source code) is well beyond the capabilities of today's verification tools.

In this short paper, we discuss some possible approaches for these problems. First, in order to the address the difficulties in writing specifications, we believe that there are ways by which we can ask programmers for high-level guidelines about the structure of specifications, and use statistical techniques to automatically generate detailed specifications. Second, in order to address scalability, we believe that we can exploit the continuum between verification and testing, and design hybrid algorithms that combine testing and verification. Since the latter topic is closer to the "Tests and Proofs" community we discuss it first.

C. Dubois (Ed.): TAP 2009, LNCS 5668, pp. 6–9, 2009.

1   Combining Verification and Testing

Suppose a specification is given to us, and we are interested in finding either a test input that violates the specification, or prove that the specification is satisfied for all inputs. For simplicity, let us consider assertional specifications that are expressed as assert statements of the form **assert**(e), where e is a predicate on the state of the program. Such a specification fails if execution reaches an assert statement **assert**(e) in a state S such that predicate e does not hold in state S.

For the past few years, we have been investigating methods for combining static analysis in the style of counter-example driven refinement ala SLAM [1], with runtime testing and automatic test case generation approaches in the style of concolic execution ala DART [3]. Our first attempt in this direction was the SYNERGY algorithm [5], which handled single procedure programs with only integer variables. Then, we proposed DASH [2], which had new ideas to handle pointer aliasing and procedure calls in programs.

The DASH algorithm simultaneously maintains a forest of test runs and a region-graph abstraction of the program. Tests are used to find bugs and abstractions are used to prove their absence. During every iteration, if a concrete test has managed to reach the error region, a bug has been found. If no path in the abstract region graph exists from the initial region to the error region, a proof of correctness has been found. If neither of the above two cases are true, then we have an abstract counterexample, which is a sequence of regions in the abstract region graph, along which a test can be potentially driven to reveal a bug. The DASH algorithm crucially relies on the notion of a frontier [5,2], which is the boundary between tested and untested regions along an abstract counterexample that a concrete test has managed to reach. In every iteration, the algorithm first attempts to extend the frontier using test case generation techniques similar to DART. If test case generation fails, then the algorithm refines the abstract region graph so as to eliminate the abstract counterexample.

Most program analyses scale to large programs by building so called "summaries" at procedure boundaries. Summaries memoize analysis findings at procedure boundaries, and enable reusing these findings at other appropriate calling contexts of a procedure. Recently, we have proposed a new algorithm to combine so-called "may-summaries" which arises from verification tools like SLAM with so-called "must-summaries" from testing tools like DART [4].

All of the above ideas have been implemented in a tool called YOGI, and empirical results from running and using the tool have been very promising [7].

2   Inferring Specifications Using Statistics

One of the difficulties with writing specifications is that they are very detailed — sometimes as detailed as the code itself. It will be useful if general guidelines can be given by the user at a high level, and tools infer detailed specifications from these guidelines.

As an example, consider the problem of detecting information flow vulnerabilities in programs. Here, certain data elements in the software (such as ones entered by the user, are passed from some untrusted program) are deemed to be "tainted", and the software is required to inspect these data and "sanitize" it before using it in a trusted context such as a database query. A formal specification of information flow security consists of classifying methods in a program into (a) *sources*: these nodes originate taint or lack of trust, (b) *sinks*: these nodes have the property that it is erroneous to pass tainted data to them, (c) *sanitizers*: these nodes cleanse or untaint the input (even if input is tainted, output is not tainted), (d) *regular nodes*: these nodes do not taint data, do not untaint data, and propagate input taint to output without mediation. In this setting an *information flow vulnerability* is a path from a source to a sink that has not been sanitized.

Since typical applications have tens of thousands of methods, it takes intensive (and error-prone) manual effort to give a detailed specification that classifies each method into a source, sanitizer, sink or regular node. Consider a data propagation graph of the program, whose nodes are methods and whose edges indicate flow of information. That is, an edge exists from node (method) m_1 to node (method) m_2 iff data flows from m_1 to m_2 either using an argument or return value of a procedure call, or using global variables.

We do not know which nodes in the propagation graph are sources, sinks or sanitizers. However, we can give higher-level guidelines about the specification such as the following. It is reasonable to assume that errors are rare and that most paths in propagation graphs are secure. That is, the probability that a path goes from a source to a sink with no intervening sanitizer is very low. Also, it is unlikely that a path between a source and a sink contains two or more sanitizers. If information flows from method m_1 to m_2, then m_1 is more likely to be a source than m_2, and m_1 is more likely to be a sink than m_1. However, all the above guidelines are not absolute. If we were to treat them as boolean constraints which all need to be satisfied, they could even be mutually contradictory. Thus, we represent all these guidelines as probabilistic constraints, and use probabilistic inference techniques to compute the probability of each node being a source, sink or sanitizer. We have built a tool called MERLIN with this approach, and we find that the tool automatically infers useful information flow specifications [6].

3   Summary

In summary, we have discussed two main challenges with formal verification. The first challenge is the difficulty in writing detailed specifications, and the second challenge is in scaling verification tools to analyze large systems. In this short paper, we have proposed approaches for these problems. To alleviate the difficulty in writing detailed specifications, we propose that users only give high-level guidelines about the shape of specification, and that statistical techniques be used to derive detailed specifications. To alleviate the difficulty of scaling, we propose new algorithms combining verification and testing. Our experience with both approaches has been promising. Our specification inference tool MERLIN, has discovered hundreds of new specifications, and this has led to discovery of several hundred vulnerabilities in large web applications. Our analysis tool YOGI, which combines verification and testing, performs much better than existing tools that use either verification or testing in isolation.

Acknowledgment. We thank our collaborators Anindya Banerjee, Nels Beckman, Bhargav Gulavani, Patrice Godefroid, Tom Henzinger, Yamini Kannan, Ben Livshits, Rob Simmons, Sai Tetali and Aditya Thakur.

References

1. Ball, T., Rajamani, S.K.: Automatically validating temporal safety properties of interfaces. In: Dwyer, M.B. (ed.) SPIN 2001. LNCS, vol. 2057, pp. 103–122. Springer, Heidelberg (2001)
2. Beckman, N.E., Nori, A.V., Rajamani, S.K., Simmons, R.J.: Proofs from tests. In: ISSTA 2008: International Symposium on Software Testing and Analysis, pp. 3–14. ACM Press, New York (2008)
3. Godefroid, P., Klarlund, N., Sen, K.: DART: Directed automated random testing. In: PLDI 2005: Programming Language Design and Implementation, pp. 213–223. ACM Press, New York (2005)
4. Godefroid, P., Nori, A.V., Rajamani, S.K., Tetali, S.: Compositional May-Must Program Analysis: Unleashing The Power of Alternation. Microsoft Research Technical Report MSR-TR-2009-2, Microsoft Research (2009)
5. Gulavani, B.S., Henzinger, T.A., Kannan, Y., Nori, A.V., Rajamani, S.K.: SYNERGY: A new algorithm for property checking. In: FSE 2006: Foundations of Software Engineering, pp. 117–127. ACM Press, New York (2006)
6. Livshits, B., Nori, A.V., Rajamani, S.K., Banerjee, A.: Merlin: Specification Inference for Explicit Information Flow Problems. In: PLDI 2009: Programming Language Design and Implementation. ACM Press, New York (to appear, 2009)
7. Nori, A.V., Rajamani, S.K., Tetali, S., Thakur, A.V.: The Yogi Project: Software Property Checking via Static Analysis and Testing. In: TACAS 2009: Tools and Algorithms for Constuction and Analysis of Systems. LNCS, vol. 5509, pp. 178–181. Springer, Heidelberg (2009)

Development of a Generic Voter under FoCaL*

Philippe Ayrault[1], Thérèse Hardin[2], and François Pessaux[2]

[1] Etersafe, 43, Allée du pont des beaunes F-91120 Palaiseau
philippe.ayrault@etersafe.com
[2] Semantics, Proofs and Implementation, Laboratoire Informatique de Paris 6,
Pierre & Marie Curie University, F-75005 Paris
{therese.hardin, francois.pessaux}@lip6.fr

Abstract. Safety and security are claimed major concerns by the formal FoCaL development environment. In [7] we introduced a safety development cycle customised to FoCaL. In this paper, we examine how to specify and implement a concrete example following this cycle. We show that indeed it is feasible and we present how FoCaL features fit with software best practises like modularity, reuse, fault confinement and maintenance.

Keywords: formal methods, development cycle, voter, FoCaL.

1 Introduction

Development of safety related systems has to be strictly compliant with applicable standards. This is required by any safety authority before commissioning of a system. Safety demonstration is greatly helped by using a formally based framework to express requirements, design, code and to ensure that this code meets specification requirements. Unfortunately, this is not sufficient. Safety authorities also require an independent verification process which must follow the different stages of a strict development cycle. Thus, any tool claiming to be dedicated to formal developments should not only provide a formal paradigm to model and prove the system but must also strongly support a well defined development cycle and must produce adequate documentation at each stage of the development. Moreover, such a tool should help to identify impacts of modifications during the whole life of the system (frequently more than 20 years). The purpose of the FoCaL tool is to bring some answers to this problem area. FoCaL provides a unified language to express requirements (declaration and properties) as well as source code and proofs while only using concepts largely accessible to engineers.

In [7], we introduced a safety development cycle customised for FoCaL. Our problem now is to study its feasibility and to understand how practically FoCaL can help to answer safety and good practise requirements. We have chosen to fully treat the example of a voter. Indeed a voter is a central equipment of all redundant architectures, widely used for safety related systems. A voter is a process or a device whereby a number of similar signals are monitored for discrepancies and are voted upon to obtain the selected output which is most probably correct. It is highly safety critical because in

---

* This work is supported in part by the *Agence Nationale de la Recherche* under grant ANR-06-SETI-016 for the *SSURF* Project (Safety and Security UndeR FoCaL).

many cases, the voter is the last barrier able to eliminate failure effects and answers a part of the safety principles underlining the whole system. As these ones strongly depend of the aim and domain of the system, for the re-usability sake, a voter should be conceived as a very generic equipment. Thus choosing a voter seems a good balance between the exemplary nature of the development and the length of the paper.

The rest of the paper is organised as follows. We present the main features of the FoCaL tool in Section 2. Section 3 exposes the rules of a voter and its textual specification. The Section 4 comments the development of the voter using the FoCaL tool. We conclude and comment possible further works in Section 5.

2   The FoCaL Environment

We give here an informal presentation of near all FoCaL features, to help further reading of this paper. For more details and the new release[1].

2.1   The Basic Brick

The primitive entity of a FoCaL development is the *species*. Like in most modular systems (i.e. objected oriented, algebraic abstract types), it can be viewed as a record grouping a data structure with its related operations. Since FoCaL does not only address data type and operations, species may contain the declarations (specifications) of these operations, some properties (which may represent requirements) and their proofs. All these components of a species are called *methods* and we briefly describe them.

- The *method* introduced by the keyword `representation` gives the data representation of entities manipulated by the *species*. It is defined by a type expression, which is roughly a ML-like pure type (with restricted polymorphism). The *representation* may be not-yet-defined in a *species*, meaning that the real structure of the data-type the *species* embeds does not need to be known at this point. However, to obtain an implementation, the *representation* has to be defined later either explicitly or by inheritance.
- Declarations (keyword `signature` followed by a name and a type) introduce *methods* to be defined later: they only specify types without implementation yet. Declarations serve to express specifications, properties. Thanks to late-binding, as soon as a name is declared, it can be used in definitions.
- Definitions (keyword `let`, followed by a name, a type and an expression) introduce constants or functions, i.e. computational operations. The expressions are roughly pure ML-like expressions with an auxiliary construction (`S!m`) to call the *method* m from a given *species* S.
- Statements (keyword `property` followed by a name and a first-order formula) may serve to express requirements (i.e. facts that the system must hold to conform to the Statement of Work) and then can be viewed as a specification purpose *method*, like *signatures* were for `let`-*methods*. They entail a proof obligation later in the development. Like *signatures*, even if no proof is yet given, the name of the *property* can be used to prove other theorems or lemmas.

---

[1] see : http://focalize.inria.fr

- Theorems (`theorem`) made of a name, a statement and a proof are *properties* together with the formal proof that their statement holds in the context of the *species*. This proof will be processed by FoCaL and ultimately checked with the theorem prover Coq.

In addition, FoCaL provides a powerful mechanism for documentation by allowing special kind of commentaries (called annotations) kept along the compiler process.

2.2 Type of Species, Interfaces and Collections

The *type* of a *species* is obtained by removing definitions and proofs. Thus, it is a kind of record type, made of all the method types of the species. If the `representation` is still a type variable say α, then the *species* type is prefixed with an existential binder $\exists\alpha$. This binder will be eliminated as soon as the `representation` will be instantiated (defined) and must be eliminated to obtain executable code. Species types remain totally implicit to users and serve only to introduce interfaces.

The *interface* of a species is obtained by abstracting the *representation* type in the *species type* and this abstraction, which hides the representation, is permanent. Interfaces play an important role. They are simply denoted by the species name. Interfaces can be ordered by inclusion, a point providing a very simple notion of sub-typing.

A species is said to be *complete* if all declarations have received definitions and all properties have received proofs. When *complete*, a species can be submitted to an abstraction process of its representation to create a *collection*. Thus the *interface* of the collection is just the *interface* of the complete species underlying it. A collection can hence be seen as an abstract data-type, only usable through the methods of its interface, but with the guarantee that all methods/theorems are defined/proved.

2.3 Combining Bricks

A FoCaL development is organised as a hierarchy which may have several roots. Usually the upper levels of the hierarchy are built during the specification stage while the lower ones correspond to implementation. Each node of the hierarchy, i.e. each *species* (or *collection* as terminal ends), is a progress to a complete implementation. There are two ways to build new species from previously built species: inheritance and parametrisation.

In FoCaL **inheritance** serves two kinds of evolutions, which can be freely mixed. One may create a new *species* by extending the inherited ones with new operations and properties while keeping those of the inherited ones (or redefining some of them). One may create a new *species* by giving explicit definitions to *signatures* and *proofs* to *properties* of the inherited species, to be closer to a "executable" implementation.

Multiple inheritance is available in FoCaL. In case of inheriting a *method* from several parents, the order of parents in the `inherits` clause serves to determine the chosen *method*.

The *type* of a *species* built using inheritance is defined like for other *species*, the *methods* types retained inside it being those of the *methods* present in the *species* after inheritance is resolved.

A strong constraint in inheritance is that the type of inherited, and/or redefined *methods* must not change. This is required to ensure logical consistency of the FoCaL model.

FoCaL allows two flavors of parametrisation: parametrisation by *collection parameters* and parametrisation by *entity parameters*. For instance a pair is a structure which is built upon its two components and is described by a *species* parametrised by its two components. *Entity parameters* are not introduced as we do not use them within this paper.

The parametrised *species* can use *collection parameters' methods* to define its own ones. A *collection parameter* is given a name C and an interface I. The name C serves to call the *methods* of C which figure in I. C can be instantiated by an effective parameter CE of interface IE. CE is a collection and its interface IE must contain I. Note that species (without abstraction) are not allowed as parameters. Indeed, if an incomplete species were used as an effective parameter run-time error due to linkage of libraries can occur and properties stated in I can not be safely used as an hypothesis. In contrast, the collection and late-binding mechanisms ensure that all methods appearing in I are indeed implemented in CE.

2.4 The Final Brick

As briefly introduced, a *species* needs to be *complete* to lead to executable code for its functions and checkable proofs for its theorems and then, can be turned into a *collection*. Hence, a *collection* represents the final stage of the inheritance tree of a *species* and leads to an effective data representation with executable functions processing it. As said before, to ensure modularity and abstraction, the *representation* of a *collection* turns hidden. This means that any software component dealing with a *collection* will only be able to manipulate it through the operations (*methods*) its interface provides. This point is especially important since it prevents other software components from possibly breaking invariants required by the internals of the *collection*.

2.5 Properties, Theorems and Proofs

FoCaL intends to encompass both the executable model (i.e. program) and properties this model must satisfy. For this reason, *theorems*, *properties* and *proofs* are *methods* dealing with logical instead of purely behavioural aspects of the system. Stating a *property* entails that a *proof* of it will be finally built. For *theorems*, the *proof* is directly embedded in the *theorem*. The compilation process submits proofs to the formal proof assistant Coq which automatically checks that they are consistent.

No syntax is offered to express high-order properties as they are rather difficult to manage by engineers not experts in logic theory. But special instances for induction and termination proofs are to be provided.

Proofs are done by the developer as follows. It can be written in "FoCaLProof Language", a hierarchical proof language that allows to give hints and directions for a proof. This script is submitted to an external theorem prover, Zenon[2] developed by D. Doligez. Zenon is a first order theorem prover based on the Tableaux method incorporating implementation novelties such as sharing[4]. From these hints Zenon attempts

---

[2] see : http://focal.inria.fr/zenon/

to automatically generate a proof and if it succeeds, expresses its proof as a Coq term verified by Coq during the compilation process. Basic hints given by the developer to Zenon are: "prove by definition of a *method*" (i.e. looking inside its body) and "prove by *property*" (i.e. using the logical statement of a *theorem* or *property*". Surrounding this hints mechanism, the language allows to build the proof by stating assumptions (that must obviously be demonstrated next) which can be used to prove lemmas or parts for the whole property. We show below an example of such a demonstration.

```
theorem order_inf_is_infimum: all x y i in Self,
   !order_inf(i, x) -> !order_inf(i, y) ->
     !order_inf(i, !inf(x, y))
 proof:
   <1>1 assume x in Self, assume y in Self, assume i in Self,
        assume H1: !order_inf(i, x), assume H2: !order_inf(i, y),
        prove !order_inf(i, !inf(x, y))
     <2>1 prove !equal(i, !inf(!inf(i, x), y))
       by hypothesis H1, H2
          property inf_left_substitution_rule,
             equal_symmetric, equal_transitive
          definition of order_inf
     <2>f qed
       by step <2>1
          property inf_is_associative, equal_transitive
          definition of order_inf
   <1>f conclude
 ;
```

Like any automatic theorem prover, Zenon may fail finding a demonstration. In this case, FoCaL allows to write verbatim Coq proofs. The compiler provides a Coq script "with a hole" which can be filled with the proof done by hand, then imported back to the FoCaL source code as verbatim Coq code.

Finally, the `assumed` keyword is the ultimate proof backdoor, telling that no proof is given thus the property is considered as an axiom. Obviously, a really safe development should not make usage of such "proofs" since they bypass the formal verification of software's model and can break the global consistency. However, a development may use external (trusted or not) code no property of which can be proved. Moreover, whatever the reason, the user may choose to admit some properties. But any "assumed" lemma should always be at least receive a textual justification inside an annotation. A good practise is to submit such lemma to the FoCaL test tool to increase confidence.

2.6 Around the Language

All along the development cycle of a FoCaL program, the compiler keeps track of dependencies between *species*, their *methods*, the *proofs*, ... to ensure any modification of component will be detected and its impact will be reported on those depending of it.

FoCaL considers two types of dependencies:

- The **decl**-dependency: a *method* A decl-depends on a *method* B if the **declaration** of B is required to express A.
- The **def**-dependency: a *method* (and more especially a *theorem*) A def-depends on a *method* B if the **definition** of B is required to state A (and more especially, to prove the property stated by the *theorem* A).

The redefinition of a function may invalidate the proofs that use properties of the body of the redefined function. All the proofs which truly depend on the definition are then erased by the compiler and must be done again in the context updated with the new definition. Hence an important point is the choice of the most interesting level in the hierarchy where to write a proof.

FoCaL currently supports two target languages: OCaml[10] and Coq[11]. Code generation towards OCaml allows to build an executable: all the logical aspects are discarded since they can't be expressed in this language and don't lead to executable code. Code generation towards Coq provides a formal model of the program, including computational and logical aspects: all computational *methods* and logical *methods* with their proofs are compiled. Thus the consistency of the whole FoCaL development can be checked by Coq.

However the compilation model (i.e. the structure of a collection, of a species, of a method) remains very simple. It is the same in both target languages and uses a few set of basic constructs: records (i.e. structures), functions and simple modules (not even functors).

Note that references are not currently allowed as it is not so easy to handle memory management at the proof level. However functional views of memory are used in several developments. We currently consider to add data-flow programming features and their logical counterparts to ease reactive systems development.

The tool called FOCDOC [3] automatically generates documentation, ensuring that the documentation of a component is always consistent with respect to its implementation. This tool uses its own XML format that contains information coming not only from structured comments (that are parsed and kept in the program's abstract syntax tree) and FoCaL concrete syntax but also from type inference and dependence analysis. From this XML representation and thanks to some XSLT style-sheets, it is possible to generate HTML or LaTeX files. In the same way, it is possible to produce UML models [5] as means to provide a graphical documentation (class diagrams) for FoCaL specifications. The use of graphical notations appears quite useful when interacting with end-users, as these tend to be more intuitive and easier to grasp than their formal (or textual) counterparts. This transformation is based on a formal scheme and captures every aspect of the FoCaL language, so that it has been possible to prove the soundness of this transformation (semantic preservation).

Although this documentation is not the complete safety case, it can helpfully contribute to its elaboration.

As a conclusion of this presentation, FoCaL is not at all a "All-in-One" language, it helps to define strict boundaries between phases of a development. Consistency between phases is ensured by a powerful dependency calculus and a proof system. FoCaL user is guided to maintain the global consistency of a complete development, even during the maintenance phase.

There exist several systems and languages having the same purposes like B[16], CASL[13], RAISE[15]... True comparison with these systems is out of the scope of this paper (but is considered in a forthcoming paper). It seems to us that the originality of FoCaL is its unified language along the different phases which allows to provide the assessor a complete package built in conformity with the related standards.

Differently from CASL[13] that is strongly oriented towards ADT, hence without effective representation of data and computation, FoCaL lets the user go until specifying them (and adds an abstraction layer to prevent users from having access to internal effective implementation). FoCaL produces executable code and related proofs whereas CASL emphasises on the specification phase despite the fact that institutions are provided to link specifications to some SML or Java code[14]. RAISE[15] provides a large range of specification and programming concepts. In contrast, FoCaL offers a limited set of concepts but they can be altogether translated to Coq to ensure a global consistency of the whole development.

2.7 FoCaL Development Cycle

As recalled in the introduction, the development of a critical system must follow a strict development cycle, compliant with standards. In [7] we proposed a development life cycle taking advantages of all features of FoCaL and compliant with the main Standards in the field of critical software development ([1], [2],...). It is based on a V-cycle, decomposed into five (mandatory) phases: requirements/specification, architecture/design, implementation and low level testing, integration/validation testing and the longest one, the maintenance phase. It also covers some transverse processes like generation of the documentation or formal traceability between phases. Transverse processes are processes that should be applied once during all phases. The main characteristics of this life cycle are :

- a strong boundary between phases, especially between the specification phase and the architecture/design one. Specification phase ends when all safety requirements can be proved using the functional requirements and the glue assumptions (see below). Architecture/design phase ends with the implementation of the functional requirements into executable code.
- the implementation phase consists in assembling collections and proving the glue assumptions made on the parametrised species.
- the use of the FoCaL dependencies calculus and documentation generation to generate formal traceability and to help maintenance.

In this paper, we mainly focus on requirements specification, architecture/design and implementation phases as we build the voter. Integration/validation testing phase is considered in the work of M. Carlier [6].

The development cycle is strongly based on the establishment of the specification through requirements expression. We distinguish four kinds of requirements:

- *Functional requirements* describe the relations between inputs and outputs of the system and what is expected on the behaviour of the system without referring to any specific solution.
- *Non-functional requirements* describe all constraints that the system must meet, like time and space bounds, safety integrity levels to achieve, portability needs... These requirements are pretty difficult to express by a first-order formula. They are put inside annotations, so are kept along the compilation process and figure in the compiled documentation.

- *Safety requirements* coming from the results of the safety studies. They ensure that the functional requirements will never trigger a Feared Event. They are considered as requirements on functional requirements.
- As a species can be parametrised, proofs of functional and/or safety requirements sometimes need assumptions on the functions and properties of the collection parameters. These assumptions are called *glue assumptions*. They are proved at the coding level just before final building of the whole system.

All the requirements but some non-functional ones are expressed as FoCaL properties.

3 Overview of the Voter

3.1 Generic Definition

Sensors may exhibit various kinds of errors like bias offset, scale factor or transient faults due to sensitivity to spurious or environmental factors (temperature, pressure,...). Redundancy is one of the major techniques used to guard safety critical systems against such transient faults. There exists many kinds of redundancy, depending on which characteristics (safety, reliability or both) should be privileged for the system. Roughly speaking, each redundant component performs the same work and, when one of them fails, the voter has to detect it and to select an output value among the other, then has to go on providing the service.

Usually, a *voter* is used to elaborate the output from the input values given by the redundant components. Voters are used, for example, for temperature acquisition by multiple sensors in a boiler, or elaboration of the emergency brake signal of a train from several computer replicas... The basic principle of a voter is to compare its input values according to a given consistency relation, and then to output one value depending on a voting policy. The point is that, in redundant systems, the voter is *the* component that must be perfect (as far as possible obviously). A failure of the voter is considered as a major weakness of the system.

A voter system must fulfil three main requirements:

- reliable and correct choice of one non faulty input among its n inputs[3]
- detection of errors on inputs
- localisation of the source of the error and report of a diagnosis related to it[4]

The elaboration of the output value follows a two-stages process:

1. the *inputs comparison*, which takes 2 or more inputs and compares them according to a "consistency law". There are many kinds of such consistency laws: strict equality, equality within a certain tolerance, most recent input, max or min values ...

---

[3] We wilfully limit the voter specification to a function that returns one of its inputs. Other more complex voters can be found in [8].

[4] The third requirement is sometimes optional depending on which dependability characteristic is emphasised.

2. the *arbitration*, by a voting policy algorithm which produces the output value. This algorithm is the heart of a voter and determines its classification and its main properties (majority vote, selection of the most restrictive vote, selection of the most recent value …).

A pre-processing of the inputs can also be performed by a *filtering process*. It analyses input values by in-line "acceptance tests" and eliminates values recognised wrong, a way to eliminate some transient faults. The inputs that succeed the filtering process are then sent to the voter[5].

In the following, we focus on voters with 3 inputs. Our choice is motivated by the fact that 3 inputs is the minimal number for a voter to deal both with safety and reliability characteristics. Taking the case where agreement between 2 sensors is sufficient to ensure the required safety level of a system. Using a voter with 2 inputs meets the safety requirements. But, in case of one failure on a sensor, you need to stop or run your application in a degraded mode. Adding a third sensor permits to continue the service in case of one fault. Most of the time, the cost of the third sensor is far less than the unavailability of the whole system. This kind of voter is a widespread voter architecture in safety critical systems (i.e. Triple Modular Redundancy).

Our choice could be even more generic. It is indeed possible to specify an "n out of m" voter and then to instantiate n and m with the needed value. But this solution needs to highly complicate the voter specification and implementation for a small added value. Indeed only some n and m values are generally used; 1oo2 for reliability, 2oo2 for safety, 2oo3 or 2oo4 for safety and reliability and the concerns are so different that this "sharing by genericity" is just useless.

3.2   The 2oo3 Voter Specification

The 2oo3 voter, used for our example, selects one value from three independent inputs if at least two of them are consistent. Moreover, we also want to detect the faulty value. So, a second output is added to the voter in order to qualify the first result. Table 1 summarises all cases, described as follows:

- **perfect_match:** the three inputs are consistent, the value and index of one of them are returned.
- **partial_match:** two of the three inputs are consistent together, but the third one is not. One of the consistent values and the index of the inconsistent one are returned. This enables identifying a failure on this input.
- **range_match:** One input is consistent with the two others which are mutually inconsistent. The consistent value and the associated index are returned. This can arise when the consistency law is not transitive (i.e. equality within a tolerance). In this case, the system can go on working with the most plausible value.
- **no_match:** all the inputs are inconsistent two per two. The voter cannot take a decision since the majority rule is not applicable.

---

[5] Filtering is different from the input comparison as it works on one single input in opposition to the consistency law which compare at least two inputs.

Table 1. Transfer function

Consistency between inputs			Returned	Diag	
v1 and v2	v1 and v3	v2 and v3	Value	Index	Qualifier
Yes	Yes	Yes	v1	sensor_1	perfect_match
Yes	Yes	No	v1	sensor_1	partial_match
Yes	No	Yes	v2	sensor_2	partial_match
No	Yes	Yes	v2	sensor_3	partial_match
Yes	No	No	v1	sensor_3	range_match
No	Yes	No	v3	sensor_2	range_match
No	No	Yes	v2	sensor_1	range_match
No	No	No	?	?	no_match

The specification of the **no_match** case seems, at first sight, satisfactory: no value is output as there is no good candidate. At the specification level, this behaviour is acceptable, but a choice has to be made during the design phase: the component connected to the voter is waiting for two values (the index of the component and the flag). It will be its own concern to decide what to do with the first output, according to the second.

3.3 The 2oo3 Properties

Functional requirements should describe the voting policy. Each line of the table 1 is transposed in a functional requirement. For example, for a perfect match, the requirement is:

$$\forall v1, v2, v3 \ in \ value, consistency(v1, v2) \wedge$$
$$consistency(v1, v3) \wedge consistency(v2, v3)$$
$$\Rightarrow voter(v1, v2, v3) = (v1, 1, perfect\_match)$$

Table 1 makes also assumptions on symmetry and reflexivity of the consistency law[6]. This leads to define the following glue assumptions:

$$\forall v1, v2 \ in \ value, consistency(v1, v2) \Rightarrow consistency(v2, v1)$$
and
$$\forall v \ in \ value, consistency(v, v)$$

A voter should also meet some safety requirements. Whatever is the order of the input values, the voter has to return a compatible output value. Thus a notion of "compatible output value" is introduced by properties P1 and P2. P1 says that if input values can be compared and output values are consistent and qualifiers are the same then the output values are compatible. P2 says that by default all output values are compatible for inconsistent input values (i.e. there is no choice made for inconsistent input values).

---

[6] Note that the voter does not need transitivity for the consistency law. Use of a transitive consistency law will remove the partial_match qualifier.

$$P1 : \forall val_a, val_b \text{ in } value, \forall qual \text{ in } qualifier,$$
$$qual \neq no\_match \wedge consistency(val_a, val_b)$$
$$\Rightarrow compatible(val_a, val_b, qual, qual)$$
$$P2 : \forall val_a, val_b \text{ in } value,$$
$$compatible(val_a, val_b, no\_match, no\_match)$$
and
$$\forall v1, v2, v3, val_a, val_b \text{ in } value, qual_a, qual_b \text{ in } qualifier$$
$$voter(v1, v2, v3) = (val_a, \_, qual_a) \Rightarrow$$
$$voter(v2, v1, v3) = (val_b, \_, qual_b) \Rightarrow$$
$$compatible(val_a, val_b, qual_a, qual_b)$$

Another safety requirement allocated to a voter is that the output value is always one of the inputs.

$$\forall v1, v2, v3 \text{ in } value,$$
$$vote(v1, v2, v3) = v1 \vee vote(v1, v2, v3) = v2 \vee vote(v1, v2, v3) = v3$$

4   Development of the Voter

4.1   Global Architecture

The voter specification closely follows the description given in Section 3. Indeed separation of the voting policy and the inputs management eases reuse and independent evolution of parts of the voter. The whole specification of the voter is thus split into two major parts. The part concerning the voting policy is introduced by the species Voter (see fig. 1) which specifies the voting policy algorithm and the glue assumptions made on the inputs of the voter, represented by parameters. The second part, which concerns values, is itself split into two parts, the first one describing what is supposed/needed on the "basic" types (like naturals, integers, booleans) and functions on them, the second one (the species Values) specifying inputs as "complex values" (like integers with tolerance, integers modulo n) built upon basic types and ensuring that glue assumptions could be satisfied. Consistency between the two parts is guaranteed by the FoCaL dependency and proof mechanisms.

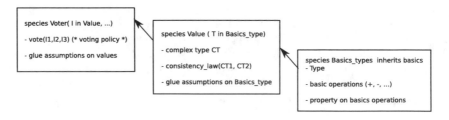

Fig. 1. Voter decomposition

4.2   The Voting Policy

Specification phase. The aim is to specify the data-flow interfaces and the requirements for the system without referring to any specific solution. In FoCaL, data-flow interfaces are encoded by functions declarations and requirements by properties on these
functions.

Specification of the voting policy is performed with a two levels approach. The first
level corresponds to the specification of a most general voter. It gives the signatures and
the generic properties of all 2oo3 voters, making no assumption on the voting policy.
The second level, derived from the first one, specifies the voting policy and gives the
proof of the generic properties.

```
species Gen_2oo3_voter( V is Value, Diag is Basics_object) =

signature vote in V -> V -> V -> (V * Diag);

(* Shortcut to extract the value *)
let output_value(p in V * Diag) in V = basics#fst(p);

(* Safety requirements of a voter *)
property voter_returns_an_input_value:
all v1 v2 v3 in V,
   output_value(vote(v1, v2, v3)) = v1
\/ output_value(vote(v1, v2, v3)) = v2
\/ output_value(vote(v1, v2, v3)) = v3
end;;
```

```
(* Specification of the diagnostics output *)
species My_diag(C is Sensor, Q is Qualifier) inherits Basics_object =
... end;;

(* Specification of the majority voter *)
species Majority_voter(V is Value, C is Sensor, Q is Qualifier, Diag
is My_diag(C, Q)) inherits
Gen_2oo3_voter(V, Diag) =

(* Functional requirements of the majority vote               *)
(* Vote with 3 consistent values returns a perfect_match and  *)
(* the value of the first sensor.                             *)
property perfect_vote :
  all v1 v2 v3 in V,
    (V!consistency_law(v1, v2) /\  V!consistency_law(v2, v3) /\
     V!consistency_law(v1, v3))
  ->
    (output_value(vote( v1, v2, v3)) = v1) /\
    (output_diag(vote( v1, v2, v3)) = Diag!constr(C!sensor_1, Q!perfect_match)))
...
(* Glue assumptions on parametrized species *)
property consistency_law_is_symmetric :
  all v1 v2 in V,
  V!consistency_law(v1, v2) -> V!consistency_law(v2, v1);
...
(* Proof of the safety requirements *)
proof of voter_returns_an_input_value =
...
end;;
```

The specification of the generic 2oo3 voter is represented by a species "Voter_2oo3"
with two parameters: a collection V for the values submitted to the vote, a collection

`Diag` for diagnosis prescriptions. The species provides a single signature `vote`. It also gives the safety requirements allocated to the voter. In order to ease reading, we add a shortcut to extract the value from of output value.

A species can be derived from this generic species for any choice of a voting policy. These derived species define the "voting policy", the glue properties required on the input values (through the collection parameter of interface `Value`) and give a proof of the generic properties. As an example, see the specification of a majority voter with identification of the faulty inputs as defined in section 3.

To create the specification of the "majority voter", we use two main features of the FoCaL language. First, we use the FoCaL inheritance mechanism to create a species having all declarations, definitions and properties defined in the species `Gen_2oo3_voter`. Then, we instantiate parameters of `Gen_2oo3_voter` with a more specific species (i.e. `My_diag`). Note that, the dependency calculus ensures consistence between the different occurrences of formal and effective parameters.

The new species contains the functional specification of the 2oo3 majority voter, the glue assumptions on parameters and the proof of safety properties under those assumptions (done with Zenon). We can compile the FoCaL model to an OCaml file and a Coq file. The first one contains only typed functions declarations that can be used as an external interface for a development. The second one contains a proof term of the safety properties that can already be checked by the Coq prover.

Architecture/design phase. This phase introduces the architectural choices to answer the specification requirements. It provides definition of the functions and the representation of the species. From the majority voter specification, we have sufficient information to propose an implementation of the functional requirements and to provide a proof that this code fulfils them.

```
species Imp_Majority_voter(V is Value, C is Sensor, Q is Qualifier,
Diag is My_diag(C, Q)) inherits Majority_voteur(V, C, Q, Diag) =
(* Implementation of the vote function *)
let vote( v1 in V, v2 in V, v3 in V) in V * Diag =
  let c1 = V!consistency_law( v1, v2) in
  let c2 = V!consistency_law( v1, v3) in
  let c3 = V!consistency_law( v2, v3) in
  if c1 then
    if c2 then
      if c3 then
        (v1, Diag!constr(C!sensor_1, Q!perfect_match))
...
(* Proof of the vote property *)
proof of perfect_vote  =
  by property V!consistency_law_reflexive, Diag!equal_reflexive
     definition of vote, output_diag, output_value;
end;;
```

Transition between specification and design is also made using inheritance. Here parameters are kept while a definition is provided to the declaration, using the FoCaL functional language. Proofs of the functional properties are made using Zenon. Giving a FoCaL interface (and thus at least a specification species) for the input values, the sensor and the qualifier, this species can be compiled: type-checking can be done and a translation of the whole species contents (including Zenon proofs) into a Coq term can be obtained to be immediately assessed. Thus we have a species that implements a 2oo3 majority voter, which can be used with any kind of input values respecting the required glue properties.

Multiple inheritance can be used at design level to provide an existing representation to a specification species. For instance the implementation species Imp_vote_status is a "merge" of two species: the specification species Sp_vote_status which provides the functional requirements and the species Integers which provides the representation and its basic properties. The dependency calculus ensures compatibility between these inherited species.

```
(* Specification species for a set of vote status *)
species Sp_vote_status inherits Setoid =

  (** The 3 values are inconsistent *)
  signature no_match : Self;
  (** 1 value is consistent with the two other which are mutually inconsistent
      *)
  signature range_match : Self;
...
end;;

(* Design of the vote status *)
species Imp_vote_status inherits Sp_vote_status, Integers =

(* Definition of the set elements *)
let no_match = 0;;
...
end;;
```

Definitions can also be changed at any level to fit new needs. In this case, the FoCaL compiler computes all definitions and properties impacted by the redefinitions and asks to provide a new proof of the impacted properties.

4.3 Building a Voter

At this stage, we have several species representing all components of the voter. In order to obtain runnable code a species should be transformed into a collection. Thus a voter collection has to be created from the voter species and collections representing the values and the diagnosis. Firstly, we choose the nature of input values (here the collection Coll_int_with_tol), finalise the diagnosis (here the collection Coll_my_diag). Secondly, we create a species which inherits from the implementation of the voter applied to effective parameters and we provide a proof for the glue assumptions. This step ensures "compatibility" between species. Then, as the new species is now complete, we can create a collection.

```
species Majority_voter_on_int_with_tol inherits
Imp_Majority_voter(Coll_value, Coll_sensor, Coll_int_with_tol, Coll_my_diag) =
  proof of consistency_law_is_symmetric =
    by property Coll_int_with_tol!consistency_law_symmetric;
...
end ;;

collection Coll_int_imp_vote_tol implements Sp_int_imp_vote_tol ;;
```

The collection `Coll_int_imp_vote_tol` is ready to use.

```
let s = Coll_int_imp_vote_tol!output_value(voter( 1, 3, 5));;

(* Results of several calls *)
Voter for integer with a tolerance of 2
v1 : 1, v2 : 3, v3 : 5 --> val : sensor_2 , res : partial_match
v1 : 1, v2 : 2, v3 : 5 --> val : sensor_3 , res : range_match
v1 : 4, v2 : 5, v3 : 5 --> val : sensor_1 , res : perfect_match
v1 : 1, v2 : 4, v3 : 7 --> val : sensor_1 , res : no_match
```

When a component is a COTS (Commercial Off The Shelf) or a very low level component as I/O drivers, one cannot produce a proof of its functional properties. In the same way, we do not want to prove well known or highly used components. In order to consolidate our confidence level of such components, works are currently performed by M. Carlier[6] to generate test cases from FoCaL functional requirements. These test cases can be ran on the external component to validate it. Verification of the voter using M. Carlier tool has been achieved. It shows that the FoCaL life cycle we propose is fully compliant with the validation of external components.

4.4   Re-usability

Many other implementations can fit the generic voter. For example, S. Dajani-Brown proposes a 2oo3 voter for avionics purpose[9]. This voter is based on a classical 2oo3 architecture with an high availability (voter provides an output even when only one input is available). Following our development cycle, we implemented this voter within FoCaL by changing the voting policy and the value representation. Then we carried out successfully all the proof of the generic voter properties (voter always returns one of the input values, voter is insensitive to inputs order).

5   Conclusion and Further Works

This paper illustrates how a safety life cycle can be developed using FoCaL features like inheritance, parametrisation by collections, properties and proofs. This development process respects boundaries between development phases, produces a certified and efficient code, is compliant with standards and thus, eases the assessment process required before commissioning. Several other examples have been developed following the same methodology like hierarchical automata's, physical input acquisition. . . These developments give similar results on the development process.

In this paper, due to a lack of space, we only gave a short glimpse on FoCaL testing. However we used the testing tool (still in development), not only to do classical tests on outputs of the voter but also when encountering some difficulties in proofs, to validate expression of some requirements. We appreciated a lot to have at our disposal, at any stage of the development cycle, a proof tool and a test tool working on the same expressions. This is indeed a FoCaL feature which is of great help when expressing some requirements, when wondering about the validity of some lemmas, when some proofs are out of reach. In this last case, some of the corresponding statements are considered as axioms during proof process, a point which weaknesses the logical approach but is unavoidable in practice, thus increasing confidence by testing the statement is welcomed.

More generally, we emphasise the great facilities given by the coordination of FoCaL programming features (typing, inheritance, late binding, etc.) and FoCaL logical features (statements, proofs) through syntactical means controlled by dependency calculus. Indeed, having the possibility to introduce a statement using names not yet associated to a definition and to prove it under hypothesis submitted to a delayed proof obligation, allows to detect anomalies sooner in the life cycle and the diagnostic provided by the compiler helps to repair them. Yet it is possible to criticise the choice of a functional language for source code. Having no notion of internal state for species can be considered as a weakness. But first, there is no difficulty to translate, if needed, FoCaL definitions into some imperative language: the compiler uses only very basic features of programming languages (simple records and modules). Second, a lot of static analysers rebuild a functional version of imperative code to perform their analyses. In FoCaL this functional version is directly at hand, a point which will be exploited to integrate static analysers in FoCaL, in the near future as the new compiler was conceived to easily include such extensions.

Using the theorem prover Coq as an assessor while having near all proofs quite automatically done with Zenon and having the choice of either doing the remaining ones directly in the Coq environment build by the FoCaL compiler or assuming their statement appears as a good compromise between the confidence level and the cost of the development. Yet the choice of Coq can be questioned. As the compiler does not use truly specific features of Coq, other theorem provers based on type theories and a flavor of Curry-Howard isomorphism can be chosen.

References

1. Railway Applications - Communications, Signalling and Processing Systems - Software for Railway Control and Protection Systems, Standard Cenelec EN 50128 (1999)
2. Functional safety of electrical/electronic/programmable electronic safety-related systems, Standard IEC-61508, International Electrotechnical Commission (1998)
3. Maarek, M., Prevosto, V.: FoCDoC: the documentation system of FoC. In: Proceedings of Calculemus (September 2003)
4. Bonichon, R., Delahaye, D., Doligez, D.: Zenon: An Extensible Automated Theorem Prover Producing Checkable Proofs. In: Dershowitz, N., Voronkov, A. (eds.) LPAR 2007. LNCS, vol. 4790, pp. 151–165. Springer, Heidelberg (2007)
5. Delahaye, D., Etienne, J.F., Donzeau-Gouge, V.: Producing UML Models from Focal Specifications: An Application to Airport Security Regulations. In: 2nd IFIP/IEEE International Symposium on Theoretical Aspects of Software Engineering, pp. 121–124 (2008)
6. Carlier, M., Dubois, C.: Functional Testing in the Focal environment. In: Beckert, B., Hähnle, R. (eds.) TAP 2008. LNCS, vol. 4966, pp. 84–98. Springer, Heidelberg (2008)
7. Ayrault, P., Hardin, T., Pessaux, F.: Development life cycle of critical software under FoCaL. In: TTSS 2008, harnessing Theories for Tools Support in Software, Istanbul (2008)
8. Lorczack, P.R., et al.: Theoretical Investigation of Generalized Voters for Redundant Systems. In: Digest of Papers FTCS-19: The Nineteenth International Symposium on Fault-Tolerant Computing, pp. 444–451 (1989)

9. Dajani-Brown, S., Cofer, D., Bouali, A.: Formal verification of an avionics sensor voter using SCADE. In: Lakhnech, Y., Yovine, S. (eds.) FORMATS 2004 and FTRTFT 2004. LNCS, vol. 3253, pp. 5–20. Springer, Heidelberg (2004)
10. Leroy, X., Doligez, D., Garrigue, J., Rémy, D., Vouillon, J.: The Objective Caml system, documentation and user manual. release 3.11. Documents include with the Objective Caml distribution, INRIA (November 2008)
11. Bertot, Y., Castéran, P.: Coq'Art: The Calculus of Inductive Constructions. Series: Texts in Theoretical Computer Science. An EATCS Series
12. Dubois, C., Hardin, T., Donzeau-Gouge, V.V.: Building a certified component within FoCaL. Trends in Functional Programming 5, 33–48 (2006)
13. Astesiano, E., Bidoit, M., Kirchner, H., Krieg-Brückner, B., Moss, P.D., Sannella, D., Tarlecki, A.: CASL: the Common Algebraic Specification Language. Theorical Computer Science 286, 153–196 (2002)
14. Aspinall, D., Sannella, D.: From specification to code in CASL. In: Kirchner, H., Ringeissen, C. (eds.) AMAST 2002. LNCS, vol. 2422, p. 1. Springer, Heidelberg (2002)
15. The RAISE Method Group: The RAISE Development Method. Prentice Hall International, Englewood Cliffs (1995)
16. Abrial, J.R.: The B-Book - Assigning Programs to meanings. Cambridge University Press, Cambridge (1996)

Combining Satisfiability Solving and Heuristics to Constrained Combinatorial Interaction Testing

Andrea Calvagna[1] and Angelo Gargantini[2]

[1] University of Catania, Italy
Dip. Ingegneria Informatica e delle Telecomunicazioni
andrea.calvagna@unict.it
[2] University of Bergamo, Italy
Dip. Metodi Matematici e Ingegneria dell'Informazione
angelo.gargantini@unibg.it

Abstract. Combinatorial interaction testing aims at revealing errors inside a system under test triggered by unintended interaction between values of its input parameters. In this context we defined a new greedy approach to generate a combinatorial interaction test suites in the presence of constraints, based on integration of an SMT solver, and ordered processing of test goals. Based on the observation that the processing order of required combinations determines the size of the final test suite, this approach has been then used as a framework to evaluate a set of deterministic ordering strategies, each based on a different heuristic optimization criteria. Their performance has been assessed and contrasted also with those of random and dummy ordering strategies. Results of experimental assessment are presented and compared with well-known combinatorial tools.

1 Introduction

Verification and validation of highly-configurable software systems, such as those supporting many optional or customizable features, is a challenging activity. In fact, due to its intrinsic complexity, formal specification of the whole system may require a great effort. Modeling activities may become extremely expensive and time consuming, and the tester may decide to model (at least initially) only the inputs and require they are sufficiently covered by tests.

To this aim, combinatorial interaction testing (CIT) techniques [11,19,25] can be effectively applied in practice [1,29,24]. CIT consists in employing combination strategies to select values for inputs and combine them to form test cases. The tests can then be used to check how the interaction among the inputs influences the behavior of the original system under test. The most used combinatorial testing approach is to systematically sample the set of inputs in such a way that all t-way combinations of inputs are included. This approach exhaustively explores t-strength interaction between input parameters, generally in the smallest possible test executions. For instance, pairwise interaction testing aims at generating a reduced size test suite which covers all *pairs* of input values. Significant time savings can be achieved by implementing this kind of approach,

C. Dubois (Ed.): TAP 2009, LNCS 5668, pp. 27–42, 2009.

as well as in general with t-wise interaction testing. As an example, exhaustive testing of a system with a hundred boolean configuration options would require 2^{100} test cases, while pairwise coverage for it can be accomplished with only 10 test cases. Similarly, pairwise coverage of a system with twenty ten-valued inputs (10^{20} distinct input assignments possible) requires a test suite sized less than 200 tests cases only.

CIT requires just specification of the input model, thus it could be defined as an *input-based* testing technique. Since it is also possible to model the output of a system under test as a boolean variable describing only the (success or failure) outcome of each applied test. It is then clear that CIT actually implements a particular type of *functional* (I/O based) testing [26], focused just on the coverage of *interactions* between the inputs, at various degrees of depth. The importance of such functional testing criteria is more evident if we think at the inputs as actually modelling interactions between system components, as it is the case for testing of GUIs or protocols, where we aim at testing just combinations of possible interaction sequences. Nevertheless, several case studies [25,33] have proved the general effectiveness of such functional approach by showing that unintended interaction between optional features can lead to incorrect behaviors which may not be detected by traditional testing.

CIT is also widely recognized as effective in revealing software defects [23]. In particular, experimental research work [25] showed that usually 100% of faults in a software system are already triggered by just a relatively low degree of feature interaction, typically 4-way to 6-way. Dalal et al. [12], showed that testing of all pairwise interactions of a set of software system was able to detect a significant percentage of the existing faults (between 50% and 75%). Dunietz *et al.* [13] compared t-wise coverage to random input testing with respect to structural (block) coverage achieved, with results showing higher reliability of the former in achieving block coverage if compared to random test suites of the same size. Burr and Young [3] report 93% code coverage as a result from applying pairwise testing of a commercial software system. For these reasons combinatorial testing, besides being an active research area, is largely used in practice and supported today by many tools (see [27] for an up to date listing).

Combinatorial testing is applied to a wide variety of problems: highly configurable software systems, software product lines which define a family of softwares, hardware systems, and so on. As an example, Table 1 reports the input domain of a simple telephone switch billing system [26], which processes telephone call data with four call properties, each of which has three possible values: the `access` parameter tells how the calling party's phone is connected to the switch, the `billing` parameter says who pays for the call, the `calltype` parameter tells the type of call, and the last parameter, `status` tells whether or not the call was successful or failed either because the calling party's phone was busy or the call was blocked in the phone network. While covering all the possible combinations for the BBS inputs shown in Table 1 would require $3^4 = 81$ tests, the pairwise coverage of the BBS can be obtained by the test suite reported in Table 2 which contains only 11 tests.

Table 1. Input domain of a basic billing system (BBS) for phone calls

access	billing	calltype	status
LOOP	CALLER	LOCALCALL	SUCCESS
ISDN	COLLECT	LONGDISTANCE	BUSY
PBX	EIGHT_HUNDRED	INTERNATIONAL	BLOCKED

Table 2. A test suite for pairwise coverage of BBS

#	billing	calltype	status	access
1	EIGHT_HUNDRED	LOCALCALL	BUSY	PBX
2	CALLER	LONGDISTANCE	BLOCKED	LOOP
3	EIGHT_HUNDRED	INTERNATIONAL	SUCCESS	ISDN
4	COLLECT	LOCALCALL	SUCCESS	LOOP
5	COLLECT	LONGDISTANCE	BUSY	ISDN
6	COLLECT	INTERNATIONAL	BLOCKED	PBX
7	CALLER	LOCALCALL	SUCCESS	ISDN
8	CALLER	LOCALCALL	BUSY	PBX
9	EIGHT_HUNDRED	LONGDISTANCE	BLOCKED	ISDN
10	COLLECT	LONGDISTANCE	BUSY	LOOP
11	COLLECT	LONGDISTANCE	SUCCESS	LOOP

In most cases, constraints or dependencies exist between the system inputs. They normally model assumptions about the environment or about the system components or about the system interface and they are normally described in natural language. If constraints are considered, then the combinatorial testing becomes constrained combinatorial interaction testing (CCIT). However, as explained in sections 2 and 5, most combinatorial testing techniques either ignore the constraints which the environment may impose on the inputs or require the user to modify the original specifications and add extra information to take into account the constraints.

Based on a CCIT construction approach which extends our own previous work [4,5], in this paper we present a study focused on the use of heuristics to order the test goals and assess their impact on the size of generated test suites. Moreover, in contrast to our previous experience, in the proposed approach we experimented implementing the support for constraints by means of integrating the well known satisfiability solver Yices [14] in the construction process.

The paper is organized as follows: Sect. 2 presents our approach and its key points, Sect. 2.1 discusses how the Yices tool is used to generate constrained combinatorial tests, Sect. 3 introduces a set of heuristic strategies for which Sect. 4 reports and discusses results of their experimental evaluation. A comparison with other techniques and tools is reported in Sect. 5, and finally Sect.6 draws our conclusions.

2 Background

Our approach to combinatorial testing can be classified as *logic-based*, since it formalizes the combinatorial coverage in the presence of constraints by means of logical predicates and applies techniques normally used for solving logical problems to it. To formalize pairwise testing, which aims at validating each possible pair of input values for a given system under test, we can formally express each pair as a corresponding logical expression, a *test predicate* (or test goal), e.g.: $p_1 = v_1 \land p_2 = v_2$, where p_1 and p_2 are two input variables and v_1 and v_2 are two possible values of $p1$ and $p2$ respectively. Similarly, the t-wise coverage can be modeled by a set of test predicates, each of the type:

$$p_1 = v_1 \land p_2 = v_2 \land \ldots \land p_t = v_t \equiv \land_{i=1}^{t} p_i = v_i$$

where $p_1, p_2 \ldots p_t$ are t inputs and $v_1, v_2 \ldots v_t$ are their possible values. We define a *test* as an assignment to all the inputs of the system. We say that a test ts covers a test predicate tp if and only if it is a model of tp, and we formally represent this fact as $ts \models tp$. Note that while a test binds *every* variable to one of its possible values, a test predicate binds only t variables. We say that a test suite achieves the t-wise combinatorial coverage if all the test predicates for the t-wise coverage are covered by at least one test in the suite. The main goal of combinatorial testing is to find a possibly small test suite able to achieve the t-wise coverage.

In order to generate the test predicates, we assume the availability of a formal description of the system under test. This description should include at least the input parameters together with their domains[1], but could also include constraints over the inputs expressed as axioms. By formalizing the t-wise testing by means of logical predicates, finding a test that satisfies a given predicate reduces to a logical problem of finding a complete[2] model for a logical formula representing the test predicate and the constraints. Formally, the first task is to find the test ts that solves the equation $ts \models tp \land c_1 \land \ldots \land c_n$, where c_i represent the constraints. To this aim, many techniques like constraint solvers and model checkers can be applied. In this approach the constraints become first class citizens and they can be represented by logical expressions.

To generate the complete test suite, one can generate all the test predicates by a simple combinatorial algorithm and then proceed *incrementally* to generate the tests, that is choosing one test predicate at the time and trying to generate a test that covers it and satisfies the constraints. In [4] we already proposed three enhancements of this approach, which have been applied also in the present context. The first consists in *monitoring* the test generation, i.e. marking the test predicates covered by the found test, and skipping them in the next runs. The second consists in conjoining as many as possible *compatible* test predicates, and using this bigger, extended test predicate to derive the test case, in order

---

[1] Currently, only finite, discrete enumerable domains are supported.
[2] We say that a model is *complete* if it assigns a value to every input variable.

to increase coverage more quickly and also reduce the number of runs of the external solver. This stage of the construction process can be referred to as *composition* of the test predicates and precedes every run of the external test generation which in [4] was a model checker. The third enhancement consists in further reducing the size of the overall test suite by searching for existence of any redundant test case, that is a test whose predicates are all already covered by other tests, and deleting such tests from the final suite. This optimization stage is performed a posteriori on the built test suite by a dedicated *reduction* greedy algorithm. Results from empirical studies [32] indicate that as minimization is applied (while keeping constant coverage), there is little or no reduction in the fault detection effectiveness. For this reason, although the reduction stage is optional, it is always applied in this paper.

The process proposed by our method is implemented by the *ASM Test Generation Tool* (ATGT)[3]. ATGT was originally developed to support structural [18] and fault based testing [16] of *Abstract State Machines* (ASMs), and it has been then extended to support also combinatorial testing.

In [4] we discussed the main advantages of our approach with respect to other approaches to CCIT, namely (1) the ability to deal with user specific requirements on the test suite, in form of both specific test predicates representing critical combinations and particular tests already generated, (2) the integration with other testing techniques like the structural coverage presented in [17] and the fault based coverage of [16], (3) the integration with the entire system development process, since the user can initially model only the input and later add also the behavior and other formal properties, and apply other analysis techniques like simulation, formal verification, and model checking, and (4) the complete support of constraints, which can be given as generic boolean predicates over the inputs. Indeed, as discussed again in Sect. 5, most methods for combinatorial testing focus only on finding very efficient algorithms able to generate small test suites, while they normally neglect all the other issues listed above. In [5] we presented an extension of this approach able to deal with temporal constraints.

2.1   Implementing Support for Constraints by Yices

One important difference introduced in this work over the methodology defined in our previous work [4,5] and summarized in Section 2 is the use of the SMT solver Yices [14] instead of the model checker SAL to support constraints over the input domain. Yices is an efficient SMT solver that decides the satisfiability of arbitrary formulas containing uninterpreted function symbols with equality, linear real and integer arithmetic, scalar types, recursive datatypes, tuples, records, extensional arrays, fixed-size bit-vectors, quantifiers, and lambda expressions. With respect to a SAT solver, Yices offers a more expressive language for the specification and for the properties and it uses several algorithms for satisfiability checking. For example, we are able to directly encode constraints over enumerative variables without the burden of their translation to SAT, which is itself an open research problem [31]. We plan in the future to exploit other features of

---

[3] ATGT is available at http://cs.unibg.it/gargantini/software/atgt/

```
;; (1) define the types and the variables for the BBS example
(define—type AccessT (scalar LOOP ISDN PBX))
(define—type BillingT (scalar CALLER COLLECT EIGHT_HUNDRED))
(define—type CallTypeT (scalar LOCALCALL LONGDISTANCE INTERNATIONAL))
(define—type StatusT (scalar SUCCESS BUSY BLOCKED))
(define access :: AccessT) (define billing :: BillingT)
(define callType :: CallTypeT) (define status :: StatusT)
;; add the constraints
(assert (=> (= billing COLLECT) (/= callType INTERNATIONAL)))
;; add the test predicate
(assert (and (= access LOOP) (= billing COLLECT)))
;; find and print a model (if any)
(set—evidence! true) (check)
```

```
;; (2) second BBS example using an uninterpreted function modelling the cost
;; Cost as uninterpreted type with a constant for FREE calls
(define—type Cost) (define FREE::Cost)
;; Two Cost functions of billing and of callType
(define CB::(—> BillingT Cost)) (define CCT::(—> CallTypeT Cost))
;; add some constraints about free calls
(assert (= (CB EIGHT_HUNDRED) FREE))
(assert (/= (CCT INTERNATIONAL) FREE))
(assert (= (CB billing) (CCT callType)))
;; add the test predicate
(assert (and (= billing EIGHT_HUNDRED) (= callType INTERNATIONAL)))
;; find and print a model (if any)
(set—evidence! true) (check) ;; ———> unsat
```

Fig. 1. BBS in Yices (1) base version (2) using uninterpreted functions

Yices to deal with more complex systems, but for now we simply use booleans and enumerative variables since we apply our tool to case studies taken from other approaches which support only that. With respect to a model checker, Yices cannot deal with state transformations (although it can be used as front end for bounded model checking) and for this reason it cannot be used in the presence of temporal constraints, where instead, model checkers can be efficiently employed [5]. Since Yices does not perform model checking and SAL uses Yices as default SMT solver, directly using Yices should be faster than using SAL. Moreover, we can use the Yices API library instead of the more expensive data exchange through files we used for SAL. Experimental work results presented in Section 4 confirmed that Yices is much faster than SAL.

The translation of the logical problem of finding a model for a given problem is straightforward. For instance, the translation of the BBS problem for the test predicate $access = LOOP \land billing = COLLECT$ is reported in Fig. 1. As second example, we show how the advanced features of Yices allow to easily model partial specifications by using uninterpreted functions.

While a model checker always finds and outputs a counter example, a SMT solver normally only checks if a formula is satisfiable or not, and it is not mandatory to print the model in case a model exists. Yices can print the model (if any) if explicitly requested by the user (with a set-evidence command). However, the model found by Yices may not bind all the variables: it specifies only the values of variables whose values are fixed by the found model, leaving the others unspecified. To be used as test, the model must be completed with values for all the variables and this can be done by choosing random values for unbound variables. In our case, the number of unbound variables should be very low, since we compose as many test predicates as possible, so to bind as many variables as possible and to leave free only the variables which are not referred by uncovered test predicates that could be composed. Therefore, the effect of this random completion of tests should negligibly affect the final test suite.

3 Sorting the Test Predicates

The order in which the test predicates are selected during test generation may affect the size of the final test suite. In our previous work [4], we found that processing the test predicates in random order generally leads to good results, provided that one runs the generation process several times and then he/she takes the best outcome as final test suite. This approach is widely used: existing tools based on greedy, non deterministic search heuristics (i.e. like AETG, SA-SAT, ATGT, PICT[4]) are commonly benchmarked over a series of fifty executions. The main disadvantage of the random based approach, is that the user must run several times the test generation process to be sure to obtain a *statistically* good result. In order to obtain a reasonably short test suite with just one run of the tool, a deterministic construction algorithm can be applied. In this case, the incremental construction algorithm will process the pool of test predicates always in the same order, determined with respect to some optimization criterion. Several orderings can be defined to this aim, based on the observation that in an optimal covering array all the combinations of variables to values assignments are evenly used. In fact, when adding a new test case to the test suite, it should cover as many new combinations as possible, that is, it should include test predicates which give a more original contribution to the test suite. To this aim, we defined several comparison criteria to evaluate which test predicate is more original between two candidates tp_1 and tp_2, given a test suite containing already several test cases. These are:

Counting explored assignments (touch). This counts the number of assignment *variable* = *value* contained in the tps which are already contained in a test of the test suite. In this way, tp_1 is preferable if it contains fewer assignment already *touched* in the test suite than tp_2.

---

[4] The PICT tool core algorithm does make pseudo-random choices but, unless a user specifies otherwise, the pseudo-random generator is always initialized with the same seed value.

Least used assignment (min). In this case, the algorithm keeps track of the number each *variable = value* assignment has already been included in the test suite, and tp_1 is preferable to tp_2 if its least used assignment is less used than the least used assignment of tp_2. The rationale behind this sorting criteria is that the novelty of a single assignment has here priority over the novelty of the whole test predicate.

Most used assignment (max). As opposite to the former, this comparison criteria prefers tp_1 to tp_2 if its most used combination has lower usage count than that of tp_2. Note that this produce a totally different ordering with respect to the former, and not just its reversal.

Even usage of assignments (dev). In this criteria, a test predicate tp_1 is preferable if the usage of its assignments is more evenly distributed than how it is for tp_2. This is actually quantified by computing the *standard deviation* of the usage counts for the assignments in the considered test predicate. The rationale is that the even usage of combinations, which is a global requirement of a good test suite, can be imposed also locally in each newly added test predicate, and throughout the incremental construction process this can help preventing the introduction of unbalanced test cases.

Accounting for tp composition. Four additional ordering strategies have been defined (*touch/c, min/c, max/c, dev/c*), which are variants of their respective original ordering strategies, modified according to the test predicate composition principle, that is, they account also for all the assignments in the composed test predicate, instead of just for those already in the test suite.

4   Evaluation and Discussion

In this section a comparison of experimental results is presented, obtained by applying the ATGT tool to a set of example tasks available from the literature [8,9], and listed in the leftmost columns of Table 3. While the tasks #[1..5,11..13] have been generated artificially with increasing size, all other tasks encode example combinatorial problems derived from real systems of various sizes. Third and fourth column of Table 3 report the input domain size and the complexity of the imposed constraints. The notation used to express the problem domain size is the exponential notation introduced in [21], while the constraints complexity is expressed by converting the constraints into DNF and then apply the following function δ:

$$\delta(a \wedge b) = \delta(a) \cdot \delta(b) \qquad\qquad \delta(a \vee b) = \delta(a) + \delta(b)$$
$$\delta(x = b) = range(x) - 1 \qquad\qquad \delta(x \neq b) = 1$$

For forbidden combinations, δ is equal to the constraints measure proposed in [9], which simply counts a forbidden combination of t variables as t and multiply all the forbidden combinations. For instance, the forbidden pair $x = a, y = b$, would be represented in our approach by the constraint $\neg(x = a \wedge$

Table 3. Suite sizes and average times for random heuristic

	task			size					time	
#	name	size	δ	min	avg	1stQ	3rdQ	max	Yices	SAL
1	CCA1	3^3	$2^5 3^1$	9	9.43	9	10	11	0,89	9,7
2	CCA2	4^3	$2^3 3^1$	17	19.16	19	20	22	1,43	15,58
3	CCA3	5^3	$2^5 3^1$	27	30.06	29	31	34	2,23	23,77
4	CCA4	6^3	$2^6 3^1$	40	42.92	42	44	47	3,13	33,67
5	CCA5	7^3	$2^5 3^1$	55	59.74	59	61	64	4,17	45,49
6	MobilePhone	$3^3 2^2$	$2^5 3^1 5^1$	10	11.48	11	12	14	1,8	19,95
7	CruiseControl	$4^1 3^1 2^4$	2^2	8	8.41	8	9	10	1,07	11,68
8	TCAS2Boolean	$10^2 4^1 3^2 2^7$	224	10	11.15	11	11	13	4,9	57,74
9	BBS	3^4	2^1	12	12.98	12	14	15	1,08	11,89
10	SpinSimulator	$4^5 2^{13}$	$2^{47} 3^2$	26	29.45	29	30	33	12,49	137,09
11	CCA6	5^4	$2^3 3^1$	34	36.76	36	38	40	3,15	32,66
12	CCA7	6^4	$2^3 3^1$	49	52.81	52	54	57	4,46	46,3
13	CCA8	7^4	$2^5 3^1$	68	73.14	72	74	79	6,09	70,36

$y = b$), which in DNF becomes $x \neq a \vee y \neq b$ which is evaluated by δ to 2. In case of forbidden combinations, quantities expressed with this criteria can take advantage of exponential layout, e.g., $2^5 \cdot 3^1$ will read also as five pairwise constraints plus one tree-wise. All the specifications shown in Table 3 contains constraints easily expressed as forbidden combinations, except task#8, which has only boolean variables and contains a single complex boolean constraint, which converted to DNF has 224 conjunctions, so the complexity is 224.

A set of fifty instances of the test suite based on the policy of random[5] processing order have been generated for each of the tasks, and Table 3 reports the resulting best, average, and worst test suite size obtained, together with the values of the first and third quartiles computed from the gathered set of sizes. Table 3 also reports the computing times for the considered tasks when using Yices or SAL respectively. They show a performance improvement by a factor of about eleven times using Yices over SAL model checker. Although these computing times correspond to the random policy experiments only, the computing times observed for the other policies were similar, irrespective of the considered processing policy, and the performance improvement observed in all experiments has shown to be constant, irrespective the task too. Thus, we decided not to report them here.

All the previously introduced deterministic ordering policies have also been applied, and the resulting test suite sizes are reported in Table 4. In the performed experiments an additional deterministic ordering policy has been applied too, which consisted in processing all the test predicates just in the same order they where enumerated by straight nested loops. This dummy ordering policy, named *as generated (asg)* has been included to have a scenario where no ordering is applied at all and the corresponding outcomes are in the rightmost column of Table 4. All results reported in tables 3 and 4 are intentionally reported prior

---

[5] An uniform distribution among test predicates has been applied.

Table 4. Comparison of suite sizes for deterministic heuristics

task#	min	min/c	touch	touch/c	max	max/c	dev	dev/c	asg
1	10	9	9	9	10	11	9	10	10
2	20	21	18	18	21	20	21	21	21
3	36	33	31	30	33	35	32	32	37
4	58	52	46	45	47	48	49	46	58
5	77	68	63	63	70	66	67	65	80
6	11	14	11	10	10	12	11	11	13
7	9	10	9	9	10	9	9	9	9
8	12	12	12	10	12	14	12	13	15
9	18	15	13	14	20	14	14	15	20
10	39	31	29	28	37	31	31	33	40
11	45	40	37	38	42	39	42	41	55
12	68	59	58	54	63	61	64	62	81
13	106	88	79	79	92	81	83	81	123

to eventual application of the suite reduction stage. Indeed, applying reduction would have improved the results but could have also masked the relative performance differences between the policies.

Figure 2 allows the reader to visually compare altogether the data in both tables 4 and 3, and especially to figure out how the considered deterministic policies perform with respect to random processing, before applying the test suite reduction algorithm. On the horizontal axis are the task numbers, split in two graphs with different scaling of the y axis, for improved readability.

While random policy has always reached better (smaller) sizes than all the considered deterministic policies, it is interesting to note that its worst (bigger) performance is also worse than many of the proposed deterministic policies in all the tasks in Figure 2(a), and in tasks #{3,4,5,10} of Figure 2(b). In many tasks there have been deterministic strategies performing even better than average random result, like i.e. in tasks # {1,2,7,8,3,4}, or comparable to average, like i.e. tasks #{9, 3, 5}. It can be observed that the *touch/c* processing policy is constantly the best performing among all the observed deterministic policies, with the exception of tasks #9 and #5, where it is only slightly outperformed by its sibling policy *touch*. Also, it is interesting to note that the *touch/c* policy is always performing better that the worst random policy performance in all tasks, with the sole exception of task #13, where they are equal, and as good as the best random result, in tasks #{1,7,8}. It is relevant to note that the time cost to achieve the best random performance has to be multiplied by the number of runs necessary to obtain it. This result encourages the use of a deterministic processing strategy, like *touch/c* over the random based alternative, at least in specific cases where time performance is a strict priority over the test suite size optimization.

Figure 2(b) also shows that the performance of deterministic policies degrades faster with respect to random policy average, when scaling up the task size. Note that the performances of the non deterministic strategy span in an interval

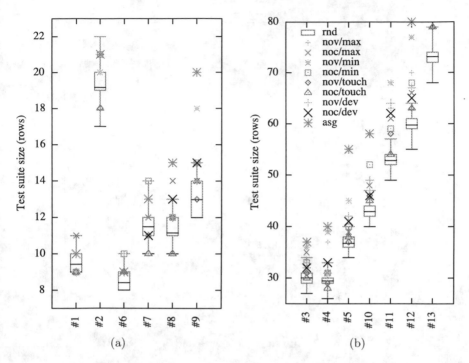

Fig. 2. Suite sizes computed for tasks #1-13, prior to reduction

which become wider for big specifications, from the best performance to the worse performance possible since such strategy has no constraints except those theoretical. The performance of a deterministic strategy will fall in this interval, but it will never perform better than the best result of the random policy. For this reason finding a deterministic strategy which performs at least better than the average is a challenging activity. Indeed, there is no guarantee about the quality of a single performance of a non deterministic strategy, requiring for this reason multiple runs. After the application of reduction stage, the performance gap reduces significantly, as shown in Figure 3, which compares the suites sizes of random and the best deterministic policy. In this case, for all considered tasks the performance of deterministic is never worse than the random worst result, and in nine out of thirteen tasks is better than average random result, supporting the adoption of deterministic heuristic as a fairly good option.

Finally, in Table 5 we contrasted the best results of our approach, from both random and best deterministic ordering policy, with those of some tools from the literature. The mAETG-SAT [8] and PICT [10] tools are AETG-like [6] greedy construction algorithms, with a random-heuristic based core, even though the PICT tool can be forced to behave deterministically by initializing its internal random seed always with the same constant value. The SA-SAT [8] tool is a meta-heuristic search algorithm inspired on simulated annealing [7], which

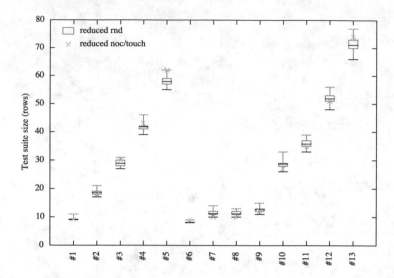

Fig. 3. Reduced suite sizes, of random and touch policies, for tasks #1-13

Table 5. Comparison of suite sizes for 2-wise and 3-wise constrained models

Task #	ATGT $touch/c^{red}$	rnd_{min}^{red}	mAETG-SAT	SA-SAT	PICT	TestCover
			t = 2, pair wise			
1	9	9	10	10	10	10
2	18	17	17	17	19	17
3	30	27	26	26	27	30
4	45	40	37	36	39	38
5	63	55	52	52	56	54
10	28	26	25	24	16	19
			t = 3, three wise			
10	135	127	108	95		
11	164	159	138	140	143	-
12	283	282	241	251	250	-
13	502	449	383	438	401	-

exhibit random behavior too. Testcover [30][28] tool builds a test suite by recursively composing together sub-blocks which are already optimal orthogonal
arrays or covering arrays. This latter is the sole tool which has no random
heuristic inside. The results from our tool ATGT are here reported inclusive
of the ex-post reduction optimization, showing that both for pairwise and for
three-wise combinatorial tasks the difference between random and deterministic
performance is always moderate, and often negligible. The shown performance
compares also fairly good with that of the other available tools.

5 Related Work

To the best of our knowledge, little work has already be done in literature about the ordering of test goals for test generation. In [15], the authors show that taking the test predicates in the same order in which they are built is generally a bad policy, while randomly choosing them leads to good results. They also define some ordering criteria, which however are not suitable to combinatorial testing. Although their approach differs with respect to that presented here, since they generate one test case for each test predicate while we collect as many test predicates as possible to generate one test, our experiments confirm that a random order is better than the order in which test predicates are generated. In [2], Bryce et al. presented a general framework of *greedy* construction algorithms, in order to study the impact of each *type* of decision on the effectiveness of the resulting heuristic construction process. To this aim, they designed the framework as a nested structure of four decision layers, regarding respectively: (1) the number of instances of the process to be run, (2) the size of the pool of candidate rows from which select each new row, (3) the factor ordering selection criteria and (4) the level ordering selection criteria. The approach presented in this work fits exactly in the *greedy* category of algorithms modeled by that framework, and it is structured in order to be parametric with respect to the desired number of repetitions and the factor and level ordering strategies. The major contribution of this study is then the evaluation of the original strategies presented in Sect. 3, which actually implement variants of a novel *hybrid* heuristic based on defining ordering selection criteria for the test predicates, instead. Building the next row around a test predicate means that both a set of *fixed* factors and their levels (values) will be determined at the same time, in contrast with Bryce et al. study which focused on separate rules for the factor and level selection layers. Their study concluded that factor ordering is predominant on the resulting test suite size, and that *density*-based level ordering selection criteria was the best performing one out of those tested. In the present work, all the strategies proposed and tested actually implement this common optimization principle of controlling the *density* of feature levels, but we explored original ways of redefining the *density* concept. In fact, while Bryce et al. compute it as the expected number of uncovered pairs, in contrast we define many measures somewhat related to the current frequency of appearance of each predicate in the test suite, and lexicographically sort with respect to that.

As a second aspect, research on combinatorial testing approaches featuring support for constraints deserves further investigation. Some methods require to remodel the original specification, very few directly support constraints in an integrated manner. For instance, AETG [6,26] requires to separate the inputs in a way they become unconstrained, and only simple constraints of type **if then else** (or **requires** in [8]) can be directly modeled in the specification. Other methods [20] require to explicitly list all the forbidden combinations. As the number of input grows, the explicit list may explode and it may become practically infeasible to find for a user. Cohen et al. [8] found that just one tool, PICT [10], was able to handle *full* constraints specification, that is, without requiring remodeling of inputs or explicit expansion of each forbidden test cases. However, there is no detail on how the constraints are actually implemented in PICT, limiting the reuse of its technique. Others propose to deal with the constraints only after the test suite has been generated by deleting tests which violate the constraints and then regenerate the missing combinations. By this approach, any classical algorithm for CIT may be extended to support constraints. However, this is usable only if the number of combinations to be regenerate is small and all the constraints are explicitly listed. Experiments show that the number of tests violating the constraints can be very high if they are simply ignored, and the number of implicit constraints can exponentially grow with the number of variables [9]. In our work we address the use of full constraints as suggested in [8] and a more expressive language for them through the expressions supported by Yices.

Several papers recently investigated the use of verification methods for combinatorial testing. Hnich et al. [22] translates the problem of building covering arrays to a Boolean satisfiability problem and then they use a SAT solver to generate their solution. In their paper, they leave the treatment of auxiliary constraints over the inputs as future work. Note that in their approach, the whole problem of finding an *entire* covering array is solved by SAT, while in our approach only the generation of a single test case is solved by Yices. To this respect, our approach is similar to that presented by Cohen et al. [8,9], where a mix of logical solvers and heuristic algorithms is used to find the final test suite. Kuhn and Okun [23] try to integrate combinatorial testing with model checking (SMV) to provide automated specification based testing, with no support for constraints. Conversely, Cohen et al. propose a framework to incorporating constraints into established greedy and simulating annealing combinatorial testing algorithm. They exclusively focus on handling constraints and present a SAT-based constraint solving technique that has to be integrated with external algorithms for combinatorial testing like IPO or AETG. Their framework is general and fully supports the presence of constraints, even if they can be modeled only in a canonical form of boolean formulae as forbidden tuples.

6   Conclusion

In this paper we have defined a pool of eight metrics to sort the test predicates prior to processing, in order to assess the impact of their processing order on the size of the resulting test suite and on the generation time. The investigation of such aspect of deterministic combinatorial construction algorithms is an original contribution. The results have been contrasted with those of random and dummy orderings and also with available results from some well-known combinatorial tools. It has been shown that even though random based heuristics can achieve better (lower) absolute results in terms of the size of the computed test suite, the performance of deterministic heuristics is still acceptable, it does not require multiple runs as the random policy, and thus it is preferable if the computing time requirements are an issue. In order to support our study we implemented a combinatorial construction technique that supports constrained combinatorial testing, by using the Yices SMT solver in order to generate models. The proposed approach is able to support not just pairwise but also n-wise CCIT, and the presented comparative evaluation with respect to other existing tools suggest that the presented methodology is fairly good approach to CCIT. To the best of our knowledge, this is also the first approach to CCIT exploiting an existing SMT solver. Work is undergoing to integrate this technique with structural and fault based testing, and to extend it in order to support constraints with universal and existential quantifications, which would be very useful to express complex constraints in a very compact style.

References

1. Brownlie, R., Prowse, J., Phadke, M.: Robust testing of AT&T PMX/starMAIL using OATS. AT&T Technical Journal 71(3), 41–47 (1992)
2. Bryce, R.C., Colbourn, C.J., Cohen, M.B.: A framework of greedy methods for constructing interaction test suites. In: ICSE 2005: Proceedings of the 27th international conference on Software engineering, pp. 146–155. ACM, New York (2005)
3. Burr, K., Young, W.: Combinatorial test techniques: Table-based automation, test generation, and code coverage. In: Proceedings of the Intl. Conf. on Software Testing Analysis and Review, October 1998, pp. 503–513 (1998)
4. Calvagna, A., Gargantini, A.: A logic-based approach to combinatorial testing with constraints. In: Beckert, B., Hähnle, R. (eds.) TAP 2008. LNCS, vol. 4966, pp. 66–83. Springer, Heidelberg (2008)
5. Calvagna, A., Gargantini, A.: Using SRI SAL model checker for combinatorial tests generation in the presence of temporal constraints. In: Rushby, J., Shankar, N. (eds.) AFM 2008: Third Workshop on Automated Formal Methods (satellite of CAV), pp. 43–52 (2008)
6. Cohen, D.M., Dalal, S.R., Fredman, M.L., Patton, G.C.: The AETG system: An approach to testing based on combinatorial design. IEEE Transactions On Software Engineering 23(7), 437–444 (1997)
7. Cohen, M.B., Colbourn, C.J., Ling, A.C.H.: Augmenting simulated annealing to build interaction test suites. In: ISSRE 2003: Proceedings of the 14th International Symposium on Software Reliability Engineering, Washington, DC, USA, p. 394. IEEE Computer Society Press, Los Alamitos (2003)
8. Cohen, M.B., Dwyer, M.B., Shi, J.: Interaction testing of highly-configurable systems in the presence of constraints. In: ISSTA International symposium on Software testing and analysis, New York, NY, USA, pp. 129–139 (2007)
9. Cohen, M.B., Dwyer, M.B., Shi, J.: Constructing interaction test suites for highly-configurable systems in the presence of constraints: a greedy approach. IEEE Transactions on Software Engineering (2008) (to appear)
10. Czerwonka, J.: Pairwise testing in real world. In: 24th Pacific Northwest Software Quality Conference (2006)
11. Dalal, S., Jain, A., Karunanithi, N., Leaton, J., Lott, C.: Model-based testing of a highly programmable system. In: The Ninth International Symposium on Software Reliability Engineering, pp. 174–179. IEEE Computer Society, Los Alamitos (1998)
12. Dalal, S.R., Jain, A., Karunanithi, N., Leaton, J.M., Lott, C.M., Patton, G.C., Horowitz, B.M.: Model-based testing in practice. In: International Conference on Software Engineering ICSE, pp. 285–295. Association for Computing Machinery, New York (1999)

13. Dunietz, I.S., Ehrlich, W.K., Szablak, B., Mallows, C., Iannino, A.: Applying design of experiments to software testing. In: Society, I. (ed.) Proc. Int'l. Conf. Software Eng. (ICSE), pp. 205–215 (1997)
14. Dutertre, B., de Moura, L.: The Yices SMT solver. Technical report, SRI (2006), http://yices.csl.sri.com/tool-paper.pdf
15. Fraser, G., Gargantini, A., Wotawa, F.: On the order of test goals in specification-based testing. Journal of Logic and Algebraic Programming (2009) (in press)
16. Gargantini, A.: Using model checking to generate fault detecting tests. In: Gurevich, Y., Meyer, B. (eds.) TAP 2007. LNCS, vol. 4454, pp. 189–206. Springer, Heidelberg (2007)
17. Gargantini, A., Riccobene, E.: Asm-based testing: Coverage criteria and automatic test sequence generation. JUCS 10(8) (November 2001)
18. Gargantini, A., Riccobene, E., Rinzivillo, S.: Using spin to generate tests from ASM specifications. In: Börger, E., Gargantini, A., Riccobene, E. (eds.) ASM 2003. LNCS, vol. 2589, pp. 263–277. Springer, Heidelberg (2003)
19. Grindal, M., Offutt, J., Andler, S.F.: Combination testing strategies: a survey. Softw. Test, Verif. Reliab. 15(3), 167–199 (2005)
20. Hartman, A.: IBM intelligent test case handler: Whitch
21. Hartman, A., Raskin, L.: Problems and algorithms for covering arrays. DMATH: Discrete Mathematics 284(1-3), 149–156 (2004)
22. Hnich, B., Prestwich, S.D., Selensky, E., Smith, B.M.: Constraint models for the covering test problem. Constraints 11(2-3), 199–219 (2006)
23. Kuhn, D.R., Okum, V.: Pseudo-exhaustive testing for software. In: SEW 2006: IEEE/NASA Software Engineering Workshop, vol. 0, pp. 153–158. IEEE Computer Society Press, Los Alamitos (2006)
24. Kuhn, D.R., Reilly, M.J.: An investigation of the applicability of design of experiments to software testing. In: 27th NASA/IEEE Software Engineering workshop, pp. 91–95. IEEE Computer Society, Los Alamitos (2002)
25. Kuhn, D.R., Wallace, D.R., Gallo, A.M.: Software fault interactions and implications for software testing. IEEE Trans. Software Eng. 30(6), 418–421 (2004)
26. Lott, C., Jain, A., Dalal, S.: Modeling requirements for combinatorial software testing. In: A-MOST 2005: Proceedings of the 1st international workshop on Advances in model-based testing, pp. 1–7. ACM Press, New York (2005)
27. Pairwise web site, http://www.pairwise.org/
28. Sherwood, G.B.: Optimal and near-optimal mixed covering arrays by column expansion. Discrete Mathematics 308(24), 6022–6035 (2008)
29. Smith, B.D., Feather, M.S., Muscettola, N.: Challenges and methods in validating the remote agent planner. In: Breckenridge, C. (ed.) Fifth International conference on Artificial Intelligence Planning Systems (AIPS) (2000)
30. TestCover tool, http://www.testcover.com/
31. Walsh, T.: SAT v CSP. In: Dechter, R. (ed.) CP 2000. LNCS, vol. 1894, pp. 441–456. Springer, Heidelberg (2000)
32. Wong, W.E., Horgan, J.R., Mathur, A.P., Pasquini, A.: Test set size minimization and fault detection effectiveness: A case study in a space application. Journal of Systems and Software 48(2), 79–89 (1999)
33. Yilmaz, C., Cohen, M.B., Porter, A.A.: Covering arrays for efficient fault characterization in complex configuration spaces. IEEE Trans. Software Eng. 32(1), 20–34 (2006)

Incorporating Historical Test Case Performance Data and Resource Constraints into Test Case Prioritization

Yalda Fazlalizadeh, Alireza Khalilian,
Mohammad Abdollahi Azgomi, and Saeed Parsa

Iran University of Science and Technology, Tehran, Iran
{ya_alizadeh,khalilian}@comp.iust.ac.ir,
{azgomi,parsa}@iust.ac.ir

Abstract. Software regression testing occurs continuously during the software development process in order to detect faults as early as possible. Growing size of test suites on one hand and resource constraints on the other hand, necessitates the test case prioritization process. Test case prioritization techniques schedule test cases for regression testing in an order that increases the chances of early detection of faults. Some prior techniques used the notion of history-based test case prioritization. In this paper, we present a new approach for prioritization using historical test case performance data which considers time and resource constraints. This approach directly calculates the priority of each test case using historical information from the previous executions of the test case. The results of applying our approach to Siemens suite and Space program are also presented. Our results present interesting insights into the effectiveness of the proposed approach in terms of faster fault detection.

Keywords: Software regression test, test case prioritization, history-based prioritization, historical fault detection.

1 Introduction

Changing the software to correct faults or add new functionality can cause existing functionality to regress, introducing new faults. To avoid such defects, one can retest software after modification, a task commonly known as *regression testing* [1]. Regression testing typically involves the re-running of all test cases [2], [3] and it is often costly and sometimes even infeasible due to time and resource constraints. Hence, such a technique is considered as one of the most expensive tasks in software maintenance activities [1].

To reduce the cost of regression testing, various techniques have been proposed [3]. One technique is selecting all or a portion of the test suite to execute. This technique is referred to as *regression test selection* (RTS) [4] and can be very costly. Another approach is *test case prioritization*, which is one of the main techniques used to address the problem of regression testing. The goal of test case prioritization is to execute important test cases with respect to some criterion, at first, in order to maximize a score function [5]. This technique is commonly used to increase fault detection

C. Dubois (Ed.): TAP 2009, LNCS 5668, pp. 43–57, 2009.

rate as far as possible. It schedules the test cases based on certain criteria and then run them in the specified order according to time and resource limitations.

The problem of finding optimal execution ordering for test cases is basically NP-hard and does not have any deterministic solution [6]. Thus, prioritization techniques are necessarily heuristic and produce sub-optimal results.

Currently, most prioritization techniques are memoryless and are based only on the analysis of source code and test case profiling information taken from the current and immediately preceding software versions. These techniques ignore historical test case performance data and commonly take a one-time testing model for software regression testing. Whereas software regression testing is continuous and long life [7], and its best model is consecutive execution of test suite after each change occurs in current version of the software. To address this problem, history-based prioritization was introduced in [7] which incorporates the notion of memoryful regression testing. The weakness of this approach is that it considers only the last execution of test cases, especially in a binary manner (i.e. to execute or not) is used to calculate the selection probability of test cases.

The main contribution of this paper is to present a new equation to compute the priority of test cases in each session of regression testing. The proposed equation considers the environment time and resource constraints and incorporates three factors: historical fault detection effectiveness, each test case's execution history in regression test and finally the last priority assigned to the test case. We have also conducted empirical studies to evaluate the performance of the proposed equation.

The rest of the paper is organized as follows. In section 2, a brief description of the test case prioritization problem and existing history-based prioritization are discussed. In section 3 the proposed approach is presented. Section 4 presents an empirical study of the proposed approach. Finally, conclusions and future work are mentioned in section 5.

2   Background and Related Work

2.1   Test Case Prioritization

Test case prioritization problem [8] was first introduced by Wong et al. in 1997 as a flexible method of software regression testing. Their technique first selects test cases based on modified code coverage and then prioritizes them. Research in this context, has been followed by Rothermel, Elbaum and other researchers [5], [6], [9], [10], [11], [12], [13], [14] which resulted in various techniques for test case prioritization. The formal definition of this problem, which has been widely accepted in the literature [5], can be expressed as follows:

Given: T, a test suite, PT, the set of permutations of T, and f, a function from PT to the real numbers.

Problem: Find $T' \subseteq T$ such that $(\forall T'' \in PT)\ (T'' \neq T')\ [(f(T') \geq f(T''))]$.

In this definition, PT represents the set of all possible prioritizations (orderings) of T, and f is a function that, applies to any such ordering, yields an award value for that ordering [5].

Most of prioritization techniques are code-based, relying on information relating test cases to the coverage of code elements [3], [5], [9], [14]. Other non coverage based techniques in the literature include fault-exposing potential prioritization [5], model-based prioritization [12], history-based test prioritization [7], [15] and the incorporation of varying test costs and fault severities into test case prioritization [14], [16].

2.2 History-Based Test Case Prioritization

History-based test case prioritization is defined in [7] as follows: given test suite T, and T' be a subset of all test cases $(T' \subseteq T)$, $P_{tc,t}(H_{tc}, \alpha)$ is selection probability of each test case tc in time t, and H_{tc} is a set of t time ordered observations $\{h_1, h_2, ..., h_t\}$ drawn from the previous runs of tc which shows each test case's execution history up to now. According to this definition, selection probability of each test case in T' based upon execution history, is defined as follows:

$$P_0 = h_k$$
$$P_k = \alpha h_k + (1 - \alpha) Pk_{-1} . \qquad 0 \leq \alpha < 1 \quad k \geq 1 \tag{1}$$

In this equation, α is a smoothing constant for weighting individual history observations, which is set as close to 0 as possible in the experiments [7]. Based on different definitions of H_{tc} in (1), history-based prioritization can be performed in the following ways:

Execution history. For each test session i which tc is executed in it, h_i takes value 0 for next selection probability, otherwise it takes value 1. In other words, after execution of high priority test cases in a session, they have lower selection probabilities in next sessions. Thus, instead of discarding low priority test cases in the constraint environments, it will cycle through all test cases over multiple sessions.

The issue with this definition is that the execution of effective test cases with respect to fault detection weakens their selection probability the same as other test cases and their effectiveness does not have any effect on increasing their priority and faster selection in next executions.

Demonstrated fault detection effectiveness. For each testing session i, which tc exposes fault(s) in it (cause program to fail), h_i takes the value 1, otherwise takes value 0. This definition of H_{tc}, restricts execution of those test cases which rarely, if ever, reveal faults.

Coverage of program entities. Program entities include statement, path, function, def-use pair, etc. In this case, higher priority values are given to those test cases which cover functions that are infrequently covered in past testing sessions. This definition of H_{tc}, limits the possibility that any function goes unexecuted for long period of time.

Notice that only one of the mentioned definitions of H_{tc} could be used for test case execution history in equation (1) in order to determine test cases' selection probability.

Using h_k to determine selection probability, especially only with two values 0 and 1, and only based on the recent execution of each test case, is not an appropriate criterion to provide an execution history for the test cases. Furthermore, increasing test case selection probability only based on whether or not a test case has been executed in recent execution, or if it has exposed fault in recent execution, will not produce efficient ordering for test cases in history-based prioritization.

In a recent study [15], history based test case selection and cost-cognizant prioritization technique [11], were combined to form an approach for cost-cognizant history-based test case prioritization. This technique uses historical information of exposed faults' severity and cost, which is kept in a repository, for estimating current faults' severity and cost. Empirical studies showed that historical value-based approach is more effective than most of existing code-based approaches.

3 The Proposed Approach

There are some factors, which are effective in determining test case priority in next selections. One of these factors is test case fault detection performance in number of times it has been executed in successive tests. We assume that in each new regression test session, some test case in ordered test suite have not been executed because of time and resource constraints. For example, consider two test cases, tc_A and tc_B in a test suite, such that tc_A leads to 3 program fails in 20 sessions of execution and tc_B leads to 9 program fails in 18 sessions of its execution. We observe that in spite of the number of executions of tc_A is more than tc_B, historical performance shows that tc_B performs about 35 percent better than tc_A with respect to fault detection. Thus, it must have greater priority with respect to tc_A.

This example shows that we should not take the *number of regression test sessions the test case executes* and the *number of test sessions it reveals fault(s)* separately. But also these two factors together have effect on test cases' historical performance as a single factor. Therefore, assuming kth execution of regression test which means that the software has been modified k times, each leads to a new version of software, let fc_k be the number of times that the execution of test case tc fails and let ec_k be the number of tc executions up to now, then we can show the relation between each test case's priority with its fault detection performance in kth execution as follows:

$$PR_k \approx HFDE_k . \tag{2}$$

$$HFDE_k = \begin{cases} 0 & \text{if } tc \text{ has not been executed yet} \\ \dfrac{fc_k}{ec_k} & \text{otherwise} \end{cases} \tag{3}$$

$$fc_k = \sum_{i=1}^{k-1} f_i . \quad f_i = \begin{cases} 1 & \text{if } tc \text{ has revealed } fault(s) \text{ in test session } i \\ 0 & \text{otherwise} \end{cases} \tag{4}$$

$$ec_k = \sum_{i=1}^{k-1} e_i . \quad e_i = \begin{cases} 1 & \text{if } tc \text{ has been executed in test session } i \\ 0 & \text{otherwise} \end{cases} \tag{5}$$

The equations (2) and (3) show that the PR_k is *proportionate* to the fc_k/ec_k. In other words, for each test case in each test session, historical performance is the proportion of the test case program fails to the number of its executions up to now. Remember that program fails in this ratio indicates the number of sessions in which the test case execution causes to fault revealing. We call this ratio *historical fault detection effectiveness.*

Another effective factor in priority is a period of time that a test case is not being executed. In other words, we would like to ensure that after some sessions, all test cases in the test suite will be executed and it will cycle through all test cases over multiple sessions, so that all faults will be revealed.

Based on what was described, we define h_k in the kth execution as follows:

$$h_k = \begin{cases} 0 & \text{if tc has been executed in test session } k-1 \\ h_{k-1}+1 & \text{otherwise} \end{cases} \qquad (6)$$

Actually h_k factor in equation (6) performs similar to a *counter*. In the context of operating systems and process scheduling, there is a known problem which is *process starvation*. If during the execution of various processes in a system, a process has not been selected for execution for a long time, the job scheduler may take the number of times the process has not been executed as *process age* and increases its priority. To do this, the job scheduler assigns a counter to each of the processes. The factor h_k also performs the same job for the test cases. We will call it *test case execution history*.

Based on what was described, there is a relationship between test case priority and its execution history in the kth execution:

$$PR_k \approx h_k . \qquad (7)$$

Each time a test case is not executed, its execution history will be increased by one. Once the test case is executed, execution history becomes 0 and the operation is repeated as well. In this manner, we can ensure that none of the test cases has remained unexecuted for a long time, and the corresponding faults will be revealed.

Finally, the third factor, shown by empirical studies, is the recent priority of each test case in each test suite during past executions of the regression test. Then we have:

$$PR_k \approx PR_{k-1} . \qquad (8)$$

There are some reasons using this factor: First, it causes to *smoother* selection of test cases in successive executions of regression test. This limits *severe changes* in selection of executing test cases in test suite in each run with respect to the previous run. Second, in cases where the historical fault detection effectiveness of the test cases and their execution history are the same, we should consider another factor to establish a proper priority between them.

We define PR_0 for each test case as the percentage of code coverage of the test case and thereby various control-flow and data-flow coverage criteria can be used. Thus, the influence of test case code coverage may propagate in next prioritizations due to recursion of the equation. In code-based prioritization techniques researchers empirically showed that the code coverage of each test case properly indicates its ability with respect to fault detection [3], [5], [13]. In fact, it is a wise idea to suppose that test cases that cover more software code components are more likely to reveal faults than test cases which have less code coverage [5], [10], [14]. Thus, they should take higher priorities. It is worth to say that our proposed test case prioritization approach which performs based on the history of test case fault detection performance, could be also considered as a coverage-based approach.

Based on the equations (2), (7) and (8) we can write the equation of each test case priority in the kth execution as follows:

$$PR_0 = Percentage\ of\ code\ coverage\ of\ the\ test\ case$$

$$PR_k = \alpha\,h_k + \beta\,PR_{k-1} + \gamma\,HFDE_k\ .\quad 0 \le \alpha,\beta,\gamma < 1 \quad k \ge 1 \tag{9}$$

Changing α, β and γ in equation (9), which are smoothing constants, we can control the effect of mentioned factors in test case prioritization.

Constant α must be smaller than the other two constants (β and γ coefficients) and so close to 0. It is also preferable to set the β and γ coefficients to values between 0.5 and 1. This is because h_k increases one unit per time according to whether or not the test case executes. Moreover, fc_k/ec_k and PR_{k-1} are numbers between 0 and 1. So, it is necessary to control the effect of h_k against those two factors, such that it has not excessive effect in prioritization and do not mask other factors effect by mistake.

Unlike P_k in equation (1) that is the selection probability of each test case, PR_k in (9) is the test case priority in kth execution.

Considering test time and resource constraints the sufficient number of test cases will be executed beginning from highest priorities. Fig. 1 depicts an overview of the proposed history-based test case prioritization approach. The following explains the figure.

- In the proposed approach, each test case's demonstrated fault detection effectiveness, test case execution history and priority values are stored in the historical information repository.
- To conduct regression testing, the stored information is used to calculate the current priority of each test case in the test suite. These priority values are used to reorder the suite for each regression test session.

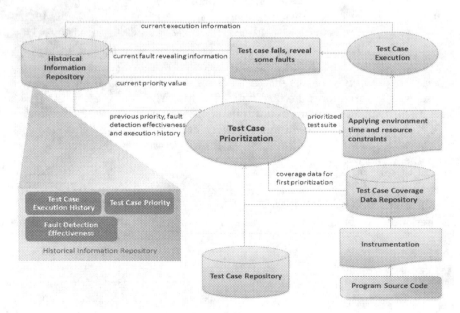

Fig. 1. Overview of our history-based test case prioritization approach

- Prioritizing test cases in the test suite, testers may face resource and time constraints when executing the whole prioritized suite.
- If a test case executes, its number of executions increases by one. Moreover, in each regression test session, the program fail count for those test cases which would fail is being increased. Also the value of execution history of not executed test cases in the test suite is being increased to help their faster selection in the next regression test sessions.

To illustrate the proposed approach's functionality, we study a simple program and its test suite as an example (Fig. 2). This program was adopted from [24] by little changes. To test the program, a branch coverage test suite with enough test cases to cover all branches in the program, is considered. This suite includes 8 test cases. The information about test cases and their coverage are displayed in Table 1. The column labeled *input* shows test cases of the program in Fig. 2. Each B^T_i and B^F_i in table columns, show *true* or *false* evaluation of branch *i*. Marked cells also show test cases' coverage in terms of *true* or *false* evaluation of a specific branch. Notice that the branch coverage is stronger than the statement coverage in which, both *true* and *false* states of all branches should be exercised.

```
B1:  if (a>0)              B3:  if (c>0)
2:           x=2;          B4:       if (d>0)
3:      else               B5:           if (e>0)
4:           begin         12:               output (1/ (b+1));
5:               x=5;      13:           else
B2:          if (b>0)      14:               output (1/(y-4));
6:               y=x+1;    15:           endif
7:           else          16:       else
8:               y=x-1;    17:           output (1/(x-5));
9:           endif         18:       endif
10:  end                   19:  else
11:  end                   20:       output (1/(x-5));
                           21:  endif
```

Fig. 2. A sample program

Table 1. A branch coverage adequate test suite

Test case	Input(a,b,c,d)	B^T_1	B^F_1	B^T_2	B^F_2	B^T_3	B^F_3	B^T_4	B^F_4	B^T_5	B^F_5	Branch coverage	Fault may detect
1	(1,1,-1,0,0)	X					X					20%	-
2	(-1,1,1,-1,0)		X	X		X			X			40%	17
3	(-1,1,-1,0,-1)		X	X			X					30%	20
4	(-1,1,1,1,1)		X	X		X		X		X		50%	-
5	(-1,-1,1,1,1)		X		X	X		X		X		50%	12
6	(1,-1,-1,-1,-1)	X					X					20%	-
7	(-1,1,-1,1,0)		X	X			X					30%	20
8	(0,0,1,1,-1)		X		X	X		X			X	50%	14

Table 2. Calculated values for test cases' priority in each regression test session

Regression test session	Detected faults	Test case priority (L to R)	tc_1	tc_2	tc_3	tc_4	tc_5	tc_6	tc_7	tc_8
1	14,12	[4,5,8,2,3,7,1,6]	0.2	0.4	0.3	0.5	0.5	0.2	0.3	0.5
2	17	[5,8,2,3,7,1,6,4]	0.24	0.28	0.26	0.1	0.8	0.24	0.26	0.8
3	-	[2,5,8,3,7,1,6,4]	0.448	0.756	0.452	0.22	0.51	0.448	0.452	0.51
4	20	[3,7,1,6,2,4,5,8]	0.689	0.501	0.690	0.444	0.335	0.689	0.690	0.335

The results of prioritization through program in Fig. 2 have been shown in Table 2. The eight right side columns of the table show calculated values by equation (**9**) for each test case in regression test.

The left side columns show regression test sessions, the number of lines including the faulty code, and execution orders for test cases, correspondingly. These execution orderings are according to priority values of test cases in each row. At the first test session, each test case's priority is the percentage of branch coverage of that test case. We assume that only a fraction of the suite could be executed (here about 40% of the test cases). Each time, the executed test cases are written in bold italic form. At first, test cases 4, 5 and 8 are executed and lead to reveal faults in lines 12 and 14. Notice that, in spite of executing test case 4, it has not revealed any faults. Thus, in the next test session, fc_1 for test case 4 is 0 and for test cases 5 and 8, is 1. Meanwhile, ec_1 for these three test cases is 1. For other test cases which have not been executed, both fc_1 and ec_1 are 0. On the other hand, the value of h_1 (execution history) is 0 for the executed test cases and 1 for other test cases. In the next test session, new priority values are calculated based on these information and test cases are prioritized and then executed on the program. We observe that the priorities of the test cases 6, 1, 7 and 3 which have not been executed in the first session have been increased. Moreover, test case 4 which has been executed in the previous session, but did not detect any fault, degrades in priority. In this session, test cases 5, 8, and 2 are executed and ec_2 for these test cases increases by one; but only test case 2 could reveal fault in line 17.

Thus, fc_2 increases just for test case 2 and holds the value of fc_1 for other test cases. Also the value of h_2 is 0 for executed test cases and increases 1 unit for unexecuted test cases. By changing priorities in the third test session, test case 2 gains the highest priority and test cases 2, 5 and 8 are executed. Test cases 3, 7, 1, 6, and 4 remain unexecuted. As other sessions, test case priorities are calculated for the forth test session. In this session, test cases 3, 7, 1 and 6 have the highest priorities. Although these test cases had lowest branch coverage and have not been executed in sessions 1 through 3, their execution history caused to increase their priorities. Thus, test cases 3, 7, and 1 are executed and finally the fault in line 20 is detected by test case 3.

4   Empirical Studies

In order to evaluate the proposed approach, we conducted empirical studies. These studies include controlled experiment with Siemens suite [17], and a case study using Space [14] program. In this section, we describe these studies. In our experiments, we would like to find the answer to the following questions:

1. Can the proposed test case prioritization technique improve fault detection effectiveness in time and resource constraint environments?
2. What is the effect of considering data-flow or control-flow coverage criteria for initial reordering of test cases and their consequent fault revealing capability?

4.1 Subject Programs

In our experiments, we used eight C programs as subjects (Table 3). Siemens suite includes seven programs in C language which are widely used in other related works, in order to evaluate various prioritization techniques. Siemens contains programs, their associated test pools, test suites for each program and scripts to run each program. Test cases for Siemens programs were generated for different testing objectives which exercise different control-flow and data-flow coverage criteria. For each program, single fault versions of the program have been created in which faults have been seeded by separate teams of programmers. The other empirical study is a case study, which we have done on Space benchmark program. Space is a big program (10KLOC) in C, with real faults which has been developed for the European Space Agency. Space has 38 associated versions, each containing a single fault.

Table 3. Subject programs used in our experiments

Program name	LOC	Faulty versions	Test pool size	Program name	LOC	Faulty versions	Test pool size
tcas	148	41	1608	print-tokens	402	7	4130
totinfo	346	23	1052	print-tokens2	483	10	4115
schedule	299	9	2650	replace	516	32	5542
schedule2	297	10	2710	space	6218	38	13585

4.2 Evaluation Metric and Analysis Tools

APFD (Average Percentage of Fault Detection) metric is used for evaluating test case prioritization techniques. It is the *weighted average percentage of fault detection in test suite lifetime*, and was introduced by Rothermel et al. [3] in 1997 to assess and compare test case prioritization techniques in terms of how quickly faults are revealed during regression testing. Basically APFD metric is calculated as follows:

$$APFD = 1 - \frac{TF_1 + TF_2 + ... + TF_m}{nm} + \frac{1}{2n} . \tag{10}$$

In equation (10), n is the number of test cases and m is the number of existing faults in the software. Each TF_i in this equation shows the place of a test case in ordered suite which first reveals the fault i.

In simple words, the higher APFD value for a prioritization technique, the faster (better) that technique reveals faults during software regression testing [14]. For better insight we usually show the percentage of detected faults versus the executed fraction of test suite, in a diagram. The area under the curve [3], [5], [13] shows the prioritized test suite's average percentage of fault detected in a session of a regression test.

We used SAS 9.1.3 [18] in our experiments to create box plots. Box plot diagrams are used to visualize the empirical results in test case prioritization studies. Using these diagrams, we can statistically analyze results and observe any differences between experiments [19].

4.3 Experiment Setup and Results

Our experiments follow a setup similar to that used by Rothermel et al. [14]. As mentioned above, each subject program has several single fault versions. For evaluating prioritization techniques, one needs versions with varying numbers of faults for each program. To this end, a set of multi-fault versions composed of non-interfering single faults (all faults that can exist simultaneously), have been created [14]. These faults are based on programmers' experience about common faults and therefore they are closer to real faults.

In our experiments, we have compared results of the proposed prioritization technique to the random ordering approach as it is common in previous studies [5], [14]. We randomly selected 29 multi-fault versions of each program in order to simulate 29 sessions of regression testing to study the proposed approach's performance during continuous executions. The 29 versions, is selected because it is the minimum number of non-interfering multi-fault versions that can be generated using single fault versions [14]. For each version, we have executed the proposed approach on 1000 branch coverage adequate test suites. α, β and γ were set to 0.04, 0.7, and 0.7, respectively. To balance individual factors' effect in test case prioritization α must be smaller than the two other coefficients since h_k increases one unit each time a test case does not execute. At the end of each test session, APFD values are calculated for the prioritized test cases.

We assumed that only a fraction of total prioritized test suite (about fifty percent) could be executed due to limitations in testing resources. Thus, this approach can be used in resource constraint testing environments, which leads to savings in resources.

For representing the efficiency of the proposed approach, we have used box plot diagram which is an ordinary way in empirical studies [3], [5], [6], [13], [14] in this area. Using box plot diagrams, we have represented the average amount of fault detection results of prioritizing 1000 branch coverage adequate test suites by the proposed approach versus random ordering approach.

In first set of our experiments (Fig. 3), we set PR_0 for each test case as the percentage of branch coverage of the test case. Branch coverage of test cases was obtained by hand-instrumentation of subjects. In second set of experiments, PR_0 was set as the percentage of all-uses coverage of each test case. We measured the all-uses coverage of test cases using the ATAC tool [21].

To have a general view of the results, we plotted an *all versions* box plot for all programs (Fig. 4). In these box plots, there are 16 plots, each for an individual program and one for each technique. The plots which have the same color compare techniques for an individual program, the left side for the proposed approach and the right side for random ordering.

Since the experiments have been performed on 29 faulty versions as regression test sessions, 29 pairs of box plots have been plotted in each eight diagrams. Fig. 3 shows theses 8 diagrams which indicate *print_tokens*, *print_tokens2*, *schedule*, *schedule2*, *tcas*, *tot_info*, *replace* and *space* from top to bottom. The box plots with same color in each diagram are respected to a specific faulty version of that program. In each same color pairs of box plots, results of APFD by prioritizing 1000 test suites using the proposed approach have been represented in the left side box and the corresponding plot for random ordering approach on the same 1000 test suites have been represented in the right side. This process has been performed for each of the 8 programs, and is displayed in 8 diagrams in Fig. 3. Obviously, the higher the place of the box plot, the faster prioritization technique reveals faults. It can be observed in Fig. 3 that the proposed approach has considerable improvements both in fault detection and stability of the results, for various test suites.

To investigate whether using different coverage criteria to reorder test cases at first session of regression testing, is effective in faster fault detection of test cases, two different coverage criteria were used; Branch coverage, which is a control-flow criterion and all-uses as a data-flow coverage criterion. All-uses coverage is generally considered to be a stronger (more fine-grained) criterion than branch coverage [20]. The results of applying these criteria have been shown in the Fig. 3 and Fig. 4. Due to lack of enough space, box plots for the all-uses criterion for *each program* have not been shown. As can be seen, using these criteria, our prioritization approach could produce reasonable orderings which lead to faster fault detection of test cases. This shows that the proposed approach is capable of prioritizing test cases in the constraint environments using historical test case performance data, such that executed test cases can detect software faults as fast as possible.

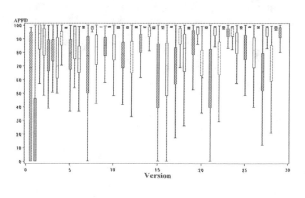

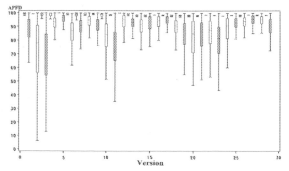

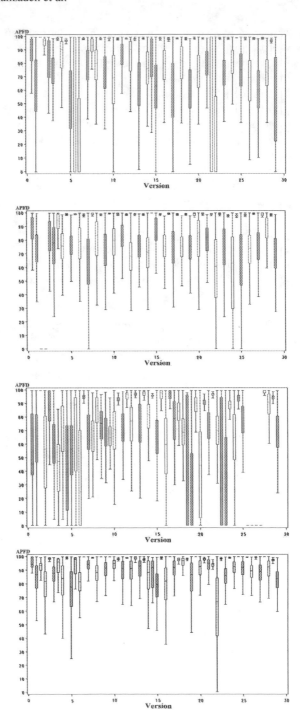

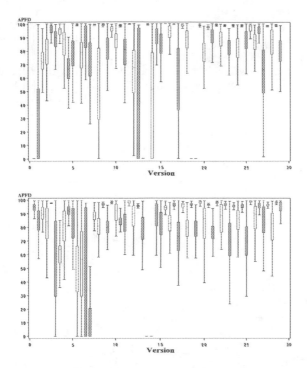

Fig. 3. Box plot diagrams to compare the proposed approach versus random ordering for each program using percent of branch coverage as initial ordering of test cases

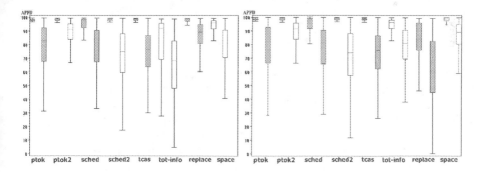

Fig. 4. All versions in each program using branch coverage (left side) and all-uses coverage (right side) as initial ordering of test cases

4.4 Threats to Validity

In this section, we describe the potential threats to validity of our study and how we can limit these threats.

Threats to construct validity arise when measurement instruments do not adequately capture the concepts they are supposed to measure [6]. In our studies, measurements for the rate of fault detection and APFD values are accurate. But it is not the only metric for measuring the rate of fault detection. Recently, $APFD_c$ has been proposed [10] which incorporates different test costs and fault severities that is not considered by APFD.

Threats to internal validity are influences that can affect the dependent variables without the researchers' knowledge and thereby affect any supposition of a causal relationship between the phenomena underlying the independent and dependent variables [6]. The most important internal threat to our study is instrumentation of programs' source code. To this end, we used ATAC tool to measure the all-uses, but branch coverage of test cases obtained by hand-instrumentation of the source code. To ensure from correctness of instrumentation, branch coverage of the test cases were verified. Another issue is the composition of the test suites. To limit this threat, we used test suites from [17] which were used in the previous studies [6], [14].

Threats to external validity are conditions that limit generalization from the results [6]. In our study, the most important threat is how subject programs can be representative of real programs. Siemens programs are small programs (average 350 LOC) and their faults are hand-seeded. Space program is a real and big program (about 11KLOC), but it is only one of such a program we used. The faulty versions in Siemens suite are single fault versions, but we needed multi-fault versions. Thus, we used faulty versions with random number of non-interfering faults. But in practice, there may be different patterns of fault occurrence.

5 Conclusions

In this paper, we proposed a new history-based approach for prioritizing test cases. Our approach considers time constraints and enormous cost of repeatedly executing all test cases in the regression test. Thus, in this approach only a fraction of the prioritized suite will be executed.

In the proposed approach, three factors are effective to determine the test case execution priority: (1) priority of the test case in previous regression test session, (2) historical demonstrated performance in fault detection during the regression test lifeline, and (3) the duration that each test case has not been executed. This approach directly uses the above three factors in prioritization. Empirical studies show considerable improvements in fault detection rate which is measured using APFD metric.

In future, we plan to setup complementary empirical studies by programs with real faults in order to study the performance of this approach in real environments more precisely. Further studies should be done using other available benchmarks. In this paper we have used C programs; however, we are going to setup experiments using Java subjects in order to investigate the proposed technique for object-oriented programs.

References

1. Mirarab, S.: A Bayesian Framework for Software Regression Testing. Master of applied science thesis, Waterloo, Ontario, Canadia (2008)
2. Burnstein, I.: Practical software testing: a process-oriented approach. Springer, New York (2003)

3. Rothermel, G., Untch, R.H., Chu, C., Harrold, M.J.: Test case prioritization: an empirical study. In: Proc. IEEE Int. Conf. on Software Maintenanc, Oxford, England, pp. 179–188 (1999)
4. Rothermel, G., Harrold, M.J.: A Safe, Efficient Regression Test Selection Technique. Proc. ACM Transactions on Software Engineering & Methodology 6(2), 173–210 (1997)
5. Rothermel, G., Untch, R.H., Chu, C., Harrold, M.J.: Prioritizing Test Cases for Regression Testing. Proc. IEEE Transactions on Software Engineering, 102–112 (2001)
6. Li, Z., Harmanand, M., Hierons, R.: Search Algorithms for Regression Test Case Prioritization. Proc. IEEE Transactions on Software Engineering 33, 225–237 (2007)
7. Kim, J.M., Porter, A.: A History-Based Test Prioritization Technique for Regression Testing in Resource Constrained Environment. In: Proc. 24th Int'l. Conf. Software Engineering, pp. 119–129 (2002)
8. Wong, W.E., Horgan, J.R., Londonm, S., Agrawal, H.: A study of effective regression testing in practice. In: Proc. 8th Int'l. Symp. Software Reliability Engineering, pp. 230–238 (1997)
9. Malishevsky, G., Elbaum, S., Rothermel, G., Kanduri, S.: Selecting a Cost-Effective Test Case Prioritization Technique. In: Proc. Software Quality Control, vol. 12, pp. 185–210 (2004)
10. Malishevsky, G., Ruthruff, J.R., Rothermel, G., Elbaum, S.: Cost-cognizant test case prioritization. Tech. Rep. Department of Computer Science and Engineering, Nebraska, Lincoln, TR-UNL-CSE-2006-0004 (March 2006)
11. Srivastava, P.R.: Test Case prioritization. Journal of Theoretical and Applied Information Technology (JATIT), BITS Pilani, India-333031
12. Korel, B., Koutsogiannakis, G., Tahat, L.H.: Model-based test prioritization heuristic methods and their evaluation. In: Proc. 3rd Int'l. Workshop on Advances in Model-Based Testing, London, UK (July 2007)
13. Elbaum, S., Malishevsky, A.G., Rothermel, G.: Prioritizing test cases for regression testing. In: Proc. 7th Int'l. Syrup. Software Testing and Analysis, August 2000, pp. 102–112 (2000)
14. Elbaum, S., Malishevsky, A.G., Rothermel, G.: Test Case Prioritization: A Family of Empirical Studies. Proc. IEEE Transactions on Software Engineering 28(2), 159–182 (2002)
15. Park, H., Ryu, H., Baik, J.: Historical Value-Based Approach for Cost-Cognizant Test Case Prioritization to Improve the Effectiveness of Regression Testing. In: 2nd Int'l. Conf. Secure System Integration and Reliability Improvement, Japan, pp. 39–46 (to appear, 2008)
16. Elbaum, S., Malishevsky, A.G., Rothermel, G.: Incorporating varying test costs and fault severities into test case prioritization. In: Proc. 23rd Int. Conf. on Software Engineering. IEEE Computer Society, Toronto (2001)
17. Rothermel, G., Elbaum, S., Kinneer, A., Do, H.: Software-artifact infrastructure repository, http://www.c-se.unl.edu/~galileo/sir
18. SAS 9.1.3 Documentation, SAS/GRAPH 9.1 Reference, http://support.sas.com/documentation/onlinedoc/91pdf/index_9 13.html
19. http://en.wikipedia.org/wiki/Box_plot
20. Jeffrey, D., Gupta, N.: Improving Fault Detection Capability by Selectively Retaining Test Cases during Test Suite Reduction. Source IEEE Transactions on Software Engineering archive, 108–123 (2007)
21. Horgan, J.R., London, S.A.: ATAC: A Data Flow Coverage Testing Tool for C. In: Proc. Symp. Assessment of Quality Software Development Tools, May 1992, pp. 2–10 (1992)

Complementary Criteria for Testing Temporal Logic Properties

Gordon Fraser* and Franz Wotawa

Institute for Software Technology
Graz University of Technology
Inffeldgasse 16b/2
A-8010 Graz, Austria
{fraser,wotawa}@ist.tugraz.at

Abstract. While traditional testing can give evidence that an implementation conforms to a specification there is no guarantee that the implementation therefore also satisfies user requirements. Consequently, it is useful to derive test cases also from requirement properties. In this paper we introduce two new test criteria to measure adequacy of existing test suites and to derive test cases with regard to requirements formalized in linear temporal logic (LTL). The first criterion is complementary to existing criteria for requirement properties in that it focuses on cases where literals in a property should not affect the outcome of the property. The second criterion uses mutation to measure the sensitivity of a test suite with regard to the implemented requirements. In addition to coverage measurement these criteria can also be used to automatically create coverage adequate test suites with a model checker. The results of a case study illustrate the feasibility of the new criteria and demonstrate that they complement existing criteria.

1   Introduction

Software testing is an important but complex task, and many different techniques have been proposed to automate certain parts of this process. Formal specifications and models can be used to automatically derive test cases and also serve as test oracles. Traditionally, these techniques derive test cases or measure the quality of existing test cases based on the structure of the specification or an automaton interpretation, but it is also important to test with regard to requirement properties.

While testing with regard to structural coverage of a specification can give evidence that an implementation conforms to such a specification it is desirable to

---

* The research herein is partially conducted within the competence network Softnet Austria (www.soft-net.at) and funded by the Austrian Federal Ministry of Economics (bm:wa), the province of Styria, the Steirische Wirtschaftsförderungsgesellschaft mbH. (SFG), and the city of Vienna in terms of the center for innovation and technology (ZIT).

also gain confidence in that the implementation satisfies high level user requirements. In order to measure adequacy and derive test cases from requirements these requirements have to be formalized. One particular scenario where this is feasible is when the requirements are formalized using temporal logic.

In this paper we assume that requirements are formalized using Linear Temporal Logic (LTL) [1]. This logic is commonly used by model checkers, which can be used to verify a formal specification against these requirements. There is a previously defined coverage criterion for LTL properties based on vacuity analysis [2], and Unique First Cause coverage (UFC) [3] is a variant of the important modified condition/decision coverage (MCDC) [4] criterion for LTL properties. We define two new criteria based on LTL properties, which serve to supplement the existing criteria:

- PICC: Property Independent Clause Coverage is based on the definition of UFC and the nomenclature given in [5]. PICC is an extension of UFC similar to the way Reinforced Condition/Decision Coverage (RCDC) [6] extends MCDC, in that it focuses on cases where literals in a property should not affect the outcome of the property. Therefore the combination of UFC and PICC could be interpreted as Reinforced UFC (RUFC).
- Property mutation: While mutation has previously been used to derive test cases with model checkers, little work has been presented on applying mutation to requirement properties. We show that mutation can serve as a test criterion for properties, and define new mutation operators for LTL.

Model checkers have also been shown to be useful in order to automatically generate test cases. In particular, any of the above mentioned coverage criteria can be formalized as a set of LTL properties, such that the model checker automatically derives test suites that satisfy the coverage criteria.

This paper is organized as follows: Section 2 introduces Linear Temporal Logic (LTL), which is the logic in which properties are assumed to be specified. The section further describes how test cases are generated with model checkers, which is usually done by formalizing test objectives as LTL properties, and discusses two previously presented coverage criteria for LTL properties that can be used to generate property based test cases. In Section 3 we introduce PICC, which is a modified version of UFC introduced in Section 2. Section 4 considers how mutation can be useful in the context of testing properties. Section 5 evaluates the new and old criteria on a case study model, Section 6 discusses related work, and finally Section 7 concludes the paper.

2 Preliminaries

This section begins with a formal definition of LTL, which is the temporal logic we assume for requirement properties as well as for formalization of test criteria for test case generation and adequacy measurement. We then show how test cases are generated with model checkers, and define coverage based on vacuity analysis [2] and Unique First Cause coverage (UFC) [3], which can be used to both measure and create test cases with model checkers.

2.1   Linear Temporal Logic

The formalism commonly used to describe model checking and to define the semantics of temporal logics is the Kripke structure.

Definition 1 (Kripke Structure). *A Kripke structure K is a tuple $K = (S, S_0, T, L)$, where AP is a countable set of atomic propositions:*

- *S is a finite set of states.*
- *$S_0 \subseteq S$ is an initial state set.*
- *$T \subseteq S \times S$ is a total transition relation, that is, for every $s \in S$ there is a $s' \in S$ such that $(s, s') \in T$.*
- *$L : S \to 2^{AP}$ is a labeling function that maps each state to a set of atomic propositions that hold in this state.*

An infinite execution sequence of this model is a *path*, and a Kripke structure defines all possible paths of a system.

Definition 2 (Path). *A path p of Kripke structure $K = (S, S_0, T, L)$ is a sequence $\langle s_0, s_1, ... \rangle$ such that $\forall\, i \geq 0 : (s_i, s_{i+1}) \in T$.*

Let $Paths(K, s)$ denote the set of paths of Kripke structure K that start in state s. We use $Paths(K)$ as an abbreviation to denote $\{Paths(K, s) \mid s \in S_0\}$.

Temporal logics are modal logics where modalities are given a temporal interpretation. While propositional logic allows reasoning about a system's state, the extension with temporal operators allows reasoning about computation paths or trees. In this paper we consider Linear Temporal Logic (LTL) [1].

An LTL formula consists of atomic propositions, Boolean operators and temporal operators. The operator "$\bigcirc$" refers to the *next* state. E.g., "$\bigcirc\ a$" expresses that a has to be true in the next state. "U" is the *until* operator, where "a U b" means that a has to hold from the current state up to a state where b is true, and such a state has to exist. "$\square$" is the *always* operator, stating that a condition has to hold at all states of a path, and "$\lozenge$" is the *eventually* operator that requires a certain condition to eventually hold at some time in the future. The syntax of LTL is given as follows, where AP denotes the set of atomic propositions:

Definition 3 (LTL Syntax). *The BNF definition of LTL formulas is:*

$$\phi ::= True \mid False \mid a \in AP \mid \neg\,\phi \mid \phi \wedge \phi \mid \phi \vee \phi \mid \phi \to \phi \mid \phi\ \mathsf{U}\ \phi \mid \bigcirc\phi \mid \square\phi \mid \lozenge\phi$$

A property ϕ satisfied by path π of model K is denoted as $K, \pi \models \phi$, which is also abbreviated as $\pi \models \phi$ if K is obvious from the context. A path π of model K violating property ϕ is denoted as $K, \pi \not\models \phi$ or $\pi \not\models \phi$. The semantics of LTL is expressed for infinite paths of a Kripke structure. π^i denotes the suffix of the path π starting from the i-th state, and π_i denotes the i-th state of the path π, with $i \in \mathbb{N}_0$. The initial state of a path π is π_0.

Definition 4 (LTL Semantics). *Satisfaction of LTL formulas by a path* $\pi \in$ *Paths(K) of a Kripke Structure* $K = (S, S_0, T, L)$ *is inductively defined as follows, where* $a \in AP$:

$$\pi \models True \qquad\qquad for\ all\ \pi \tag{1}$$

$$\pi \not\models False \qquad\qquad for\ all\ \pi \tag{2}$$

$$\pi \models a \qquad iff \qquad a \in L(\pi_0) \tag{3}$$

$$\pi \models \neg\phi \qquad iff \qquad \pi \not\models \phi \tag{4}$$

$$\pi \models \phi_1 \wedge \phi_2 \qquad iff \qquad \pi \models \phi_1 \wedge \pi \models \phi_2 \tag{5}$$

$$\pi \models \phi_1 \vee \phi_2 \qquad iff \qquad \pi \models \phi_1 \vee \pi \models \phi_2 \tag{6}$$

$$\pi \models \phi_1 \rightarrow \phi_2 \qquad iff \qquad \pi \not\models \phi_1 \vee \pi \models \phi_2 \tag{7}$$

$$\pi \models \phi_1 \ U\ \phi_2 \qquad iff \qquad \exists i \in \mathbb{N}_0 : \pi^i \models \phi_2 \wedge \forall\, 0 \le j < i : \pi^j \models \phi_1 \tag{8}$$

$$\pi \models \bigcirc\phi \qquad iff \qquad \pi^1 \models \phi \tag{9}$$

$$\pi \models \Box\phi \qquad iff \qquad \forall j \in \mathbb{N}_0 : \pi^j \models \phi \tag{10}$$

$$\pi \models \Diamond\phi \qquad iff \qquad \exists j \in \mathbb{N}_0 : \pi^j \models \phi \tag{11}$$

2.2   Test Case Generation with Model Checkers

In general, model checking [7] describes the process of determining whether an automaton model satisfies a temporal logic property. One of the most useful features of model checkers in practice is their ability to create counterexamples to illustrate how properties are violated. Under certain constraints (e.g., we assume that the system under test and its specification are deterministic) such counterexample sequences can be interpreted as test cases.

A counterexample returned by a model checker is a finite sequence of states. In this paper, we assume that a *test case* is also a sequence of states, while its interpretation depends on the type of system under test. For example, in reactive systems each state represents input and output values serving as test data and test oracle: For each state, test data is provided as input to the system under test and the returned outputs are compared to the expected output values to derive a verdict. A finite counterexample can also represent an infinite path if it contains a loopback state (i.e., it is a lasso-shaped sequence). To get a finite test case the lasso needs to be unfolded; we refer to Tan et al. [2], who describe truncation strategies to create finite test cases from lasso-shaped sequences. The length of a test case is defined as the number of states it consists of. A *test suite* is a set of test cases, and its size is the number of test cases it consists of.

Automated test case generation requires formalization of the test objective (e.g., satisfaction of a coverage criterion), which can be seen as a set of test requirements (e.g., one test requirement for each coverable item). Each test requirement can be formalized as a temporal logical *test predicate*.

Definition 5 (Test predicate). *A test predicate* ϕ *is a temporal logical predicate that is satisfied by a test case* $t = \langle s_0, ...s_n \rangle$ *if there is* $0 \le i < n$ *such that* $t^i \models \phi$.

A test predicate is *infeasible* if it cannot be satisfied by any possible test case for a given model. A coverage criterion is a rule for generating test predicates, and a test suite T satisfies a coverage criterion if and only if for each feasible test predicate ϕ there exists a test $t \in T$ such that $t \models \phi$. To quantify the degree of coverage we use the percentage of satisfied test predicates as *coverage value*.

Model checking allows generation of finite paths for logical predicates, either showing satisfaction (*witness*) or violation (*counterexample*). For test case generation counterexample generation is exploited in most cases because it is supported by all model checking techniques. In order to force the model checker to generate a counterexample the test predicates are formalized in a negated fashion, such that the counterexample satisfies the original test predicate. Such properties are known as *trap properties*:

Definition 6 (Trap property). *A trap property τ for test predicate ϕ is a temporal logic property, such that any counterexample t to τ, i.e., $t \not\models \tau$ is a test case that satisfies ϕ.*

In the simplest case, a trap property for test predicate ϕ can be derived by negating ϕ, or by stating that ϕ is never satisfied (**AG** $\neg\phi$), but there are many scenarios when further constraints are necessary (e.g., postfix sequences).

In the past, coverage criteria have for example been defined for structural coverage of specifications, mutation testing, or combinatorial testing. One of the main strengths of testing with model checkers is that once a framework has been created it is easy to apply any of these techniques or combine several at the same time. For a detailed overview of testing with model checkers we refer to [8].

2.3   Vacuity Based Coverage

A well known problem in model checking is vacuous satisfaction: A property is vacuously satisfied if the model checker reports that the property is satisfied regardless of whether the model really fulfills what the specifier originally had in mind or not. For example, the property $\square(x \rightarrow \bigcirc y)$ is vacuously satisfied by any model where x is never true. Vacuity is an indication of a problem in either the model or the property, and techniques to detect vacuity have been proposed (e.g., [9,10,11]). In the context of software testing these techniques have been used to define a coverage criterion [2] that requires that properties are exercised in 'interesting' (i.e., non vacuous) ways.

The general strategy to detect vacuity employed in [9,10,11] is to replace parts of a property and see if this has any effects on the result of the verification. In order to detect vacuity it is sufficient to replace a sub-formula ϕ of property f with *True* or *False* [10], depending on the *polarity* of ϕ in f. The polarity of a sub-formula ψ is positive, if it is nested in an even number of negations in f, otherwise it is negative, and $pol(\phi)$ is a function such that $pol(\phi) = False$ if ϕ has positive polarity in f and $pol(\phi) = True$ otherwise. The replacement of sub-formula ϕ with ψ in formula f is denoted as $f[\phi|\psi]$.

Tan et al. [2] introduced *property coverage*, which we denote as *vacuity based coverage* (VC) in this paper in order to better distinguish it from other property based criteria. VC requires that for every sub-formula ϕ of a property f (denoted as $\forall \phi \in f$) there exists a test case that non-vacuously satisfies the sub-formula:

Definition 7 (Vacuity Based Coverage [2]). *The following set of test predicates describes coverage of a property f:* $\{\neg f[\phi|\, pol\,(\phi)] \mid \forall \phi \in f\}$.

To turn these test predicates into trap properties a simple negation is sufficient (or equivalently, omitting the negation). A resulting test case is an example for a non-vacuous satisfaction of ϕ in f, and any implementation that passes such a test case cannot satisfy $f[\phi|\, pol\,(\phi)]$. For all property based criteria, if there are several properties then the criterion is applied to all of them.

2.4 Unique First Cause Coverage

An important coverage criterion for structural coverage of programs and specifications is the modified condition/decision coverage (MCDC) criterion [4], which is for example mandated in the avionic domain. Using the nomenclature of [5], given a logical predicate consisting of several clauses (i.e., predicates that do not contain logical operators) connected by logical operators, *Active Clause Coverage* (i.e., MCDC) requires that each clause (condition) is shown to independently affect the value of the predicate (decision) it is part of; there are several interpretations of varying strictness of this criterion.

Whalen et al. [3] have adapted *General Active Clause Coverage* (GACC, also known as masking MCDC) to temporal logic properties, resulting in *Unique First Cause Coverage* (UFC). Intuitively, a clause x is the unique first cause of a formula A, if in the first state along a path π where A is satisfied, it is satisfied *because* of x. For example, in a sequence $\langle(\neg x, \neg y), (x, \neg y), (\neg x, y)\rangle$, the property $\Diamond\,(x \vee y)$ is true because x is true in the second state and y is true in the third state, but x is its unique first cause.

Given a predicate A, A^+ denotes the set of test predicates necessary to show that all clauses in A positively affect the outcome of A; that is, where A evaluates to true as a consequence of a considered clause. A^- denotes the set of test predicates necessary to show that all clauses in A negatively affect the outcome of A. x denotes a clause. The set of test predicates necessary to cover a predicate is determined by recursively applying the following rules:

Definition 8 (Rules to derive test predicates for GACC [3])

$$
\begin{aligned}
x^+ &= \{x\} \\
x^- &= \{\neg x\} \\
(A \wedge B)^{+/-} &= \{a \wedge B \mid a \in A^{+/-}\} \cup \{A \wedge b \mid b \in B^{+/-}\} \\
(A \vee B)^{+/-} &= \{a \wedge \neg B \mid a \in A^{+/-}\} \cup \{\neg A \wedge b \mid b \in B^{+/-}\} \\
(\neg A)^{+/-} &= A^{-/+}
\end{aligned}
$$

For example, the predicate $p := x \vee (y \wedge z)$ results in the set $\{(x \wedge \neg (y \wedge z)), (\neg x \wedge (y \wedge z))\}$ to show positive affect, and the set for negative affect is $\{(\neg x \wedge \neg (y \wedge$

z)), $(\neg x \wedge (\neg y \wedge z))$, $(\neg x \wedge (y \wedge \neg z))$}. A requirement for a test suite to satisfy GACC of p is that each constraint in these two sets is satisfied by a test case.

As LTL formulas are defined on paths, the above rules are extended by Whalen et al. [3] for UFC to take temporal operators into consideration:

Definition 9 (Rules to derive test predicates for UFC [3])

$$\Box(A)^+ \quad = \quad \{A \, \mathsf{U} \, (a \wedge \Box(A)) \mid a \in A^+\}$$

$$\Box(A)^- \quad = \quad \{A \, \mathsf{U} \, a \mid a \in A^-\}$$

$$\Diamond(A)^+ \quad = \quad \{\neg A \, \mathsf{U} \, a \mid a \in A^+\}$$

$$\Diamond(A)^- \quad = \quad \{\neg A \, \mathsf{U} \, (a \wedge \Box(\neg A)) \mid a \in A^-\}$$

$$\bigcirc(A)^{+/-} \quad = \quad \{\bigcirc(a) \mid a \in A^{+/-}\}$$

$$(A \, \mathsf{U} \, B)^+ \quad = \quad \{(A \wedge \neg B) \, \mathsf{U} \, ((a \wedge \neg B) \wedge (A \, \mathsf{U} \, B)) \mid a \in A^+\} \cup$$
$$\{(A \wedge \neg B) \, \mathsf{U} \, b \mid b \in B^+\}$$

$$(A \, \mathsf{U} \, B)^- \quad = \quad \{(A \wedge \neg B) \, \mathsf{U} \, (a \wedge \neg B) \mid a \in A^-\} \cup$$
$$\{(A \wedge \neg B) \, \mathsf{U} \, (b \wedge \neg(A \, \mathsf{U} \, B)) \mid b \in B^-\}$$

For example, the simple property $\phi = \Box(x \wedge y)$ results in the constraints $\phi^+ = \{(x \wedge y) \, \mathsf{U} \, ((x \wedge y) \wedge \Box(x \wedge y))\}$ and $\phi^- = \{((x \wedge y) \, \mathsf{U} \, (\neg x \wedge y)), ((x \wedge y) \, \mathsf{U} \, (x \wedge \neg y))\}$. These test predicates can be used as trap properties by negating them to create counterexamples. A requirement for a test suite to satisfy UFC of ϕ is that each test predicate in the set for *positive* affect is satisfied by a test case (the rules for negative affect are still required because of the recursive definition).

3   Property Inactive Clause Coverage

A natural extension of MCDC is *Reinforced Condition/Decision Coverage* [6], or *Inactive Clause Coverage* (ICC)[5]. The idea of ICC is that it is not sufficient to show for each clause that it independently affects the predicate's outcome; it is also necessary to show that each clause independently *keeps* the outcome i.e., the value of the predicate does not change because of changes in the clause.

The motivation for ICC also applies to properties: For example, for a property $\Box((c_1 \wedge c_2) \rightarrow \bigcirc d)$ UFC covers the cases where the property is true because of c_1 ($\neg c_1$ causes the left hand side of the implication to be false while c_2 is true), because of c_2 ($\neg c_2$ causes the left hand side of the implication to be false), and because of d ($c_1 \wedge c_2$ has to be true). However, assuming that c_1, c_2, and d represent some safety critical values (e.g., a track at a railway point as in the example in [6]) it is important to also cover the cases where the property is true independently of c_1 and independently of c_2 (which is the case if the respective other value is false), and independently of d (which is the case if $c_1 \wedge c_2$ is false, a case that incidentally is also covered by UFC). Therefore, we define a similar extension for UFC: *Property Inactive Clause Coverage* (PICC) looks for changes in a clause such that the expression keeps the outcome.

Similar to the definition of UFC we give a definition of PICC as a set of rules ρ, such that applying these rules to a property results in a set of test predicates that need to be satisfied in order for a test suite to be adequate with regard to the PICC criterion. For properties consisting of only one clause UFC collapses with traditional criteria such as clause coverage. In contrast, given an expression consisting of only a single clause it is impossible for this single clause not to affect the expression. For practical reasons, PICC changes to clause coverage in that case in our definition.

Definition 10 (Rules to derive test predicates for PICC)

$$\rho(x) \quad = \quad \{x, \neg x\} \tag{12}$$
$$\rho(A \wedge B) \quad = \quad \{a \wedge \neg B \,|\, a \in \rho(A)\} \cup \{\neg A \wedge b \,|\, b \in \rho(B)\} \tag{13}$$
$$\rho(A \vee B) \quad = \quad \{a \wedge B \,|\, a \in \rho(A)\} \cup \{A \wedge b \,|\, b \in \rho(B)\} \tag{14}$$
$$\rho(\neg A) \quad = \quad \rho(A) \tag{15}$$
$$\rho(\square(A)) \quad = \quad \{A \,U\, (a \wedge \square(A)) \,|\, a \in \rho(A)\} \tag{16}$$
$$\rho(\lozenge(A)) \quad = \quad \{\neg A \,U\, (a \wedge (A \vee \lozenge A)) \,|\, a \in \rho(A)\} \tag{17}$$
$$\rho(\bigcirc(A)) \quad = \quad \{\bigcirc(a) \,|\, a \in \rho(A)\} \tag{18}$$
$$\rho(A \,U\, B) \quad = \quad \{(A \wedge \neg B) \,U\, (a \wedge (B \vee (A \,U\, B))) \,|\, a \in \rho(A)\} \cup \tag{19}$$
$$\{(A \wedge \neg B) \,U\, (b \wedge (B \vee (A \,U\, B))) \,|\, b \in \rho(B)\}$$

In a conjunction $A \wedge B$ the clause A can take on any value if B is false without changing the value of the predicate. Similarly, for $A \vee B$, A can take on any value if B is true. $\square(A)$ is true if A is true along all states within a path; Equation 16 ensures that all inactive clause values are selected at some point. For $\lozenge A$ (Eq. 17) we want the test case to actually reach A, therefore we add the disjunction with $\lozenge A$ to cover cases where $\rho(A)$ evaluates to false. For the next operator (Eq. 18) we simply require that all inactive clause values are selected in the next state. Finally, $A \,U\, B$ (Eq. 19) has to ensure that for both A and B values are chosen for inactive clauses and test cases also have to reach a state where B is true. For a property with n clauses these rules result in $2 \times n$ expressions, i.e., two for each clause, while the UFC rules result in one expression per clause.

As an example, consider the following LTL property: $\phi = \square(x \rightarrow \bigcirc y)$. The first step is to resolve the always operator using Eq. 16:

$$\rho(\phi) = \rho(\square(x \rightarrow \bigcirc y)) = \{(x \rightarrow \bigcirc y) \,U\, (a \wedge \square(x \rightarrow \bigcirc y)) \,|\, a \in \rho(x \rightarrow \bigcirc y)\}$$

Next we need all values of the rules applied to the implication within the scope of the $\square$ operator:

$$\rho(x \rightarrow \bigcirc y) = \rho(\neg x \vee \bigcirc y) = \{a \wedge \bigcirc y \,|\, a \in \rho(\neg x)\} \cup \{\neg x \wedge b \,|\, b \in \rho(\bigcirc y)\}$$

Consequently, we need all values of the rules applied to $\neg x$ and $\bigcirc y$, which is simply $\rho(\neg x) = \rho(x) = \{x, \neg x\}$ and $\rho(y) = \{y, \neg y\}$. Now we can solve the case for the next operator directly: $\rho(\bigcirc y) = \{\bigcirc(a) \,|\, a \in \rho(y)\} = \{\bigcirc(y), \bigcirc(\neg y)\}$

Finally, this gives us the following result for $\rho(\phi)$:

$$\rho(\phi) \quad = \quad \{(x \rightarrow \bigcirc y) \cup ((x \wedge \bigcirc y) \wedge \square (x \rightarrow \bigcirc y)),$$
$$(x \rightarrow \bigcirc y) \cup ((\neg x \wedge \bigcirc y) \wedge \square (x \rightarrow \bigcirc y)),$$
$$(x \rightarrow \bigcirc y) \cup ((\neg x \wedge \bigcirc (y)) \wedge \square (x \rightarrow \bigcirc y)),$$
$$(x \rightarrow \bigcirc y) \cup ((\neg x \wedge \bigcirc (\neg y)) \wedge \square (x \rightarrow \bigcirc y))\}$$

A test case satisfies PICC with regard to ϕ, if for each of the test predicates $r \in \rho(\phi)$ there is a test case t such that $t \models r$. In order to use a model checker to create a test suite that satisfied PICC with regard to ϕ one simply has to call the model checker for trap properties derived by negation of the test predicates.

4 Property Mutation

Mutation testing describes an approach where simple faults are introduced in programs or specifications and the adequacy of a test suite is measured as its ability to distinguish between the original program or specification and the mutant. Model checkers can be used to automatically create mutation adequate test suites [12,13]. However, previously mutation was only applied to logical expressions contained in the specification (or properties that reflect these expressions [12], which is essentially the same), but not to requirement properties.

For a mutant of a program or a specification it is clear that a test case that kills this mutant can distinguish between the correct program and a program that contains this fault. In contrast it is not so clear what killing a property mutant means: A test case that kills a property mutant can distinguish between an implementation that satisfies the original property and an implementation that satisfies the faulty property. In traditional mutation analysis the *competent programmer assumption* [14] expresses that the implementation is close to being correct, which we can interpret as it being close to satisfying the user requirements. In addition, we assume that the *coupling effect* [15] applies also to property mutants, meaning that test cases able to detect small errors in the implemented properties also likely detect complex errors.

Property mutation is straight forward: The specification is assumed to satisfy a given property. Consequently, also test cases for such a specification will satisfy the property (with some restrictions, see below). The property is mutated, i.e., variants that differ in small ways are created. A test case simply kills a mutant property if it does not satisfy the property. Because test cases are finite while LTL semantics is based on infinite paths some precaution has to be taken: For example, how to interpret a next operator at the last state of a test case? An example solution to this problem as presented by Ammann and Black [16] is to rewrite properties to take the final state into account explicitly; this is done with a helper variable that represents the number of the current state in the sequence, and the property is rewritten such that a violation cannot occur because of the end of the sequence (i.e., using implications on the state number). Alternatively, one can also define finite trace semantics (e.g., [3,17]), such that the value of a temporal expression defaults to true if a sequence is too short (e.g., $\bigcirc x$ would always be true at the last state of a sequence).

If the test case passes on an implementation (i.e., the implementation under test behaves as expected by the test case), then that implementation cannot implement the mutated property. This means that a test case that kills a property mutant can distinguish between an implementation that satisfies the original property and an implementation that satisfies the mutated property.

Mutation operators suitable for specifications are analyzed by [18]; these operators can be applied to any languages that use similar logical expressions, including LTL. For example, the Missing Condition mutation operator (MCO) removes a literal from a logical expression, and the Logical Operator Replacement mutation operator (LRO) replaces a logical operator with a different mutation operator. In addition to the existing operators for logical expression, which can all be applied to LTL properties, we define three new mutation operators for LTL:

Temporal Operator Insertion (TIO): Inserts a temporal operator (e.g., $\square$, $\bigcirc$, $\lozenge$, U) in a logical expression.

Temporal Operator Replacement (TRO): Replaces a temporal operator with another temporal operator.

Missing Temporal Operator (MTO): Removes a temporal operator from a temporal logic expression.

As an example, consider the LTL property $\phi = \square\,(x \rightarrow \bigcirc y)$ again. A possible mutant resulting from application of the TIO operator is $\phi' = \square\,(\bigcirc x \rightarrow \bigcirc y)$. As an example for the TRO operator the following mutant might result: $\phi' = \square\,(x \rightarrow \square y)$. As another example, a possible mutant resulting from application of the MTO operator is $\phi' = \square\,(x \rightarrow y)$.

Let $Mutants(M, \phi)$ define the set of mutant properties resulting from application of mutation operator M on property ϕ:

Definition 11 (Property Mutation). *Test predicates for mutation operator M and property ϕ are given by:* $\{\neg\phi' \mid \phi' \in Mutants(M, \phi)\}$.

Trap properties are again derived by simple negation. If a mutant is not equivalent, then a resulting counterexample kills this mutant (i.e., equivalent mutants lead to infeasible test predicates).

One problem of mutation in general is detecting equivalent mutants. In the special case of state based specifications with finite state space equivalent mutants are not a problem because they can be detected by a model checker. However, one generally expected problem of applying mutation to properties is that the number of equivalent mutants is likely to be higher than when applying mutation to specifications or programs. Our experiments have shown that to some extent this is due to vacuity in the properties. A vacuously satisfied part of a property can be replaced in any way without changing the result of the verification.

Table 1. Test predicates and test cases

Criterion	Test Predicates			Test Cases	
	Total	Infeasible	Feasible	Unique	Minimal
VC	113	18 (15,9%)	95	76	20
UFC	113	27 (23,9%)	86	72	17
PICC	226	35 (15,5%)	191	138	15
Property mutation	2405	1078 (44,8%)	1327	577	55
GACC	472	22 (4,7%)	450	65	36
GICC	944	457 (48,4%)	487	66	17
Mutation	3128	716 (22,9%)	2412	144	37

In addition, there are several mutation operators or special cases thereof that lead to a large number of equivalent mutants. For example, the Stuck At mutation operator (STO) replaces literals with true and false. This, essentially, is what the coverage criterion described in Section 2.3 represents, except that the coverage criterion only chooses either true or false. Therefore, at least every second mutant resulting from STO is equivalent; even more are equivalent in the case of vacuous satisfaction.

Consequently, a good choice of mutation operators and their mutants can serve to reduce the number of equivalent mutants, while some of the equivalent mutants will serve to illustrate vacuity and can help to improve the properties.

5 Case Study: Wiper Control

As a case study a windscreen wiper controller provided by Magna Steyr is used. The formal specification was created manually in the language of the model checker NuSMV [19]. The system controls the windscreen heating, the speed of the windscreen wiper, and provides water for cleaning upon user request. NuSMV reports a total of $2^{44.8727}$ states, 93 BDD variables and 174762 BDD nodes after model encoding. A number of textual user requirements were formalized in LTL, resulting in 23 LTL properties used in this evaluation; only some of these properties are state invariants, while many are of the type $\Box(x \rightarrow \bigcirc(y \rightarrow \bigcirc(\ldots)))$, with a number of nested next statements.

Table 1 lists the numbers of test predicates created for each of the criteria and how many of them are infeasible. The number of test cases resulting when calling the model checker on each test predicate equals the number of feasible test predicates. Some of the test cases are duplicate or prefixes of other test cases; these test cases are dropped, resulting in the unique number of test cases. Finally, a greedy heuristic is applied to minimize a test suite with regard to the coverage criterion it was created for: The heuristic selects the test case that satisfies the most test requirements and removes all test requirements satisfied by that test case. This is repeated until all test requirements are satisfied. In addition to the property based criteria we use the specification based criteria General Active Clause Coverage (GACC) and General Inactive Clause Coverage

Table 2. Cross coverage for minimized test suites (in percent %)

	VC	UFC	PICC	PMut.	GACC	GICC	Mut.
VC	-	100	97	91	85	99	88
UFC	91	-	98	83	86	96	91
PICC	83	91	-	79	82	96	87
Property mutation	100	100	99	-	93	100	94
GACC	71	76	90	61	-	99	100
GICC	51	53	86	48	69	-	69
Mutation	74	80	93	64	89	89	-

(GICC), which represent masking MCDC and its alternate version for inactive clauses, and mutation testing for comparison.

The number of infeasible test predicates is 25% on average for the four property based criteria as well as for the structural criteria. The number of infeasible test predicates for property based criteria is influenced by vacuity; from the VC criterion we know that 16% of all literals in the properties are satisfied vacuously. Consequently, roughly 16% of all test predicates for property based criteria are infeasible because of vacuity. Even so, property mutation results in more infeasible test predicates than mutation of expressions in the specification.

Table 2 lists the cross coverage of each of the criteria used for minimized test suites. Only feasible test predicates are counted for this coverage measurement. Interestingly, all property based criteria achieve very high coverage of the other property based criteria. Property mutation subsumes VC because of the Stuck-At operator, but for the other criteria there are always a few very difficult to cover test requirements.

The tables reveal that none of the specification based criteria is sufficient to cover all property based criteria and vice versa. In addition to the criteria listed in Table 2 we calculated the cross coverage with further logical coverage criteria (e.g., predicate, clause, transition pair coverage), combinatorial coverage (e.g., state, pairwise, 3-way coverage), and data-flow criteria (all-def and all-du coverage) with similar results (not shown here in detail). This suggests that structural coverage of specifications (or programs) and coverage of properties are best used complementary, which is also suggested by recent research [20].

Table 2 also demonstrates that PICC and property mutation add new test objectives that cannot simply be achieved with any of the other existing techniques. Consequently, these new criteria are well suited to complement existing criteria. Interestingly, the property coverage criteria achieve higher coverage of structural coverage criteria than the other way round. While this will always depend on the underlying properties, this seems to suggest that property based criteria result in better (i.e., covering more aspects) test cases.

Table 3 lists the results in detail for the mutation operators. In addition to the new operators introduced in Section 4, we used the following mutation operators (see [18] for details): Stuck-At (STO), Missing Condition (MCO), Simple Expression Negation (SNO), Variable Replacement (VRO), Constant Replacement (CRO), Relational Operator Replacement (RRO), and Logical Operator

Table 3. Mutation operator statistics

Operator	Mutants			Test Cases	
	Total	Equivalent	Inequivalent	Unique	Minimal
TIO	420	196 (46,7%)	224	189	27
TRO	123	96 (78%)	27	26	12
MTO	50	27 (54%)	23	20	7
STO	280	158 (56%)	122	83	20
MCO	157	34 (21,7%)	123	82	17
SNO	122	18 (14,8%)	104	83	23
VRO	722	299 (41,4%)	722	258	42
CRO	36	12 (33,3%)	24	13	6
RRO	117	22 (18,8%)	95	73	23
LRO	360	70 (19,4%)	290	151	16

Table 4. Mutation operator cross coverage for minimized test suites (in percent %)

	TIO	TRO	MTO	STO	MCO	SNO	VRO	CRO	RRO	LRO	All
TIO	-	100	95	100	100	100	85	75	100	98	95
TRO	62	-	90	81	79	81	60	71	77	88	73
MTO	60	93	-	77	75	77	56	62	73	84	69
STO	82	93	95	-	99	100	83	75	100	97	91
MCO	75	81	86	93	-	93	75	75	94	97	85
SNO	84	93	95	100	100	-	83	75	100	98	91
VRO	87	93	100	100	100	100	-	75	100	99	97
CRO	36	37	33	48	58	48	26	-	46	63	42
RRO	80	93	95	100	99	100	83	75	-	98	90
LRO	75	85	90	90	93	90	73	62	88	-	84

Replacement (LRO). There are no arithmetic expressions in our properties, therefore the Arithmetic Operator Replacement (ARO) operator was not used. CRO and VRO represent the Operand Replacement Operator (ORO) in [18].

With regard to TIO we observed that while the use of all future temporal operators leads to 53% inequivalent mutants this number can be increased by only considering the next operator (73% inequivalent mutants), while for always and eventually the numbers of inequivalent mutants are 36% and 50,7%, respectively. Some initial experiments with past time temporal operators showed that these operators result in useful test cases as well. For the TRO operator the best result can be achieved by replacing only with the always operator (54% inequivalent mutants). A further factor that contributes to the large number of equivalent mutants is vacuity. STO has more than 50% equivalent mutants: half of these mutants equals the VC test predicates, some of which are infeasible because of vacuity. The other half mostly results in equivalent mutants. From the VC criterion we know that 16% of the literals of our LTL properties are satisfied vacuously; any mutant changing one of these 16% of literals will be equivalent.

Table 4 illustrates the cross coverage for the mutation operators for the minimized test suites. The TIO and VRO operators achieve the highest mutation scores, but as shown in Table 3 they also result in the most mutants. Similar to the findings reported in [18] we observe that SNO and MCO have good coverage and result in fewer mutants. The combination of TIO, VRO, CRO, and RRO is sufficient to kill all other mutants in our experiments. This is similar to the findings in [18] with regard to ORO+ (which is VRO, CRO, and RRO), but in our case ORO+ is not sufficient to kill all mutants of TIO, TRO, and MTO (neither is the combination of all other mutation operators). Similarly, the combination of TIO, TRO, and MTO is also unable to kill all mutants, consequently a combination of these two types of mutation operators is recommendable (for example the combination of the ORO+ set and TIO).

6   Related Work

In contrast to coverage as discussed in this paper, some related approaches use mutation to derive test cases where faults might result in property violations. Ammann et al. [21] define the notion of dangerous traces, which after a mutation may immediately or eventually lead to a safety property violation. Fraser and Wotawa [22] introduce property relevance and property relevant coverage, using a mutation-like technique to direct testing efforts to potential property violations.

Fraser and Ammann [23] adapted the Reachability, Infection, and Propagation (RIP) model for faults and failures in ordinary code to requirements testing, where the reachability property amounts to the property not being vacuously true on a given test case, and the propagation property amounts to a potential violation of the property on the test case being observable. Neither any of the above mentioned techniques using mutation or coverage criteria nor the criteria introduced in this paper can guarantee propagation. Therefore, post processing of test cases is necessary in any case if propagation is required.

In other areas of formal testing it has also been realized that conformance testing might not be sufficient, but that properties verified against a specification also need to be tested against an implementation. In [24,25], test purposes are derived from CTL properties using model checking; test purposes can be used to automatically derive test cases. Rusu et al. [26] describe a method that attempts to push an implementation into violating a requirement given as a safety property, and define a relation between conformance and satisfaction of safety properties. Fernandez et al. [27] generate test cases from observers describing LTL requirements.

7   Conclusions

In this paper we considered specification based testing in the presence of temporal logic properties. While the specification can be verified against the properties, testing is necessary in addition to verification because the correctness of a specification does not guarantee that the actual realization of the specification still satisfies the same properties: The realization includes additional and refined code, is compiled and treated by different tools, and then run on different hardware and in different environments. Traditional specification based testing often only considers whether an implementation conforms to the specification, therefore it is important to also use requirement properties to derive test cases.

We considered existing coverage criteria for temporal logic properties in this paper and introduced two new criteria: PICC and property mutation. The new criteria can be seen as complementary to the existing criteria, and our evaluation shows that they are indeed difficult to satisfy with test suites created for existing criteria based on both specifications and properties.

The first new criterion, PICC, is similar in nature to the RCDC extension to the popular MCDC criterion in that it tests those cases where the change of a clause's truth value should not affect the outcome of the property. Similarly, mutation of properties allows to measure the sensitivity of an existing test suite with regard to the implemented properties. Infeasible test predicates are partially due to vacuity in the properties, and by using a restricted set of mutation operators the total number of test predicates and the number of infeasible test predicates (i.e., equivalent mutants) can be kept within bounds (similar to specification mutation). As both criteria are defined via temporal logic properties they can immediately be used to derive test cases satisfying the criteria.

References

1. Pnueli, A.: The Temporal Logic of Programs. In: 18th Annual Symposium on Foundations of Computer Science, October 31-November 2, pp. 46–57. IEEE, Providence (1977)
2. Tan, L., Sokolsky, O., Lee, I.: Specification-Based Testing with Linear Temporal Logic. In: Proceedings of IEEE International Conference on Information Reuse and Integration (IRI 2004), pp. 493–498 (2004)
3. Whalen, M.W., Rajan, A., Heimdahl, M.P., Miller, S.P.: Coverage Metrics for Requirements-Based Testing. In: ISSTA 2006: Proceedings of the 2006 International Symposium on Software Testing and Analysis, pp. 25–36. ACM Press, New York (2006)
4. Chilenski, J.J., Miller, S.P.: Applicability of modified condition/decision coverage to software testing. Software Engineering Journal, 193–200 (September 1994)
5. Ammann, P., Offutt, J.: Introduction to Software Testing. Cambridge University Press, New York (2008)
6. Vilkomir, S.A., Bowen, J.P.: Reinforced Condition/Decision Coverage (RC/DC): A New Criterion for Software Testing. In: Bert, D., Bowen, J.P., Henson, M.C., Robinson, K. (eds.) B 2002 and ZB 2002. LNCS, vol. 2272, pp. 291–308. Springer, Heidelberg (2002)
7. Clarke, E.M., Grumberg, O., Peled, D.A.: Model Checking, 1st edn. MIT Press, Cambridge (2001) (3rd printing)
8. Fraser, G., Wotawa, F., Ammann, P.E.: Testing with model checkers: a survey. In: Software Testing, Verification and Reliability (2009) (to appear)
9. Beer, I., Ben-David, S., Eisner, C., Rodeh, Y.: Efficient Detection of Vacuity in ACTL Formulas. In: Grumberg, O. (ed.) CAV 1997. LNCS, vol. 1254, pp. 279–290. Springer, Heidelberg (1997)
10. Kupferman, O., Vardi, M.Y.: Vacuity Detection in Temporal Model Checking. In: Pierre, L., Kropf, T. (eds.) CHARME 1999. LNCS, vol. 1703, pp. 82–96. Springer, Heidelberg (1999)

11. Purandare, M., Somenzi, F.: Vacuum Cleaning CTL Formulae. In: Brinksma, E., Larsen, K.G. (eds.) CAV 2002. LNCS, vol. 2404, pp. 485–499. Springer, Heidelberg (2002)
12. Ammann, P.E., Black, P.E., Majurski, W.: Using Model Checking to Generate Tests from Specifications. In: Proceedings of the Second IEEE International Conference on Formal Engineering Methods (ICFEM 1998), pp. 46–54. IEEE Computer Society, Los Alamitos (1998)
13. Gargantini, A.: Using Model Checking to Generate Fault Detecting Tests. In: Gurevich, Y., Meyer, B. (eds.) TAP 2007. LNCS, vol. 4454, pp. 189–206. Springer, Heidelberg (2007)
14. Acree, A.T., Budd, T.A., DeMillo, R.A., Lipton, R.J., Sayward, F.G.: Mutation Analysis. Technical report, School of Information and Computer Science, Georgia Inst. of Technology, Atlanta, Ga (September 1979)
15. DeMillo, R.A., Lipton, R.J., Sayward, F.G.: Hints on Test Data Selection: Help for the Practicing Programmer. Computer 11, 34–41 (1978)
16. Ammann, P., Black, P.E.: A Specification-Based Coverage Metric to Evaluate Test Sets. In: HASE 1999: The 4th IEEE International Symposium on High-Assurance Systems Engineering, Washington, DC, USA, pp. 239–248. IEEE Computer Society, Los Alamitos (1999)
17. Havelund, K., Rosu, G.: Monitoring Programs Using Rewriting. In: ASE 2001: Proceedings of the 16th IEEE Int. Conference on Automated Software Engineering, Washington, DC, USA, p. 135. IEEE Computer Society, Los Alamitos (2001)
18. Black, P.E., Okun, V., Yesha, Y.: Mutation Operators for Specifications. In: Proceedings of the Fifteenth IEEE International Conference on Automated Software Engineering (ASE 2000), Washington, DC, USA. IEEE Computer Society Press, Los Alamitos (2000)
19. Cimatti, A., Clarke, E.M., Giunchiglia, F., Roveri, M.: NUSMV: A New Symbolic Model Verifier. In: Halbwachs, N., Peled, D.A. (eds.) CAV 1999. LNCS, vol. 1633, pp. 495–499. Springer, Heidelberg (1999)
20. Rajan, A., Whalen, M., Staats, M., Heimdahl, M.P.E.: Requirements Coverage as an Adequacy Measure for Conformance Testing. In: Liu, S., Maibaum, T., Araki, K. (eds.) ICFEM 2008. LNCS, vol. 5256, pp. 86–104. Springer, Heidelberg (2008)
21. Ammann, P., Ding, W., Xu, D.: Using a Model Checker to Test Safety Properties. In: Proceedings of the 7th International Conference on Engineering of Complex Computer Systems (ICECCS 2001), pp. 212–221. IEEE, Los Alamitos (2001)
22. Fraser, G., Wotawa, F.: Using Model-Checkers to Generate and Analyze Property Relevant Test-Cases. Software Quality Journal 16(2), 161–183 (2008)
23. Fraser, G., Ammann, P.: Reachability and propagation for ltl requirements testing. In: Proceedings of the 8th International Conference on Quality Software (QSIC 2008), pp. 189–198 (2008)
24. da Silva, D.A., Machado, P.D.L.: Towards Test Purpose Generation from CTL Properties for Reactive Systems. Electrical Notes in Theoretical Computer Science, vol. 164, pp. 29–40 (2006)
25. Machado, P.D.L., Silva, D.A., Mota, A.C.: Towards Property Oriented Testing. Electrical Notes in Theoretical Computer Science, vol. 184, pp. 3–19 (2007)
26. Rusu, V., Marchand, H., Tschaen, V., Jéron, T., Jeannet, B.: From safety verification to safety testing. Testing of Communicating Systems, 160–176 (2004)
27. Fernandez, J.C., Mounier, L., Pachon, C.: Property oriented test case generation. Formal Approaches to Software Testing, 147–163 (2004)

Could We Have Chosen a Better
Loop Invariant or Method Contract?

Christoph Gladisch

University of Koblenz-Landau
Department of Computer Science
Germany
gladisch@uni-koblenz.de

Abstract. The method contract and loop invariant rules (*contract rules*) are an important software verification technique for handling method invocations and loops. However, if a verification condition resulting from using a contract rule turns out to be falsifiable, then the user does not know if she could have chosen a stronger contract to verify the program or if the program is not verifiable due to a software bug. We approach this problem and present a novel technique that unifies verification and software bug detection.

1 Introduction

Software verification is an iterative and time consuming task. A software correctness proof usually does not succeed on the first proof attempt because often a program has either a) an error, i.e. the program does not satisfy the specification (Figure 1.1), or b) the program is correct but inappropriate *auxiliary* formulas, i.e. loop invariants or method contracts, are used. The user then does not know if she should search for a bug in the program or search for a different loop invariant or method contract.

The technique described in this paper tries to show the correctness of a program and in case of verification failure it tries to show program incorrectness, i.e. it tries to exclude case (b) as the source for verification failure by showing case (a). Furthermore, we propose a unified method for verification and bug detection that is based on verification and on failed proof attempts. The idea is that even if a verification proof fails, it contains useful information that can help to find a program error, if one exists, and in this way the work for verification is reused for bug finding – subsuming testing. This is basically done by checking if an unproved verification condition has a counterexample, i.e., if it is falsifiable. The problem of existing techniques following this approach is that such counterexamples don't necessarily imply a program error but they only guide the user to find the problem.

The contribution of this paper is a method that checks if a falsifiable verification condition implies a program error. The bottlenecks that prevent from concluding the existence of program errors directly from a falsifiable verification

C. Dubois (Ed.): TAP 2009, LNCS 5668, pp. 74–89, 2009.

```
——— Java + JML (1.1) ———
/*@ public normal_behavior
  requires x>=0;
  ensures \result * \result <= x
  && (\result+1)*(\result+1)>x;
  diverges true; @*/
public int sqrtA(int x){
  int i=0;
  /*@ loop_invariant (i-1)*(i-1)<=x
  || i==0; modifies i; @*/
  while(i*i<=x){i++;}
  return i;} //bug
——————————— Java + JML ———
```

```
——— Java + JML (1.2) ———
/*@ public normal_behavior
  requires x>=0;
  ensures \result * \result <= x
  && (\result+1)*(\result+1)>x;
  diverges true; @*/
public int sqrtB(int x){
  int i=0;
  /*@ loop_invariant (i-1)*(i-1)<=x;
  modifies i; @*///weak invariant
  while(i*i<=x){i++;}
  return i-1; }
——————————— Java + JML ———
```

Fig. 1. Motivating examples

condition are the so called contract rules (loop invariant rule, method contract rule) of the verification calculus. These rules are important to reason about programs with loops and method invocation. However, in contrast to first-order logic rules and most other rules that transform the program to a first-order formula, the contract rules are *not always* falsifiability preserving. Falsifiability preservation is the property of the rules that enables us concluding that the verification condition at the beginning of the proof attempt is falsifiable. The core of our method is to check if contract rules that occur in a sequence of rule applications are falsifiability preserving for given contracts and in this way it enables us to conclude the existence of program error from falsifiable verification conditions.

For example, trying to verify the programs in listings (1.1) and (1.2) using the given loop invariants fails because the loop invariant rule, as will be shown in this paper, creates a falsifiable verification condition. The reason for the failure is however different in both cases. The method sqrtA() has a bug and cannot be verified with any loop invariant whereas method sqrtB() is correct but the loop invariant is inappropriate. The method described in this paper tries to show if a contract rule with a given loop invariant or method contract is falsifiability preserving. In listing (1.1) this is the case and indeed our approach detects that the method sqrtA() has a bug.

Whether a contract rule is falsifiability preserving or not depends on the *strength* of the auxiliary formulas, e.g. loop invariant, method contract which instantiate the loop invariant or method contract rule in the respective case. The stronger an auxiliary formula is, the more detailed information it contains about the loop or method invocation it describes. Consequently the described method is capable to detect bugs only if contracts are sufficiently strong. The method does not check if a stronger contract exists that would complete the proof or make a contract rule falsifiability preserving. In this paper we further assume the existence of a method that determines if a first-order logic formula is falsifiable. For this an SMT solver can be used or the user can simply decide if a formula is falsifiable. The latter scenario could be considered in interactive proving, for example.

Plan of the Paper. Section 2 introduces the foundation of our approach which are a logic for reasoning about programs and a verification calculus. Section 3 describes our approach in detail. In Section 3.1 the falsifiability of contract rule premises is analysed. In Section 3.2 the approach is described in a general way. Sections 3.1 and 3.2 form the basis for our main contribution that is described in Section 3.3 where also our central theorem is proved. An example of using our approach is given in Section 4. Related work is described in Section 5 and finally Section 6 concludes our work.

2   Dynamic Logic and the Verification Calculus

2.1   Overview of JAVA CARD DL

The work presented here is based on a Dynamic Logic [15] for JAVA CARD (JAVA CARD DL [4]) but it can be adapted to similar logics like Hoare Logic and for different programming languages. JAVA CARD DL is the program logic of the KeY-System [6,1], which is a combined interactive and automatic verification and test generation system with symbolic execution rules for a subset of JAVA.

Dynamic Logic is an extension of first-order logic where a formula φ can be *prepended* by the modal operators $\langle p \rangle$ and $[p]$ for every program p. The formula $[p]\varphi$ means that if p terminates, then φ holds in the state after the execution of p. As we consider only sequential and deterministic JAVA programs the meaning of $\langle p \rangle \varphi$ is that the program terminates and that $[p]\varphi$ is true. Thus $[p]\varphi \wedge \langle p \rangle true$ is equivalent to $\langle p \rangle \varphi$. In the following we denote the set of DL-formulas by *Fml*, and the set of first-order logic formulas by Fml_{FOL}. All variables in formulas are bound with quantifiers.

An implication of the form $pre \rightarrow [p]post \in Fml$ with $pre, post \in Fml_{FOL}$ corresponds to the Hoare triple $\{pre\}p\{post\}$ in Hoare logic. If the precondition *pre* is true in the state before the execution of the program and the program terminates, then the postcondition *post* holds after the execution of the program; if the precondition does not hold before the execution of the program, then no statement is made about the post-state. The implication $pre \rightarrow \langle p \rangle post$ states additionally that p terminates. Dynamic logic allows *pre* and *post* to *contain* programs in contrast to Hoare logic: if $pre, post \in Fml$ then $pre \rightarrow [p]post \in Fml$.

Program variables are modelled in JAVA CARD DL as *non-rigid* function symbols $f \in \Sigma_{nr} \subset \Sigma$ of the signature Σ. Different program states are therefore realized as different first-order interpretations of the non-rigid function symbols. For instance let $a, o, i, acc_{[]} \in \Sigma_{nr}$. In this case a program variable a is represented by a logical non-rigid constant a, an expression like o.a, that accesses an object attribute, is modeled as the term $a(o)$, and in case of an array access o.a[i] the corresponding term is $acc_{[]}(a(o), i)$. We use constant domain semantics which means that in all states terms are evaluated to values of the same universe. Logical variables are always *rigid*, i.e., they have the same value in all program states. We write $\models \varphi$ to denote that the formula φ is valid, i.e. it is true under all interpretations.

JAVA CARD DL extends classical Dynamic Logic [15] with updates [4]. An update represents a state change and has the form $\{l_1 := t_1 \,||\, \dots \,||\, l_n := t_m\}$. Each elementary update $l_i := t_i$, with $1 \leqslant i \leqslant m$, assigns the value of the term t_i (also called symbolic value) to the term l_i. The top-level function symbol of l_i must be non-rigid since the update changes its interpretation.

Updates allow an efficient way of handling the aliasing problem and making side-effects explicit. Consider the formula $i \doteq 0 \rightarrow \langle \texttt{i++;a[i]=i} \rangle acc_{[]}(a, i) \doteq 1$. Transforming the modal operator of this formula into an update yields the formula $i \doteq 0 \rightarrow \{i := i + 1 \,||\, acc_{[]}(a, i + 1) := i + 1\} acc_{[]}(a, i + 1) \doteq 1$ that can be simplified using update application to $i \doteq 0 \rightarrow i + 1 \doteq 1$.

A (quantified) update [20] of the form $\{f(x_1, \dots, x_m) := g(x_1, \dots, x_m)\}$ assigns all values of $g \in \Sigma$ to $f \in \Sigma$ at the respective argument positions and is effectively a substitution $[g/f]$. In contrast to substitutions, updates allow referring to a pre- and a post-state. We abbreviate such an update with $\{f := g\}$. Furthermore the notation $\{A := B\}\varphi$ with $A, B \subset \Sigma$ is equivalent to the substitution $[b_1/a_1, \dots, b_n/a_n]\varphi$ where the function symbols $a_1, \dots, a_n \in A$ are replaced by the function symbols $b_1, \dots, b_n \in B$ respectively.

2.2   Modifier Sets and Anonymous Updates

A modifier set for a program is a set of function symbols that model program variables. The purpose of using a modifier set as part of a specification is to specify which program variables are modified by the program.

Definition 1. *The* minimal *modifier set of a program* p *is denoted by* $Mod(p) \subset \Sigma$ *and it consists exactly of those function symbols that can be modified by* p.

A correct *modifier set* $M \subset \Sigma_{nr}$ *contains at least the function symbols that are modifiable by* p, *i.e.* $M \supseteq Mod(p)$.

A modifier set $M \subset \Sigma_{nr}$ can be used to create an *anonymous update* of the form $\{M := M_{sk}\}$ (or shorter $\{M_{sk}\}$) which replaces each function symbol $f \in M$ by a fresh function symbol $f_{sk} \in M_{sk}$. Anonymous updates enable us to replace programs by abstractions. Consider the formula $a \doteq 7 \rightarrow \langle \texttt{m();} \rangle (a \leqslant b \vee b \leqslant 7)$. If it is known that the method $\texttt{m()}$ terminates and modifies only $\texttt{b}$, then the modal operator can be replaced by the anonymous update $\{\{b_{sk}\}\}$ resulting in the formula $a \doteq 7 \rightarrow \{b := b_{sk}\}(a \leqslant b \vee b \leqslant 7)$. Update application then yields $a \doteq 7 \rightarrow a \leqslant b_{sk} \vee b_{sk} \leqslant 7$. Note that more general updates, than those used in the paper representing simple substitutions, allow also more powerful anonymous updates where the modifier set may contain terms. Then, assuming that the method $\texttt{m2()}$ modifies only $\texttt{q.x}$, i.e. $x(q)$, it is possible to prove, e.g., $a(p) \doteq 7 \wedge p \neq q \rightarrow \langle \texttt{m2()} \rangle a(p) \doteq 7$.

2.3   Specifications

Definition 2. *A specification is a triple* $(pre, post, M)$ *where* $pre \in Fml_{FOL}$ *is the precondition, post* $\in Fml_{FOL}$ *is the postcondition and* $M \in \Sigma$ *is a modifier set.*

A specification typically describes the behavior of a method but it can specify the behavior of any statement or sequence of statements. For instance a loop invariant $I \in Fml$ is the pre- and postcondition of a loop's body and the loop itself. A stronger postcondition of the loop is $I \wedge \neg lc$ where $lc \in Fml$ is the loop condition, i.e. the loop iterates while lc is true. The specification of a loop is therefore the triple $(I, I \wedge \neg lc, M)$.

2.4   The Underlying Verification Technique

The underlying software verification technique of our approach is based on a sequent calculus. The calculus consists of sequent rules of the form

$$\frac{\Gamma_1 \Rightarrow \Delta_1 \quad \dots \quad \Gamma_n \Rightarrow \Delta_n}{\Gamma_0 \Rightarrow \Delta_0}$$

where $\Gamma_i \Rightarrow \Delta_i$, with $i \in \{0, \dots, n\}$, are the sequents, or verification conditions and Γ_i and Δ_i are sets of formulas. A sequent has the form

$$\gamma_1, \dots, \gamma_k \Rightarrow \delta_1, \dots, \delta_l$$

with $\gamma_1, \dots, \gamma_k, \delta_1, \dots, \delta_l \in Fml$ and is equivalent to the implication

$$((\gamma_1) \wedge \dots \wedge (\gamma_k)) \rightarrow ((\delta_1) \vee \dots \vee (\delta_l)).$$

When the context is clear, we use Δ_i and Γ_i to denote formulas: Γ_i denotes the conjunction of the formulas it includes and Δ_i denotes respectively a disjunction. Similarly we allow combining sequents with formulas with the obvious meaning.

The sequents $\Gamma_i \Rightarrow \Delta_i$, with $i \in \{1, \dots, n\}$, are the rule premises and the sequent $\Gamma_0 \Rightarrow \Delta_0$ is the rule conclusion. Soundness of the calculus ensures that if all rule premises are valid, then also the rule conclusion is valid.

In sequent calculus, proofs are constructed by applying sequent rules bottom-up, i.e., in order to prove $\Gamma_0 \Rightarrow \Delta_0$ the new proof obligations $\Gamma_1 \Rightarrow \Delta_1 \ \dots \ \Gamma_n \Rightarrow \Delta_n$ are created by rule application that have to be proved instead. In this way a tree structure is created, also called a proof tree, consisting of proof branches of the form $S_0, \dots, S_n$ where S_0 is the root sequent of the tree and S_n is the leaf sequent of a branch. We use the notation S_i to refere to a node or the sequent contained in that node depending on the context.

In a verification proof the *root* of a proof tree has the form

$$\Gamma \Rightarrow \{U\}\langle\!\langle p \rangle\!\rangle_\pi post, \Delta \tag{1}$$

where p is the *target program*, the formula $\Gamma \wedge \neg\Delta$, with $\neg\Delta \equiv \bigwedge_{\delta \in \Delta} \neg\delta$, is the *current precondition*, and $\langle\!\langle\rangle\!\rangle$ stands for $\langle\rangle$ or $[]$ depending on whether total or partial correctness is to be proved in the respective case. The subscript π denotes the *context* which is a stack of method invocations and JAVA blocks and is needed for the handling of jump statements like `return`, `throw`, `break`, and `continue`. In the KeY-system the context is embedded inside the modal operator. We omit writing the context whenever possible. The current precondition of the root consists of the precondition of the requirement specification and U is initially empty.

For example the root in a verification attempt of the method `sqrtA()` from Figure 1 with the given requirement specification is (let $(X)^2$ denote $X * X$):

$$x \geqslant 0 \Longrightarrow \{\}[\texttt{sqrtA (x)}] \overbrace{((\backslash result)^2 \leqslant x \wedge x < (\backslash result + 1)^2)}^{E} \qquad : S_0$$

Applying *symbolic execution* rules on the program part results in the sequents

$$x \geqslant 0 \Longrightarrow [\texttt{i=0;}]_\pi[\texttt{while(c)\{i++;\}}]_\pi[\texttt{return i}]_\pi E \qquad : S_1$$

$$x \geqslant 0 \Longrightarrow \{i := 0\}[\texttt{while(c)\{i++;\}}]_\pi[\texttt{return i}]_\pi E \qquad : S_2$$

where the context π consists of `sqrtA`. At this point consider using the loop invariant rule from Figure 2 (see also [7]) with the contract

$$(\overbrace{(i-1)^2 \leqslant x \vee i \doteq 0}^{I}, \overbrace{((i-1)^2 \leqslant x \vee i \doteq 0) \wedge i^2 > x}^{I \wedge \neg c}, \overbrace{\{i\}}^{M})$$

Recall that the contract of a method is $(pre_m, post_m, M)$, the contract of a loop is $(I, I \wedge \neg c, M)$, and we assume that M is a correct modifier set in the respective case throughout the paper. The resulting rule premises are

$$\textbf{1: } x \geqslant 0 \Longrightarrow \overbrace{\{i := 0\}}^{U} \overbrace{(i-1)^2 \leqslant x \vee i \doteq 0}^{I} \qquad : PO1_{S_2}$$
$$\textbf{2: } x \geqslant 0 \Longrightarrow \{i := 0\}\{i := i_{sk1}\}(I \wedge c \rightarrow [\texttt{i++}]_\pi I) \qquad : PO2_{S_2}$$
$$\textbf{3: } x \geqslant 0 \Longrightarrow \{i := 0\}\{i := i_{sk1}\}(I \wedge \neg c \rightarrow [\texttt{return i}]_\pi E) \qquad : PO3_{S_2} = S_3$$

where the abbreviations $PO1_{S_2}$, $PO2_{S_2}$, and $PO3_{S_2}$ are defined as follows.

Definition 3. *Definition of a contract rule premise occurrence (PO):*

- $PO1_S$, $PO2_S$, and $PO3_S$ denote respectively the 1st, 2nd, and 3rd premise of the contract rule application at the sequent S in a proof tree.
- $PO12_S$ is the union $PO1_S \cup PO2_S$

The sequents $PO1_{S_2}$ and $PO2_{S_2}$ are proved by further rule applications. Symbolic execution on S_3 is continued in Section 4.

Note that in case of recursion, application of the method contract rule does not terminate unless it is combined with induction.

Method Contract Rule

1: $\Gamma \Rightarrow \{U\}pre_m, \Delta$
2: $\Gamma \Rightarrow \{U\}(pre_m \rightarrow \langle m()\rangle post_m), \Delta$
3: $\Gamma \Rightarrow \{U\}\{M\}(post_m \rightarrow post), \Delta$
$$\overline{\Gamma \Rightarrow \{U\}\langle m()\rangle post, \Delta}$$

Loop Invariant Rule

1: $\Gamma \Rightarrow \{U\}I, \Delta$
2: $\Gamma \Rightarrow \{U\}\{M\}(I \wedge c \rightarrow [\mathtt{b}]I), \Delta$
3: $\Gamma \Rightarrow \{U\}\{M\}((I \wedge \neg c) \rightarrow post), \Delta$
$$\overline{\Gamma \Rightarrow \{U\}[\mathtt{while(c)\{b;\}}]post, \Delta}$$

Fig. 2. Contract Rules

3   Unified Verification and Bug Detection

3.1   Falsifiability of Contract Rule Premises

The method contract and loop invariant rules (*contract rules*) (see Figure 2) are a software verification technique for generating verification conditions, i.e. proof obligations, for programs with method calls and loops. However, if a verification condition resulting from using a contract rule turns out to be falsifiable, then one cannot always conclude if the target program has an error or not. This section explains how to interpret falsifiable proof branches, i.e. rule premises, that these rules generate upon rule application. Both rules are considered in parallel.

Branch 1. This branch ensures that the precondition of the contract is satisfied in the prestate of the method or loop. Falsifiability of this branch can be interpreted in two ways. If the verification approach requires the precondition to be satisfied, then falsifiability of this branch implies a program bug in the calling code. Otherwise, the contract is too weak to prove anything and the user has the option to strengthen the contract by weakening the formula pre_m resp. I, or to strengthen $\Gamma \wedge \neg \Delta$ by strengthening contracts occurring earlier in the proof tree.

Branch 2. This branch ensures that the contract of the method or loop is correct. Falsifiability of this branch can be interpreted in two ways depending on the verification approach. If the contract is regarded as an auxiliary and not as a requirement specification, then falsifiability of this branch means that the contract is wrong and the user has to choose a correct contract. If the contract is regarded as a requirement specification, then falsifiability of this branch implies an error in the target program and the user has to fix the target program.

Branch 3. In this branch the postcondition of the contract plays a surrogate for the description of the state transition by the target program. If this branch is falsifiable, then either the target program is not correct or the contract is just too weak to complete the proof.

Conclusion. Whether the falsifiability of branch 1 or 2 is caused by an error in the target program or in the contract depends on the role of the contract in the particular verification approach and is clear in the respective case. Falsifiability of branch 3 in contrast has in both cases an ambiguous meaning. The contract, either auxiliary or required, may be too weak to complete the proof or the program has an error. Our main contribution, described in the next section, is to help to distinguish between these cases by checking if the program has an error if the sequent in third branch is falsifiable.

3.2 Falsifiability Preservation Checking

The approach described in this paper is to try to show the correctness of a program and in case of verification failure to show program incorrectness or to guide the user (see Algorithm 1). The main *contribution* of this paper is however a technique to find program errors based on information contained in proof trees of failed verification attempts. If a verification condition or sequent, is falsifiable, i.e. it has a counterexample, then we check a falsification preservation property of a branch (Def. 4), such that if the property is valid, then it is sound to conclude that the program has an error. The user then knows that she could *not* have chosen a better loop invariant or method contract to succeed the verification attempt and instead she should fix the bug in the program or its specification.

Definition 4. *Definition of falsifiability preservation conditions (FP):*

- *The falsifiability preservation condition FP_P of a rule premise P is the formula $\neg P \rightarrow \neg C$, where C is the rule conclusion. A rule premise is falsifiability preserving if FP_P is valid.*
- *A rule R is falsifiability preserving iff for all premises P of R, $\models FP_P$.*
- *The falsifiability preservation condition of a sequence of sequents $S_i, \ldots, S_j$, in a branch $S_0, \ldots, S_n$, with $0 \leqslant i < j \leqslant n$, is the formula $\neg S_j \rightarrow \neg S_i$ denoted by $FP_{S_i}^{S_j}$. FP_S^S is trivially true.*
- *A proof branch $S_0, \ldots, S_n$ is falsifiability preserving iff $FP_{S_0}^{S_n}$, or short FP^{S_n}*

In case a verification attempt has failed Algorithm 1 iterates via the outer loop over the open proof tree branches and analyses them in the inner loop. The inner loop (Lines 8-24) operates only on falsifiable branches and tries to prove falsifiability preservation from a leaf to the root. If premise 1 or 2 of a contract rule application is falsifiable (Lines 12-15), then the user is guided by the corresponding description in Section 3.1. The main part is the analysis of premise 3 of a contract rule application in Line 17. Checking falsifiability preservation of this premise can be done, e.g., using the formula $FP_{S_i}^{S_n}$ (see Def. 4). If the check is successful and S_n is a falsifiable sequent of a proof branch $S_0, \ldots, S_n$, then it is easy to see that also S_0 is falsifiable. Consequently, if S_0 has the form (1) then the target program has a bug. Otherwise if checking FP^{S_n} fails, then the algorithm may return further information for the user to proceed.

3.3 Special Falsifiability Preservation Checking

This section describes our main contribution. We check with a special falsifiability preservation condition whether contracts that are used in contract rule applications on a given branch are strong enough to reveal a software bug. A *conventional* proof of the formula FP^{S_n}, i.e. $\neg S_n \rightarrow \neg S_0$, that ensures falsification

---

Algorithm 1. tryToVerifyOrToFindABug(root)

Require: All rules but the contract rules are known to be falsifiability preserving.
1. Create proof tree PT for $root$
2. **if** all branches in PT are closed **then**
3.   **return** ' 'verified"
4. **end if**
5. **for all** $B \in$ open branches of PT **do**
6.   **if** B is falsifiable /*determined by user, SMT solver, or other method*/ **then**
7.   let $(S_0, \ldots, S_n) = B$
8.   **for** $i = n - 1$ to 0 **do**
9.   **if** S_i is the root **then**
10.   **return** "program has a bug on trace "+B
11.   **else if** a contract rule was applied at S_i **then**
12.   **if** S_{i+1} is $PO1_{S_i}$ /*i.e., 1st premiss of contract rule app*/ **then**
13. $msg = msg \cup$ "S_{i+1} is falsifiable" + Description Branch 1 (Sec 3.1)
14.   **else if** S_{i+1} is $PO2_{S_i}$ /*i.e., 2nd premiss of contract rule app*/ **then**
15. $msg = msg \cup$ "S_{i+1} is falsifiable" + Description Branch 2 (Sec 3.1)
16.   **else if** S_{i+1} is $PO3_{S_i}$ /*i.e., 3rd premiss of contract rule app*/ **then**
17. $fp_i^n =$ check falsifiability preservation from S_n to S_i according to Definition 4 or Definition 5.
18.   **if** fp_i^n is not true **then**
19. $msg = msg \cup$ "contract at node (i) is too weak to show program correctness or incorrectness"
20.   i=0 //terminate the inner loop
21.   **end if**
22.   **end if**
23.   **end if**
24.   **end for**
25.   **end if**
26. **end for**
27. **return** msg

---

preservation of branch S_n, would require a transformation of the program in S_0 into a first-order logic formula requiring, e.g., symbolic execution. Instead, for a unified verification and bug detection approach we regard the branch $S_0, \ldots, S_n$ that is created by the verification attempt as a *test run* with symbolic values and we reuse information contained in this branch to prove its falsifiability preservation. This is achieved by replacing in Line 17 of Algorithm 1 the formula $FP_{S_i}^{S_n}$ with the more sophisticated formula $SFP_{S}^{S_n}$ that is defined next.

Definition 5. *Let* $(S_0, \ldots, S_n) = B$ *be a branch and* S_i *with* $0 \leqslant i < n$ *be a sequent that has either the form (case 1):*

$$\Gamma_i \Longrightarrow \{U\}\langle\mathrm{p}\rangle\varphi, \Delta_i$$

or the form (case 2):

$$\Gamma_i \Longrightarrow \{U\}[\mathrm{p}]\varphi, \Delta_i$$

and on S_i a contract rule is applied with the contract $(pre, post, M)$. Let $M \supseteq mod(\mathbf{p})$. S_{i+1} is the 3rd branch of the contract rule, i.e. $S_{i+1} = PO3_{S_i}$.

The special falsifiability preservation condition $SFP^{S_n}_{S_i}$ is the conjunction of

$$(((\{M^1 := M^2\}S_n) \wedge \{U\}\{M^2\}post) \rightarrow S_n \tag{2}$$

$$(\neg S_n \wedge \Gamma_i \wedge \neg \Delta_i) \rightarrow \{U\}\Psi \tag{3}$$

$$\neg S_n \rightarrow (\Gamma_i \wedge \neg \Delta_i) \tag{4}$$

where $\Psi = \langle \mathbf{p} \rangle true$ in case 1 and $\Psi = true$ in case 2. The third formula is optional if it is known to be valid for all instances of S_n, Γ_i and Δ_i that may occur in a proof tree (as it is the case for here regarded calculus).

Theorem 1. *Assuming that R is the contract rule applied at S_i with $0 \leqslant i < n$; the 1st and 2nd premises of R are proved; and $FP^{S_n}_{S_{i+1}}$ holds, then*

$$\models SFP^{S_n}_{S_i} \text{ implies } \models FP^{S_n}_{S_i}$$

Theorem 1 is the key for using the formula SFP to prove the falsifiability preservation of a branch that contains occurrences of the third premiss of contract rules. The implication of the theorem is that the formula $SFP^{S_n}_{S_i}$, or even just Formula 2 as described below, can replace the formula $FP^{S_n}_{S_i}$, i.e. $\neg S_n \rightarrow \neg S_0$, in Line 17 of Algorithm 1. In contrast to $FP^{S_n}_{S_i}$, the formula $SFP^{S_n}_{S_i}$ contains no program parts, or it contains only program parts that have not yet been symbolically executed on the branch with the leaf S_n. This is achieved because $SFP^{S_n}_{S_i}$ has no occurrence of φ that may contain the rest of the program following $\mathbf{p}$. Since $SFP^{S_n}_{S_i}$ is mainly built from formulas in S_n, all the symbolic execution that took place up to S_n (by a verification attempt) is *reused*. These properties of $SFP^{S_n}_{S_i}$ support the idea of unified verification and bug detection.

The main subformula of $SFP^{S_n}_{S_i}$ is (2). This formula extends the leaf S_n of branch B with the conjunction $((\{M^1 := M^2\}S_n) \wedge \{U\}\{M^2\}post)$ that is mainly built from an updated version of S_n and the postcondition from the contract rule applied at S_i. Formula (3) ensures that in case of a partial correctness verification attempt non-terminating programs are recognized as correct programs. In practice, however, even if a partial correctness proof is created non-terminating programs are regarded as incorrect. Formula (3) is therefore optional. By ignoring the formula non-terminating programs in partial correctness proofs are regarded as incorrect which is not sound but usually a welcome behavior. Formula (4) is optional as well because, e.g., in the KeY calculus with the contract rules in Figure (2) the Formula (4) is always valid. The formula is however given here to increase the generality of the approach.

We regard the requirement that the 1st and 2nd branch of the respective contract rule application, i.e. $PO12_S$, must be closed, as a minor problem because trying to close these branches is part of the verification process in Algorithm 1 so that no additional work is done for bug detection. Furthermore if the branches $PO12_S$ are not proved, then the algorithm provides guidelines for the user on how to proceed. The second requirement, i.e. $\models FP^{S_n}_{S_{i+1}}$, is ensured by an induction principle of the inner loop: as the loop iterates the program variable i is decreased and the validity of $FP^{S_n}_{S_{i+1}}$, $FP^{S_n}_{S_i}$, ... is ensured.

Proof Sketch of Theorem 1. In this proof the formula $SFP^{S_n}_{S_i}$ is constructed from a formula that is equivalent to $FP^{S_n}_{S_i}$ while making use of the assumptions in Theorem 1. The construction of $SFP^{S_n}_{S_i}$ ensures that $SFP^{S_n}_{S_i}$ implies $FP^{S_n}_{S_i}$.

By assumption of the theorem, $FP^{S_n}_{S_i}$ is valid and has the form

$$\neg S_n \to \neg\overbrace{(\Gamma_i \to ((\{U\}\langle\!\langle p\rangle\!\rangle\varphi) \vee \Delta_i))}^{S_i} \tag{5}$$

Equivalence transformations yield the conjunction of the two formulas

$$\neg S_n \to (\Gamma_i \wedge \neg\Delta_i) \tag{6}$$

$$(\neg S_n \wedge (\Gamma_i \wedge \neg\Delta_i)) \to \{U\}[\langle p\rangle]\neg\varphi \tag{7}$$

where (6) is equal to (4). Formula (7) is equivalent to the conjunction of the following two formulas

$$(\neg S_n \wedge \Gamma_i \wedge \neg\Delta_i) \to \{U\}[p]\neg\varphi \tag{8}$$

$$(\neg S_n \wedge \Gamma_i \wedge \neg\Delta_i) \to \{U\}\Psi \tag{9}$$

where (9) is equal to (3) and $\Psi = \langle p\rangle true$ or $\Psi = true$ depending on the modal operator of the target program. Let $(pre, post, M)$ be the contract of R that was by assumption applied on S_i. The same contract rule with the same contract is now applied on (8). This yields three branches of which the first two are already proved. The third branch is

$$(\neg S_n \wedge \Gamma_i \wedge \neg\Delta_i) \to \{U\}\{M^2\}(post \to \neg\varphi) \tag{10}$$

and can be transformed via equivalence transformations to

$$\overbrace{((\Gamma_i \wedge \neg\Delta_i) \wedge \{U\}\{M^2\}(post \wedge \varphi))}^{\Phi} \to S_n \tag{11}$$

This formula is *implied by* the formula

$$\overbrace{(\{M^1 := M^2\}S_n \wedge \{U\}\{M^2\}post)}^{\Phi'} \to S_n \tag{12}$$

that is equal to (2). It remains to show that $\Phi \to \Phi'$. By the assumption $\models FP^{S_n}_{S_{i+1}}$ the following sequent is valid (we use sequents for a compact notation)

$$S_{i+1} \Longrightarrow S_n \tag{13}$$

This sequent is extended to the valid sequent

$$(\{M^1 := M^2\}S_{i+1}) \wedge \phi \Longrightarrow (\{M^1 := M^2\}S_n) \wedge \phi \qquad (14)$$

where $\phi = (\Gamma_i \wedge \neg\Delta_i) \wedge \{M^1 := M^2\}((\Gamma_i \wedge \neg\Delta_i) \rightarrow \{U\}\{M^1\}post)$. According to Figure 2, $\Gamma_i = \Gamma_{i+1}$ and $\Delta_i = \Delta_{i+1}$. The rule R ensures that the skolem functions in M^1 cannot occur neither in $\{U\}$ nor in $(\Gamma_{i+1} \wedge \neg\Delta_{i+1})$ and the same applies to the skolem functions in M^2. A set of equivalence transformations of (14) yields

$$(\Gamma_i \wedge \neg\Delta_i) \wedge \{U\}\{M^2\}(post \wedge \varphi) \Longrightarrow \{M^1 := M^2\}S_n \wedge \{U\}\{M^2\}post$$

showing that $\Phi \rightarrow \Phi'$. A detailed proof exists in a longer version of this paper.

∎

4 Example

The example illustrates the workflow of Algorithm 1 and in particular the construction of the formula $SFP^{S_n}_{S_i}$ from a falsifiable sequent S_n and a sequent S_i on which a contract rule was applied. From the users perspective the ordinary underlying verification process is extended with automatic or manual falsifiability checking of unproved proof obligations and automatic falsifiability preservation analysis of open proof branches. Thus the required amount of user interaction is relative to the required amount of user interaction of the underlying verification approach.

4.1 Verification Attempt

The example from Section 2.4 where Algorithm 1 is applied on the method `sqrtA()` (Fig. 1) is continued with symbolic execution of sequent S_3 (or $PO3_{S_2}$).

$$\overbrace{x \geqslant 0}^{\Gamma_2 = \Gamma_3} \Longrightarrow \overbrace{\{i := 0\}}^{U}\overbrace{\{i := i_{sk^1}\}}^{M^1}\overbrace{(I \wedge \neg c \rightarrow [\text{return } i]_\pi E)}^{\varphi} \quad : S_3$$

$$x \geqslant 0 \Longrightarrow \{i := i_{sk^1}\}(I \wedge \neg c \rightarrow [\text{return } i]_\pi E) \quad : S_4$$

$$x \geqslant 0 \Longrightarrow \{i := i_{sk^1}\}(I \wedge \neg c) \rightarrow \{i := i_{sk^1}\}[\text{return } i]_\pi E : S_5$$

$$x \geqslant 0, \{i := i_{sk^1}\}(I \wedge \neg c) \Longrightarrow \{i := i_{sk^1}\}[\text{return } i]_\pi E \quad : S_6$$

Rule applications on $\{i := i_{sk^1}\}[\text{return } i]_\pi E$ yield

$$x \geqslant 0, \{i := i_{sk^1}\}(I \wedge \neg c) \Longrightarrow \overbrace{(i_{sk^1})^2 \leqslant x \wedge (i_{sk^1} + 1)^2 > x}^{\Delta_6} \quad : S_6$$

Update simplification on $\{i := i_{sk^1}\}(I \wedge \neg c)$ yields (with $\Delta_7 = \Delta_6$)

$$x \geqslant 0, ((i_{sk^1} - 1)^2 \leqslant x \vee i_{sk^1} \doteq 0) \wedge (i_{sk^1})^2 > x) \Longrightarrow \Delta_7 \quad : S_7$$

Running this example with the KeY-system yields one open branch that extends the sequence $(S_0, \ldots, S_7)$ to $(S_0, \ldots, S_7, \ldots, S_n)$ with $n > 7$. The sequent S_n in the KeY-system is shown (copied directly from the prover with adapted notation):

$$x \geqslant 1 + i_{sk^1} * (-2),$$
$$(i_{sk^1})^2 \geqslant 0,$$
$$i_{sk^1} \geqslant 1,$$
$$(i_{sk^1})^2 \geqslant 1 + x,$$
$$(i_{sk^1}) \leqslant i_{sk^1} * 2 + x - 1,$$
$$x \geqslant 0$$
$$\Longrightarrow$$

Note that the succedent of S_n is empty. The verification attempt has failed at this point and the user does not know the reason for the failure. The description of the example continues in the following section.

4.2 Checking Falsifiability Preservation

The sequent S_n cannot be proved by the system. The next step is to decide if S_n is actually falsifiable which can be done by the user, an SMT solver or, e.g., by using the built-in satisfiability solver for test generation of KeY.

KeY finds a counterexample for the sequent S_n which implies that the sequent is falsifiable. Instead of creating a JUnit test that has to create the correct initial state and then execute the program that has already been symbolically executed, our approach is to check falsifiability preservation of the branch S_n. In contrast to traditional testing our method does not require a concrete counterexample for S_n.

Algorithm 1 proceeds in Line 5 and selects the branch $(S_0, \ldots, S_n)$. As the inner loop of the algorithm iterates it decreases the program variable i from n until it reaches the value 2 because at S_2 the first occurrence of a contract rule application is found. In Line 16 the if-condition is satisfied. In Line 17 the falsifiability preservation is checked by proving of $SFP^{S_n}_{S_2}$. According to Definition 5, $SFP^{S_n}_{S_2}$ is the conjunction of the formulas (2), (3), and (4). Note that also the side condition that $PO1_{S_2}$ and $PO2_{S_2}$ are proved must be checked. This was however done as part of the verification attempt (see Section 2.4).

The Formula (4) is always valid when using the KeY-calculus (see Section 3.3). In our concrete case, e.g., Δ_2 denotes an empty disjunction that is equivalent to false and Γ_2 is $x \geqslant 0$. The formula $\neg S_n \rightarrow (\Gamma_2 \wedge \neg \Delta_2)$ simplifies to $\Gamma_n \rightarrow x \geqslant 0$ which is valid because $(x \geqslant 0) \in \Gamma_n$.

The role of Formula (3) is to prevent the provability of $SFP^{S_n}_{S_2}$ in case the target program does not terminate because non-termination implies program correctness when using the modal operator $[]$, (case 2 in the definition). In practice the reason for using the modal operator $[]$ is, however, to simplify a verification attempt. Even when using the modal operator $[]$ the user may implicitly regard non-terminating programs as incorrect. For terminating programs this formula causes a computationally expensive proof obligation. For these reasons formula (3) can be ignored in practice.

The important formula to be proved is (2) that has the form

$$(\overbrace{\{i_{sk^1} := i_{sk^2}\}}^{M^1 := M^2} S_n \wedge \overbrace{\{i := 0\}}^{U} \overbrace{\{i := i_{sk^2}\}}^{M^2} \overbrace{((i-1)^2 \leqslant x \vee i \doteq 0) \wedge i^2 > x)}^{I \wedge \neg c}) \rightarrow S_n$$

in our example. The sequent S_n has the form $\Gamma_n \Rightarrow$, which is equivalent to $\neg\Gamma_n$. The formula can therefore be rewritten by equivalence transformations as

$$(\{i_{sk1} := i_{sk2}\}\neg\Gamma_n \wedge \{i := 0\}\{i := i_{sk2}\}((i-1)^2 \leqslant x \vee i \doteq 0) \wedge i^2 > x) \rightarrow \neg\Gamma_n$$

$$(\Gamma_n \wedge ((i_{sk2} - 1)^2 \leqslant x \vee i_{sk2} \doteq 0) \wedge (i_{sk2})^2 > x) \rightarrow \Gamma_n' \qquad (15)$$

where Γ_n' is obtained by applying the update $\{i_{sk1} := i_{sk2}\}$ on Γ_n. $SFP_{S_2}^{S_n}$ simplifies therefore to a first-order logic formula that is built based on the leaf node S_n and the post condition of the contract. KeY proves formula 15 fully automatically in 187 prove steps.

The algorithm continues with two more loop iterations until $i = 0$ and exits at line 10 with the return message "program has a bug on trace $(S_0, \ldots, S_n)$". By looking at the used symbolic execution rules the trace can be read as the program execution trace that leads to the bug. The user now knows that choosing a different contract would not have lead to a successful verification attempt because the program or the requirement specification has to be fixed.

5   Related Work

This work is an extension of the works [11,5,13,10,21] that were developed within the KeY-project [6]. In [11] verification-based testing is introduced as a method for deriving test cases from verification proofs. In [5] we present a white-box testing approach which combines verification-based specification inference and black-box testing enabling us to combine different coverage criteria. Both approaches consider the derivation of test cases based on loop invariants.

More directly this work is an extension of [13] that describes a test case generation technique for full feasible (program) branch coverage. In [13] branch coverage is ensured if contracts satisfy a *strength condition*. In this work we have extended this idea resulting in the *special falsifiability preservation condition* (*SFP*). Checking falsifiability preservation for contract rules is also possible with the *strength condition* of a contract. However, the *SFP* can be viewed as a *customized* strength condition for a contract that is valid in far more cases than the more general strength condition given in [13]. Furthermore, in contrast to the strength condition defined [13], *SFP reuses* symbolic execution that has already been performed. The latter property is the reason why we argue that our approach unifies verification and bug detection.

While our approach starts with a verification attempt, the approach in [21] tries to show program incorrectness by starting at the root of the proof tree with a formula that express program incorrectness. Thus in contrast to our approach the approach in [21] can only show program incorrectness.

Another related work that unifies verification and bug finding very closely is Synergy [14] that is an extensions of the Lee-Yannakakis algorithm [17] and is an improvement to SLAM [2] and BLAST [16]. While these approaches are based on abstraction and refinement, our approach is optimized for underlying verification techniques that are based on symbolic execution or weakest precondition computation. Furthermore, the approaches [14,16] and, e.g., [18] are more concerned with the automatic generation of annotations while in our work theorem proving and the challenges with user-provided loop invariants and method contracts are in focus. The latter applies also to [8] where in contrast to our work explicit program execution is used and also other reasons for proof failure than program error are considered. The main concern in [8] is however finding the right program input to detect a bug while in our approach we reason about the existence of such an input.

Approaches that start with a verification attempt and in case of failure generate counterexamples for the unproved verification conditions are e.g. Spec#[3], VCC [22], Caduceus [12], Krakatoa [19], Bogor/Kiasan[9]. These approaches have the problem that a counterexample for a verification condition has an ambiguous meaning, i.e. the used contracts can be too weak or the target program has an error. Our contribution in contrast deals with this problem and therefore it extends the existing approaches.

6   Summary and Conclusion

The presented work extends existing approaches that try to verify a program and in case of verification failure generate counterexamples for verification conditions. In contrast to existing approach our approach allows us to conclude the existence of a program bug from falsifiable verifications even if contract rules were used during the verification attempt. Furthermore, checking the existence of a program bug after the verification attempt does not require explicit program testing, symbolic execution, or weakest precondition computation. Instead we *reuse* information obtained from the verification attempt to reason about the existence of a program bug. In this way our technique unifies verification and bug detection. We have successfully tested several small example programs and specifications using KeY with some manual interaction. An extended evaluation of this approach is planned as future work.

References

1. Ahrendt, W., Baar, T., Beckert, B., Bubel, R., Giese, M., Hähnle, R., Menzel, W., Mostowski, W., Roth, A., Schlager, S., Schmitt, P.H.: The KeY tool. Software and System Modeling 4, 32–54 (2005)
2. Ball, T., Rajamani, S.K.: Automatically validating temporal safety properties of interfaces. In: Dwyer, M.B. (ed.) SPIN 2001. LNCS, vol. 2057, pp. 103–122. Springer, Heidelberg (2001)
3. Barnett, M., DeLine, R., Fähndrich, M., Jacobs, B., Leino, K.R.M., Schulte, W., Venter, H.: The SPEC# programming system: Challenges and directions. In: Meyer, B., Woodcock, J. (eds.) VSTTE 2005. LNCS, vol. 4171, pp. 144–152. Springer, Heidelberg (2008)
4. Beckert, B.: A dynamic logic for the formal verification of Java Card programs. In: Attali, I., Jensen, T. (eds.) JavaCard 2000. LNCS, vol. 2041, pp. 6–24. Springer, Heidelberg (2001)

5. Beckert, B., Gladisch, C.: White-box Testing by Combining Deduction-based Specification Extraction and Black-box Testing. In: Gurevich, Y., Meyer, B. (eds.) TAP 2007. LNCS, vol. 4454, pp. 207–216. Springer, Heidelberg (2007)
6. Beckert, B., Hähnle, R., Schmitt, P.H. (eds.): Verification of Object-Oriented Software. LNCS, vol. 4334. Springer, Heidelberg (2007)
7. Beckert, B., Schlager, S., Schmitt, P.H.: An improved rule for while loops in deductive program verification. In: Lau, K.-K., Banach, R. (eds.) ICFEM 2005. LNCS, vol. 3785, pp. 315–329. Springer, Heidelberg (2005)
8. Claessen, K., Svensson, H.: Finding counter examples in induction proofs. In: Beckert, B., Hähnle, R. (eds.) TAP 2008. LNCS, vol. 4966, pp. 48–65. Springer, Heidelberg (2008)
9. Deng, X., Lee, J., Robby: Bogor/Kiasan: A k-bounded Symbolic Execution for Checking Strong Heap Properties of Open Systems. In: ASE, pp. 157–166 (2006)
10. Engel, C., Gladisch, C., Klebanov, V., Rümmer, P.: Integrating verification and testing of object-oriented software. In: Beckert, B., Hähnle, R. (eds.) TAP 2008. LNCS, vol. 4966, pp. 182–191. Springer, Heidelberg (2008)
11. Engel, C., Hähnle, R.: Generating Unit Tests from Formal Proofs. In: Gurevich, Y., Meyer, B. (eds.) TAP 2007. LNCS, vol. 4454, pp. 169–188. Springer, Heidelberg (2007)
12. Filliâtre, J.-C., Marché, C.: Multi-prover Verification of C Programs. In: Davies, J., Schulte, W., Barnett, M. (eds.) ICFEM 2004. LNCS, vol. 3308, pp. 15–29. Springer, Heidelberg (2004)
13. Gladisch, C.: Verification-based testing for full feasible branch coverage. In: Proc. 6th IEEE Int. Conf. Software Engineering and Formal Methods (SEFM 2008). IEEE Computer Society Press, Los Alamitos (2008)
14. Gulavani, B.S., Henzinger, T.A., Kannan, Y., Nori, A.V., Rajamani, S.K.: Synergy: a new algorithm for property checking. In: SIGSOFT FSE, pp. 117–127 (2006)
15. Harel, D.: Dynamic logic. In: Gabbay, D., Guenthner, F. (eds.) Handbook of Philosophical Logic, Extensions of Classical Logic, ch. 10, vol. II, pp. 497–604. Reidel, Dordrecht (1984)
16. Henzinger, T.A., Jhala, R., Majumdar, R., Sutre, G.: Lazy abstraction. In: POPL, pp. 58–70 (2002)
17. Lee, D., Yannakakis, M.: Online minimization of transition systems (extended abstract). In: STOC, pp. 264–274 (1992)
18. Leino, K.R.M., Logozzo, F.: Loop invariants on demand. In: Yi, K. (ed.) APLAS 2005. LNCS, vol. 3780, pp. 119–134. Springer, Heidelberg (2005)
19. Marché, C., Paulin, C., Urbain, X.: The Krakatoa tool for JML/Java program certification (2003), http://krakatoa.lri.fr
20. Rümmer, P.: Sequential, parallel, and quantified updates of first-order structures. In: Hermann, M., Voronkov, A. (eds.) LPAR 2006. LNCS, vol. 4246, pp. 422–436. Springer, Heidelberg (2006)
21. Rümmer, P., Shah, M.A.: Proving programs incorrect using a sequent calculus for java dynamic logic. In: Gurevich, Y., Meyer, B. (eds.) TAP 2007. LNCS, vol. 4454, pp. 41–60. Springer, Heidelberg (2007)
22. Schulte, W., Songtao, X., Smans, J., Piessens, F.: A glimpse of a verifying C compiler. In: C/C++ Verification Workshop (2007)

Consistency, Independence and Consequences in UML and OCL Models

Martin Gogolla, Mirco Kuhlmann, and Lars Hamann

University of Bremen, Computer Science Department
Database Systems Group, D-28334 Bremen, Germany
{gogolla,mk,lhamann}@informatik.uni-bremen.de

Abstract. Properties in UML models are frequently formulated as OCL invariants or OCL pre- and postconditions. The UML-based Specification Environment (USE) supports validation and to a certain degree verification of such properties. USE allows the developer to prove the consistency and independence of invariants by building automatically generated test cases. USE also assists the developer in checking consequences and making deductions from invariants by automatically constructing a set of test cases in form of model scenarios. Suspected deductions are either falsified by a counter test case or are shown to be valid in a fixed finite search space.

1   Introduction

In recent years, many proposals for improving software quality have put forward model-centric development in contrast to code-centric development. Modeling languages and standards like UML [15] including the OCL [19] and QVT [16] are cornerstones of model-driven approaches. Our work concentrates on OCL and UML class diagram features. Our tool USE (UML-based Specification Environment) supports the validation of UML models by building prototypical test cases in form of scenarios comprising UML object or sequence diagrams [10,11]. One goal of USE is to derive properties of a UML design from these test scenarios.

In particular, USE is able to support the consistency and the independence of OCL constraints. USE also supports deductions from OCL constraints. *Consistency* of OCL invariants can be shown in USE by constructing a positive test case in form of an object or sequence diagram such that all invariants do hold. *Independence* of invariants means that no single invariant can be concluded from other stated invariants. This a property which helps to keep UML models small and focussed. Independence can be shown in a systematic way within USE by the construction of counter test cases. Checking *consequences* and drawing conclusions from OCL invariants is often needed when only basic properties are formulated as invariants and other more advanced properties are consequences from the more basic ones. Checking consequences is supported in USE also by building counter test scenarios or by showing that a property is valid in a fixed search space consisting of a possibly large number of UML object diagrams.

C. Dubois (Ed.): TAP 2009, LNCS 5668, pp. 90–104, 2009.

Our work has connections to other relevant approaches. Basic concepts for formal testing can be found in the pioneering paper [8]. It introduces essential concepts, e.g., the formal definition of test data selection. The tool presented in [17] allows the developer to perform static and dynamic model checking with focus on UML statecharts. UMLAnT [18] allows designers and testers to validate UML models in a way similar to xUnit tests. UMLAnT delegates the validation of invariants, pre- and postconditions to USE [11]. Automatic test generation based on subsets of UML and OCL are examined in [5] and [2], whereas runtime checking of JML assertions transformed from OCL constraints is treated in [1]. Approaches for static UML and OCL model verification without generating a system state can be found in [14], [4] and [6]. In [14], UML models and corresponding OCL expressions are translated into B specifications and, for OCL expressions, into B formal expressions. The transformation result is analyzed by an external tool which provides information about specification errors, e.g., a contradiction between invariants. The work in [4] focuses on static verification of dynamic model parts (sequence diagrams) with respect to the static specification. The KeY approach [6] targets Java Card applications which can be verified against UML and OCL models. Our approach for checking model properties and in particular for finding models has many similarities with the Alloy [13] approach. The approach in [12] is closely related to ours because it also deals with state spaces for testing purposes.

The structure of the rest of the paper is as follows. Section 2 introduces the running example we are going to use throughout. Section 3, 4 and 5 discuss in detail consistency, independence, and checking consequences within USE, respectively. The paper is finished with concluding remarks and future work.

2   Running Example

Our considerations regarding completeness, consistency and checking consequences in UML and OCL models are illustrated and motivated by an example model [3,9] which describes trains, wagons and their formation. The model allows that trains can consist of ordered wagons, i.e., a wagon may have predecessor and successor wagons.

Figure 1 displays the user interface of USE which is divided into a project browser (left frame), a main window and a log window (lower frame). The project browser displays all model elements, i.e., UML classes and associations as well as OCL constraints which can be invariants or pre- and postconditions. Details of items selected in the project browser are shown below the project browser.

The main window may contain several views for inspecting the model and particularly its system states. The class diagram view depicts the structural part of the model. It gives an overview on the defined classes, their associations and the constraining multiplicities.

The object diagram view visualizes the system state resulting from the commands shown right beside it. In this case it presents a valid state of the train

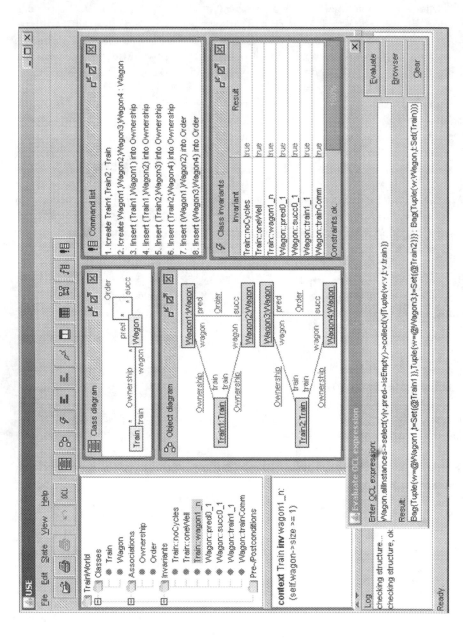

Fig. 1. USE Scenario Proving Consistency in the Example

model, because no constraint is violated. Each invariant expression evaluates to true and all links between the objects comply with the UML multiplicities which is stated in the log window.

USE allows the developer to query the system state interactively by entering an OCL expression into the OCL evaluation window. The result is directly reported. The example query asks for all wagons which do not have preceding wagons and collects their object identifiers together with the train identifiers which the wagon is part of.

As shown in the class diagram the class Train is related to the class Wagon via the association Ownership. A reflexive association Order permits connections between wagons. There are no restrictions concerning the multiplicities, although some of the invariants explained below express properties which could be stated in the class diagram as multiplicities. We have preferred to denote them explicitly as invariants, because this gives us the possibility to compare these multiplicities with other stated properties. The valid system state comprises two trains each connected with two ordered wagons.

Seven OCL invariants enrich the class diagram. All constraints are evaluated in context of a specific class. Accordingly an invariant is fulfilled if its body expression evaluates to true for each instance of the respective class, e.g., the invariant wagon1_n has to be fulfilled for the objects Train1 and Train2.

The first four invariants add restrictions to the most general allowed multiplicities stated in the class diagram. Trains own one or more wagons (invariant Train::wagon1_n). Wagons belong to exactly one train (invariant Wagon::train1_1) and have at most one successor resp. one predecessor (invariants Wagon::succ0_1 resp. Wagon::pred0_1).

```
context Train inv wagon1_n: self.wagon->size>=1
context Wagon inv train1_1: self.train->size=1
context Wagon inv succ0_1: self.succ->size<=1
context Wagon inv pred0_1: self.pred->size<=1
```

Three additional invariants characterize and restrict the train formation. Each train must have exactly one wagon (variable well) whose direct and indirect successors (operation succPlus) form a superset of the direct and indirect successors of all wagons in the train (invariant Train::oneWell). No wagon is allowed to appear in the set of its direct or indirect predecessors (invariant Train::noCycles). Finally, a commutativity property for wagons has to hold for each pair of wagons, i.e., if a wagon succeeds another, both have to be owned by the same train (invariant Wagon::trainComm).

```
context Train inv oneWell:
  self.wagon->one(well| self.wagon->forAll(w|
    well.succPlus()->includesAll(w.succPlus())))
context Train inv noCycles:
  self.wagon->forAll(w|w.predPlus()->excludes(w))
context w1:Wagon inv trainComm:
  Wagon.allInstances->forAll(w2|
    w1.succ->includes(w2) implies w1.train=w2.train)
```

All invariants make use of side effect free operations described within the classes `Train` and `Wagon`. The operation `succPlus` computes the direct and indirect wagon successors, i.e., the transitive closure of the successors of a wagon. It invokes the recursive auxiliary operation `succPlusOnSet` which collects the successors step-by-step. The operation `predPlus` is defined analogously. Later on we will introduce further, dynamically loaded invariants using the operation `allWagons` in the class `Train` which returns all wagons reachable from the owned wagons.

```
Wagon::succPlus():Set(Wagon)=
  self.succPlusOnSet(self.succ)
Wagon::succPlusOnSet(s:Set(Wagon)):Set(Wagon)=
  let oneStep:Set(Wagon)=s.succ->asSet in
  if oneStep=s
    then s else succPlusOnSet(s->union(oneStep)) endif

Train::allWagons():Set(Wagon)=
  self.wagon->union(self.wagon.predPlus()->asSet())->
    union(self.wagon.succPlus()->asSet())
```

In practice such models, especially more complex ones, are developed incrementally, i.e., the system properties are added one after the other, possibly by different developers. Ideally, the developer has to clarify after each addition or modification whether the model is still consistent and whether each invariant adds new information. Emerging correlations are often overlooked. This might result in models without clear borders between the model elements. In the following sections we discuss these elementary questions and the possibilities to answer them automatically by taking advantage of the USE tool.

3   Consistency

A consistent model is a desirable premise for further considerations. Consistency characterizes a model with no conflicts between any constraints, i.e., no constraint or set of constraints rules out other constraints. Within this paper we concentrate on relationships between OCL invariants.

We will continue with a more formal description. Each model M defines a set $I = (i_1, \ldots i_n)$ of invariants. An invariant is evaluated in the context of a specific system state σ, i.e., the evaluation $\sigma(i)$ of invariant i yields true or false. We denote the set of all possible system states by $\sigma(M)$. A consistent model satisfies the following property.

$$\neg \exists i \in I \; (\exists J \subseteq I (\forall \sigma \in \sigma(M)(\bigwedge_{j \in J} \sigma(j) \Rightarrow \neg \sigma(i))))$$

There must be no invariant i and no set of invariants J such that the invariant i is false whenever the invariants in J are true. The formula is equivalent to

$\forall i \in I(\forall J \subseteq I(\exists \sigma \in \sigma(M)(\bigwedge_{j \in J} \sigma(j) \wedge \sigma(i))))$ which can be simplified to the basis of the subsequent proof of consistency.

$$\exists \sigma \in \sigma(M)(\sigma(i_1) \wedge \ldots \wedge \sigma(i_n))$$

Consequently we have to find a system state which fulfills all invariants in order to prove consistency. Due to the fact that each invariant expression is implicitly universally quantified, the empty system state always fulfills all invariants. Thus the formula is never false. A common way for avoiding this problem is to narrow the set of possible states by demanding the existence of at least one object for each class in each system state [7].

With the aid of the USE system and in particular the USE snapshot generator, it is possible to search a given state space for a non-empty state which fulfills all invariants. The generator executes user-defined ASSL (A Snapshot Sequence Language) procedures which make it possible to build up system states in a (pseudo) non-deterministic way. This feature can be applied for specifying a well-delimited set of system states (the set of states which can possibly be reached after invoking the procedure). These general considerations are made now more concrete by means of examples.

USE constructs a collection of system states (search space) as follows: After creating one system state the USE generator checks whether the state is valid in context of the UML and OCL constraints; if not, it backtracks and tries another way until a valid state was found or all possible search paths were considered. In our example, the following procedure is used for proving the consistency of the train model.

```
 1 procedure genTrainsWagonsOwnershipOrder
 2   (countTrains:Integer,countWagons:Integer,
 3    countOwnership:Integer,countOrder:Integer)
 4 var theTrains:Sequence(Train), aTrain:Train,
 5     theWagons:Sequence(Wagon),
 6     aWagon:Wagon, aWagon2:Wagon;
 7 begin
 8 theTrains:=CreateN(Train,[countTrains]);
 9 theWagons:=CreateN(Wagon,[countWagons]);
10 for i:Integer in [Sequence{1..countOwnership}]
11    begin
12    aTrain:=Try([theTrains]);
13    aWagon:=Try([theWagons->reject(w|w.train->includes(aTrain))]);
14    Insert(Ownership,[aTrain],[aWagon]);
15    end;
16 for i:Integer in [Sequence{1..countOrder}]
17    begin
18    aWagon:=Try([theWagons]);
19    aWagon2:=Try([theWagons->reject(w|w.pred->includes(aWagon))]);
20    Insert(Order,[aWagon],[aWagon2]);
21    end;
22 end;
```

The procedure `genTrainsWagonsOwnershipOrder` has parameters for the number of trains, wagons, ownership links and order links to be created. After defining local variables (lines 4–6) the executable code begins. The generator is directed to create the specified number of trains and wagons (lines 8–9). With the following `for` loop, the specified number of ownership links is created. The generator selects a train and a wagon and inserts an ownership link between them in each iteration step.

The keyword `Try` indicates a backtrack point. The generator backtracks to it if the selected values prohibit the construction of a valid state. If the procedure results in an invalid state the generator backtracks to the last `Try` statement and chooses another value. If all alternative values for a `Try` were checked and no valid state was found, the generator backtracks to the next (outer) `Try`, e.g., when no wagon allows the creation of a valid system state (line 13) the generator jumps back to the upper `Try` and chooses another train (line 12).

For avoiding multiple link insertions between the same (train,wagon) pairs, wagons which are already connected to the train are rejected before the selection. Order links are inserted analogously. Here the links are established between wagon pairs.

The USE generator provides the possibility to load invariants which are not part of the model before starting the generation process. Through this it is possible to direct the result by adding respective constraints. The invariant `trainSizeBalanced` forbids system states with unbalanced trains: Two trains must own the same number of wagons or the numbers of wagons in two trains differ by one.

```
context t1:Train inv trainSizeBalanced: Train.allInstances->forAll(t2|
    t1<>t2 implies (t1.wagon->size-t2.wagon->size).abs<=1)
```

We use this constraint during the generation process to achieve a more attractive object diagram. If the generator does not find any valid state, we must start a run without the additional constraint to ensure that our considerations were not influenced by this additional constraint. A USE protocol explaining the invocation of the procedure `genTrainsWagonsOwnershipOrder` is shown below. The lines starting with `use>` indicate user input, the rest are responses from USE.

```
use> open train_wagon.use

use> gen load trainSizeBalanced.invs
     Added invariants: Train::trainSizeBalanced

use> gen start train_wagon.assl genTrainsWagonsOwnershipOrder(2,4,4,2)
use> gen result
     Random number generator was initialized with 6315.
     Checked 5786 snapshots.
     Result: Valid state found.
     Commands to produce the valid state:
     !create Train1,Train2 : Train
     !create Wagon1,Wagon2,Wagon3,Wagon4 : Wagon
```

```
    !insert (Train1,Wagon1) into Ownership
    !insert (Train1,Wagon2) into Ownership
    !insert (Train2,Wagon3) into Ownership
    !insert (Train2,Wagon4) into Ownership
    !insert (Wagon1,Wagon2) into Order
    !insert (Wagon3,Wagon4) into Order
use> gen result accept
    Generated result (system state) accepted.
```

After loading the train model, the USE generator is instructed to load the external invariant. Thereafter the procedure is invoked. The state space is controlled by the arguments. In the above case, the generator should only consider states with two trains, four wagons, four ownership links and two order links. When the generation process has finished the result can be checked. In this case, the generator has found a state fulfilling all model invariants in conjunction with the external one after checking 5786 states. The command sequence creating the state is shown afterwards. Once the result is accepted the state can be displayed in the object diagram view as pictured in Fig. 1. By this, the consistency of the train model has been proven.

This approach can be carried over to any UML model concentrating on a class diagram and OCL invariants. Depending on the state of knowledge about the constraints and their relations, an adequate procedure may be more general or more specific. The procedure above incorporates some knowledge about the model and its purpose. In the next section we use a more general procedure which results in a larger state space.

4   Independence

During development, the possibility of creating dependencies in the set of the constraints cannot be excluded. Dependent constraints, i.e., constraints whose fulfillment or violation depends on other constraints, can occur through the work of different developers or even through a single developer when the model evolves over a long time period.

Developers should aim for independent constraints in their models, because this allows them to concentrate on the essential properties. Regarding OCL constraints, independence implies that each invariant is essential, i.e., the constraint cannot be removed from the model without loss of information. Formally, an invariant $i_k \in I$ is independent if and only if there is no set $J \subseteq I$ of invariants which implies i_k. Naturally, the invariant i_k which has to be proved to be independent should not be part of J.

$$\neg \exists J \subseteq I \; (i_k \notin J \wedge \forall \sigma \in \sigma(M)(\bigwedge_{j \in J} \sigma(j) \Rightarrow \sigma(i_k)))$$

This is equivalent to $\forall J \subseteq I \; (i_k \in J \vee \exists \sigma \in \sigma(M)(\bigwedge_{j \in J} \sigma(j) \wedge \neg \sigma(i_k)))$ which can again be simplified to the following statement.

$$\exists \sigma \in \sigma(M) \; (\sigma(i_1) \wedge \ldots \wedge \sigma(i_{k-1}) \wedge \sigma(i_{k+1}) \wedge \ldots \wedge \sigma(i_n) \wedge \neg \sigma(i_k))$$

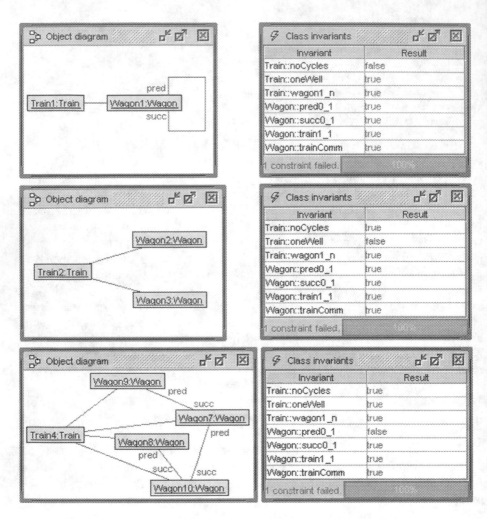

Fig. 2. USE Scenarios Proving Independence in the Example (Part A)

This means, we have to find a system state which conforms to all invariants except i_k and which also conforms to $\neg i_k$. If we are not sure whether an invariant is independent, it is not easy to find such a state. The USE generator can help again by searching a given state space.

Figures 2 and 3 show the proof results for six invariants of the train model. The generator has been configured to find system states violating one invariant at a time. The states are visualized on the left side and the invariant evaluation on the right side.

As mentioned before, the underlying ASSL procedure `genMaxCountTrains-MaxCountWagons` represents a generalized form of `genTrainsWagonsOwnership-Order`. The formal parameters determine the maximum number of trains and wagons. The number of links cannot be affected manually.

```
 1 procedure genMaxCountTrainsMaxCountWagons
 2   (maxCountTrains:Integer,maxCountWagons:Integer)
 3 var theWagons:Sequence(Wagon), theTrains:Sequence(Train),
 4     actualCountTrains:Integer, actualCountWagons:Integer;
 5 begin
 6 actualCountTrains:=Try([Sequence{1..maxCountTrains}]);
 7 actualCountWagons:=Try([Sequence{1..maxCountWagons}]);
 8 theTrains:=CreateN(Train,[actualCountTrains]);
 9 theWagons:=CreateN(Wagon,[actualCountWagons]);
10 Try(Ownership,[theTrains],[theWagons]);
11 Try(Order,[theWagons],[theWagons]);
12 end;
```

First, the generator has to choose the actual number of trains and wagons, i.e.,
a number between one and the specified maximum number (lines 6–7). The generator takes different values if the chosen numbers turn out to be inappropriate
for finding a valid state. The corresponding sets of trains and wagons are created in lines 8 and 9. Afterwards the keyword Try is used for the link insertion
process. With line 10 all possible Ownership link configurations are tried. The
generator starts with the empty link set, then it tries all link sets with one link,
then all links sets with two links and so on. Line 11 describes the same approach
for Order links. These Try statements are crucial, because in the worst case the
generator has to try all possible combinations.

Before we turn to further considerations concerning the ASSL procedure,
we use it for proving in an exemplary way the independence of the invariant
Train::noCycles and thus demonstrate the general approach.

```
use> open train_wagon.use

use> gen flags Train::noCycles +n

use> gen start train_wagon.assl genMaxCountTrainsMaxCountWagons(2,4)
use> gen result
    Random number generator was initialized with 9864.
    Checked 4 snapshots.
    Result: Valid state found.
    Commands to produce the valid state:
    !create Train1 : Train
    !create Wagon1 : Wagon
    !insert (Train1,Wagon1) into Ownership
    !insert (Wagon1,Wagon1) into Order
use> gen result accept
    Generated result (system state) accepted.
```

The first generator command sets a flag which negates the invariant
Train::noCycles. After that, the generator is invoked with a small state
space (at most two trains and four wagons). The result shows that this space
was adequate for the proof as shown in the upper object diagram in Fig. 2.
The invariant Train::noCycles is independent, because it is the only invariant

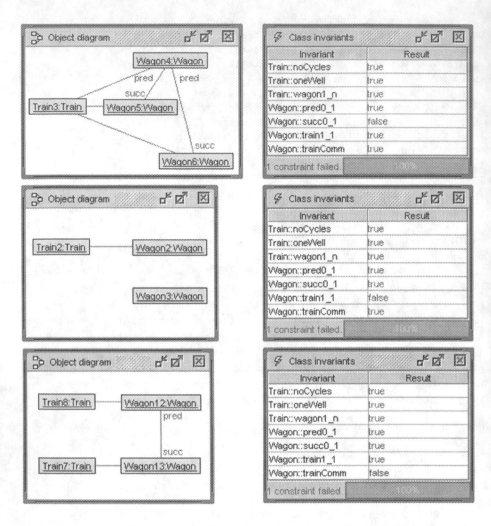

Fig. 3. USE Scenarios Proving Independence in the Example (Part B)

which forbids the created system state (a train with one wagon which is its own predecessor). The invariant adds essential information to the model.

The independence proofs for five other invariants are treated analogously to `Train::noCycles`. The ASSL procedure is always invoked with the same arguments. Figures 2 and 3 show all proof results in form of specific system states.

For the invariant `Train::wagon1_n` it is not possible to find an appropriate system state with the aforementioned configuration. The generator has checked 17862988 states representing the defined state space.

```
use> open train_wagon.use

use> gen flags Train::wagon1_n +n
```

```
use> gen start train_wagon.assl genMaxCountTrainsMaxCountWagons(2,4)
use> gen result
     Random number generator was initialized with 5785.
     Checked 17862988 snapshots.
     Result: No valid state found.
```

The size of the state space results from the procedure's arguments. See the formula below for an exact calculation. The generator tries all numbers for trains and wagons from 1 to maxCountTrains resp. maxCountWagons. The variables t and w represent the actual number of trains and wagons. There are 2^w possibilities to connect a train with w wagons. t trains result in a total of 2^{wt} combinations. Analogously each wagon can be a predecessor of another one. Altogether this fact results in 2^{w^w} possible combinations.

$$\sum_{t=1}^{t=maxCountTrains} \left(\sum_{w=1}^{w=maxCountWagons} 2^{wt} \cdot 2^{w^w} \right)$$

The fact that no valid state was found does not prove a dependence in general, but for the given state space. So we get a strong indication for the dependence between Train::wagon1_n and a subset of the other invariants.

A closer examination of the invariants reveals a direct implication of Train::wagon1_n by Train::oneWell. The latter requires exactly one wagon of the current train to fulfill a specific boolean OCL expression. This implies the existence of at least one wagon linked to the train. It is possible to check this dependence by running again the procedure with the following generator configuration.

```
use> open train_wagon.use

use> gen flags Train::wagon1_n   +n

use> gen flags Train::noCycles   +d
use> gen flags Wagon::pred0_1    +d
use> gen flags Wagon::succ0_1    +d
use> gen flags Wagon::train1_1   +d
use> gen flags Wagon::trainComm  +d

use> gen flags Train::oneWell    -d

use> gen start train_wagon.assl genMaxCountTrainsMaxCountWagons(2,4)

use> gen result
     Random number generator was initialized with 4575.
     Checked 17862988 snapshots.
     Result: No valid state found.
```

The invariant Train::wagon1_n was negated and the rest of the invariants were deactivated except for Train::oneWell. After the generation process the generator shows the same result as in the former run in which all invariants were embraced. This result strongly supports the assumption that the considered invariant is not independent, i.e., that `Train::wagon1_n` is a consequence of `Train::oneWell`.

5   Checking Consequences

The USE generator feature for loading external OCL invariants can be utilized yet in a different way. Besides using it to load constraints for guiding the search, it can be used for checking consequences from the model.

In general, only essential constraints, which have no dependencies, should be formulated within a model. But the constraints do not necessarily represent all important properties of the model directly. Instead, other important properties may follow from the defined constraints. For example, the important property written down below as the invariant `Train::distinctTrainsDistinctWagons` is assumed to be always fulfilled when a valid state is produced. The constraint forbids wagons from being shared between two trains.

```
context t1:Train inv distinctTrainsDistinctWagons:
  Train.allInstances->forAll(t2| t1<>t2 implies
    t1.allWagons()->intersection(t2.allWagons())->isEmpty())
```

The following USE protocol shows how the relationship between the explicit model constraints and the property under consideration can be explored with the USE generator. The corresponding additional invariant is negated directly after it has been loaded. After starting the search, the generator reports that it does not find a valid state.

```
use> open train_wagon.use

use> gen load distinctTrainsDistinctWagons.invs
    Added invariants: Train::distinctTrainsDistinctWagons

use> gen flags Train::distinctTrainsDistinctWagons +n

use> gen start train_wagon.assl genMaxCountTrainsMaxCountWagons(2,4)
use> gen result
    Random number generator was initialized with 9261.
    Checked 17862988 snapshots.
    Result: No valid state found.
```

Therefore, within the scope of a state space with at most two trains and four wagons, the added invariant has been proven to be not independent, i.e., to be implied by the model. In this example, this conclusion may be generalized, because additional trains and wagons do not entail significant changes to the state space except for its size.

Standard OCL does not distinguish between a basic invariant and an invariant which is an implication from other invariants. However, in order to label such implications one could introduce a special stereotype to express this.

6 Conclusion

This paper explains how consistency, independence and checking consequences in UML and OCL models can be handled with the USE tool on the basis of test scenarios. The OCL plays a central role in our approach: OCL is used for formulating constraints, for reducing the test search space (in ASSL procedures), for formulating search space properties (by employing dynamically loaded invariants) and for focusing deductions (by switching off unneeded invariants). Our approach is based on an interaction between building scenarios (through test cases) and studying system properties (through formulating properties and giving proofs).

A number of open questions remain for future work. We have to improve our approach by reducing the search space. Currently we are investigating how to guide the ASSL search by allowing constraints to be stated so that the ASSL search can be finished earlier in negative cases. Furthermore it is necessary to show more information about the search space as well as valid and invalid invariants during the search. The user interface of the ASSL search could be improved by allowing for a direct interaction. General ASSL procedures like `genMaxCountTrainsMaxCountWagons` with a universal scheme for state constructing could be generated in an automatic way. Last but not least, we want to employ efficient SAT solver technology for checking properties like consistency or independence.

Acknowledgement

The constructive remarks of the referees have helped us to improve and to polish our work.

References

1. Avila, C., Flores, G., Cheon, Y.: A Library-Based Approach to Translating OCL Constraints to JML Assertions for Runtime Checking. In: Arabnia, H.R., Reza, H. (eds.) Software Engineering Research and Practice, pp. 403–408. CSREA Press (2008)
2. Aichernig, B.K., Salas, P.A.: Test Case Generation by OCL Mutation and Constraint Solving. In: QSIC, pp. 64–71. IEEE Computer Society, Los Alamitos (2005)
3. Bohling, J.: Snapshot Generation for Validating UML Class Diagrams. Diploma Thesis, University of Bremen, Computer Science Department (2001) (in German)
4. Baruzzo, A., Comini, M.: Static Verification of UML Model Consistency. In: Hearnden, D., Süß, J.G., Baudry, B., Rapin, N. (eds.) Proc. 3rd Workshop Model Design and Validation, October 2006, pp. 111–126. University of Queensland (2006)
5. Bouquet, F., Grandpierre, C., Legeard, B., Peureux, F., Vacelet, N., Utting, M.: A Subset of Precise UML for Model-Based Testing. In: A-MOST, pp. 95–104. ACM, New York (2007)
6. Beckert, B., Hähnle, R., Schmitt, P.H. (eds.): Verification of Object-Oriented Software. LNCS, vol. 4334. Springer, Heidelberg (2007)

7. Cabot, J., Clarisó, R.: UML/OCL Verification in Practice. In: Van Baelen, S., Van Der Straeten, R., Mens, T. (eds.) ChaMDE 2008, 1st Int. Workshop Challenges in Model Driven Software Engineering, pp. 31–35 (2008), http://ssel.vub.ac.be/ChaMDE08/

8. Gaudel, M.-C.: Testing can be Formal, Too. In: Mosses, P.D., Schwartzbach, M.I., Nielsen, M. (eds.) CAAP 1995, FASE 1995, and TAPSOFT 1995. LNCS, vol. 915, pp. 82–96. Springer, Heidelberg (1995)

9. Gogolla, M., Richters, M., Bohling, J.: Tool Support for Validating UML and OCL Models through Automatic Snapshot Generation. In: Eloff, J., Engelbrecht, A., Kotze, P., Eloff, M. (eds.) Proc. Annual Research Conf. South African Institute of Computer Scientists and Information Technologists, pp. 248–257. ACM, New York (2003)

10. Gogolla, M., Bohling, J., Richters, M.: Validating UML and OCL Models in USE by Automatic Snapshot Generation. Journal on Software and System Modeling 4(4), 386–398 (2005)

11. Gogolla, M., Büttner, F., Richters, M.: USE: A UML-Based Specification Environment for Validating UML and OCL. Science of Computer Programming 69, 27–34 (2007)

12. Hughes, J.: QuickCheck Testing for Fun and Profit. In: Hanus, M. (ed.) PADL 2007. LNCS, vol. 4354, pp. 1–32. Springer, Heidelberg (2006)

13. Jackson, D.: Software Abstractions: Logic, Language, and Analysis. MIT Press, Cambridge (2006)

14. Marcano-Kamenoff, R., Lévy, N.: Transformation Rules of OCL Constraints into B Formal Expressions. In: CSDUML 2002, Workshop Critical Systems Development with UML. 5th Int. Conf. Unified Modeling Language, Dresden, Germany (September 2002)

15. OMG, (ed.): OMG Unified Modeling Language Specification, Version 2.0. OMG (2004)

16. OMG (ed.): OMG Query, View and Transformation Specification (QVT). OMG (2005)

17. Shen, W., Compton, K., Huggins, J.: A Toolset for Supporting UML Static and Dynamic Model Checking. In: Proc. 16th IEEE Int. Conf. Automated Software Engineering (ASE), pp. 147–152. IEEE Computer Society, Los Alamitos (2001)

18. Trong, T.D., Ghosh, S., France, R.B., Hamilton, M., Wilkins, B.: UMLAnT: An Eclipse Plugin for Animating and Testing UML Designs. In: Eclipse 2005, Proc. 2005 OOPSLA Workshop Eclipse Technology eXchange, pp. 120–124. ACM Press, New York (2005)

19. Warmer, J., Kleppe, A.: The Object Constraint Language: Precise Modeling with UML, 2nd edn. Addison-Wesley, Reading (2003)

Dynamic Symbolic Execution
for Testing Distributed Objects[*]

Andreas Griesmayer[1], Bernhard Aichernig [1,2],
Einar Broch Johnsen [3], and Rudolf Schlatte [1,2]

[1] International Institute for Software Technology, United Nations University
(UNU-IIST), Macao S.A.R., China
{agriesma,bka,rschlatte}@iist.unu.edu
[2] Institute for Software Technology, Graz University of Technology, Austria
{aichernig,rschlatte}@ist.tugraz.at
[3] Department of Informatics, University of Oslo, Norway
einarj@ifi.uio.no

Abstract. This paper extends dynamic symbolic execution to distributed and concurrent systems. Dynamic symbolic execution can be used
in software testing to systematically identify equivalence classes of input values and has been shown to scale well to large systems. Although
mainly applied to sequential programs, this scalability makes it interesting to consider the technique in the distributed and concurrent setting as
well. In order to extend the technique to concurrent systems, it is necessary to obtain sufficient control over the scheduling of concurrent activities to avoid race conditions. Creol, a modeling language for distributed
concurrent objects, solves this problem by abstracting from a particular
scheduling policy but explicitly defining scheduling points. This provides
sufficient control to apply the technique of dynamic symbolic execution
for model based testing of interleaved processes. The technique has been
formalized in rewriting logic, executes in Maude, and applied to non-
trivial examples, including an industrial case study.

1 Introduction

Distributed and concurrent systems, e.g. web services, are becoming increas-
ingly important for long-running infrastructure and applications. They typically
consist of loosely coupled components which communicate asynchronously, potentially running on different hardware systems. For critical distributed systems,
the use of formal methods, both for design and verification, remains a challenge.
In the general case, the complexity of such systems makes full verification seem
impossible, even for medium sized examples. In this paper we consider model-
based testing of distributed concurrent systems, where we use an object oriented,
distributed model as specification.

[*] This research was carried out as part of the EU FP6 project *Credo*: Modeling and
analysis of evolutionary structures for distributed services (IST-33826).

C. Dubois (Ed.): TAP 2009, LNCS 5668, pp. 105–120, 2009.

We present a tool which identifies adequate test cases from such a formal model. In order to test the different communication patterns, we focus on architectural models which reflect the distributed nature of the systems under test. Hence, the models themselves are complex in the sense that they have to capture distribution, concurrency, and asynchronous communication. The challenge is to find a test generation technique that scales to the combinatorial explosion in the number of possible runs in such models. A promising technique that seems to scale well to large systems is *dynamic symbolic execution* [2,8,18,19]. The idea is to calculate a symbolic execution in parallel with the concrete test run of a given formal model. The result is a set of conditions over symbolic input values representing the path of the last run. The conjunction of these conditions form the equivalence class of inputs that could take the same path.

The problem is that dynamic symbolic execution cannot deal with common concurrency models as present in today's programming languages. The reason is that dynamic symbolic execution does not work in the context of arbitrary non-deterministic interleavings of executions. Hence, its main application so far has been limited to single-threaded (sequential) programs and to client-server applications with simple serialized communication flows. In this work we overcome this limitation by choosing a modeling language that provides the appropriate level of concurrency control: Creol [10].

Creol is an executable object oriented modeling language whose execution model was designed to assist in the development of distributed systems. An object in Creol describes an execution unit that executes a dynamic number of processes, a single process at a time. Features like asynchronous method calls and conditional release points allow to model complex interactions between distributed components or objects.

We have implemented dynamic symbolic execution in Maude [4], which is the execution platform of Creol, allowing us to perform the symbolic run dynamically while the concrete run is executed. The tool computes the equivalence classes of test inputs covering the paths already taken, allowing the tester to systematically find new test stimuli for non-covered parts. The generated test cases are used to check the conformance of implementations of the distributed systems with their Creol models as presented in previous work in [1]. The presented technique forms part of a new design process for distributed systems that has been developed in the EU FP6 CREDO project. The feasibility of the approach has been shown by application to the ASK system, an industrial distributed agent-based information system.

To summarize, the *contributions* of this work are as follows:

- This is the first time dynamic symbolic execution is applied to distributed systems involving asynchronous method calls and non-deterministic scheduling of interleaved processes.
- The technique has been formalized in terms of rewriting logic and implemented in the Maude rewriting system.
- It has been applied to an industrial case study.

In the remainder of this section we give an overview of related work, followed by a short introduction to dynamic symbolic execution in the next section and an introduction to Creol in Section 3. Dynamic symbolic execution is extended to distributed systems in Section 4 and applied to testing in Section 5, before showing examples in Section 6. Finally, in Section 7 we draw our conclusions.

1.1   Related Work

Symbolic execution is a widely used program analysis technique that represents the values of variables as symbolic expressions instead of concrete data. An execution of a program is performed by manipulating those expressions instead of computing concrete values. Application of symbolic execution to testing was already proposed in 1976 by King [12], who shows symbolic execution for a simple sequential language and presents an interactive tool EFFIGY to traverse the execution tree.

Much more recently, symbolic execution has been used for various applications in the area of testing. Khurshid et al. [11] perform source to source transformation on Java programs to allow explicit state model checkers like the Java PathFinder [21] to exploit the succinct representation of the state space by symbolic representation. They generate test cases by checking the reachability of a testing criterion. Analysis of the counter example gives the input for test cases similar to [22,7,9]. In [23], Xie et al. introduce SYMSTRA, a tool that uses symbolic execution to explore different sequences of method calls in order to generate unit tests for object oriented systems. These applications use symbolic execution mainly to compress the representation of the state space while performing an exhaustive search. However, there are limits to the feasibility of executing complex concurrent systems purely symbolically, due to the sheer number of possible execution paths induced by non-determinism.

There are basically two possibilities to make the process feasible for large systems: (1) reducing the amount of information which needs to be tracked and (2) reducing the number of paths to search. An example for the first kind are static analysis tools like ARCHER from Engler et al. [24], which very successfully concentrate on certain properties of interest for the analysis (memory and array access). To derive input values that drive a run to certain areas in the program, however, we want to consider all information available. We therefore reduce the number of paths that are searched at the same time to make symbolic execution feasible. The latter technique is called *dynamic symbolic execution* (DSE).

To our knowledge, the first to use symbolic execution on single runs were Boyer et al. in 1975 [2] who developed the interactive tool SELECT that computes input values for a run selected by the user. One of the first automated DSE tools for testing was DART (Directed Automated Random Testing) from Godefroid et al. [8]. DART automatically extracts a program's interface and generates a test driver to perform random testing. While DART only evaluates integer variables, the CUTE and jCUTE tools from Sen at al. [18] extend this approach to include pointers and generate dynamic data structures. Several extensions to these approaches exist, among the most notable the PEX tool from

Tillmann et al. [19] for computing test cases using *parameterized unit tests* for single-threaded .NET programs.

We extend this approaches to a model-based testing method that targets distributed and concurrent systems and deals with interacting processes and asynchronous communication between components. Model-based testing uses models of the system under test (SUT) to derive test cases. Evaluations, e.g., from Pretschner et al. [17], have shown their usefulness in software development. Tools for reactive systems, like TorX from Tretmans et al. [20], observe the inputs of the SUT and perform on-the-fly testing by generating new inputs for the SUT according to the model and a test purpose. In contrast to this applications, distributed systems are only loosely coupled, close synchronization between SUT and tester is not useful as we discussed in more detail in previous work [1]. In our setting, the specification is given as Creol model. Creole is a modeling language whose semantics is defined in rewrite logic, which is executable in Maude. The definition of the language in rewrite logic therefore directly gives an interpreter, an approach that also was used by Chen et al. [3] for their framework for "rapid prototyping" of new languages. In this work, we extend the semantic rules to perform DSE on Creol models in order to find test cases with optimal coverage of this specification. We compute test suites to check the conformance between an implementation and the specification. Our previous work [1] also shows how to use a Creol model as an oracle for a test run on the implementation.

Recent work from Kirner [13] gives criteria to ensure that a coverage metric on the model also holds on the actual implementation. In this work we assume that these criteria hold. There are a number of techniques that help in testing of concurrent systems by either controlling the scheduling to make the test results more deterministic [14,16] or by repeating test cases multiple times with a different (randomized) scheduling to gain a good coverage of the code [6]. These methods are complementary to the approach shown here as they handle the actual test execution rather then the computation of test cases and should be combined with the test case generation shown in this paper for optimal results.

2   Dynamic Symbolic Execution for Testing

This section gives a brief introduction to dynamic symbolic execution (DSE) and its application to conventional test case generation, before we proceed with extensions for distributed and concurrent systems. Conventional symbolic execution uses symbols to represent arbitrary values during execution. When encountering a conditional branch statement, the run is forked. This results in a tree covering all paths in the program. Decisions on branch statements are recorded, resulting in a set of conditions over the symbolic values that have to evaluate to *true* for a path to be taken. We call the conjunction of these conditions the *path condition*; it represents an equivalence class of concrete input values that could have taken the same path. In contrast, *dynamic* symbolic execution calculates the symbolic execution *in parallel* with a concrete run that is actually taken, avoiding the usual problem of eliminating infeasible paths and maintaining the call stack of the whole run tree.

We use DSE to compute test cases on the model that are then used on the actual implementation. The inputs of the model are treated as symbolic values and a path condition describing the equivalence class of inputs that can perform the same run is computed. Concrete input values from *outside* this equivalence class are selected to force new execution paths, and thereby new test cases. Consider the following piece of code from an agent system calculating the number of threads needed to handle job requests (taken from Figure 5).

```
1    amountToCreate:= tasks − idlethreads +  ...  ;
2    if (amountToCreate > (maxthreads − threads)) then
3      amountToCreate:= maxthreads − threads;
4    end;
5    if (amountToCreate > 0) then ... end;
```

Testers usually analyze the control flow in order to achieve a certain coverage. For example, a run evaluating both conditions above to **true** is sufficient to ensure *statement coverage*; *branch coverage* needs at least two cases and *path coverage* all four combinations. Dynamic symbolic computation gives a condition for each conditional statement in terms of symbolic input values. For better readability, we mark the symbolic values of an input parameter by appending s to the parameter's variable name. Let threads, idlethreads, and tasks denote the input parameters for testing, and maxthreads being a constant with a concrete value. Assume that we have a first concrete run in which both conditions evaluate to **true**. This single run already fulfills statement coverage. DSE gives us following path condition that has to be fulfilled to obtain the run (for constant maxthreads $= 10$)

$$(tasks_S - idlethreads_S) > (10 - threads_S)$$
$$\wedge (maxthreads_S - threads_S) > 0$$

In this example, DSE replaces the variable amountToCreate by its symbolic value $maxthreads_S - threads_S$. To create a new test case that follows a different path, one or more of the sub-conditions are negated and inputs that fulfill the new condition are selected. If the path condition is not satisfiable, the corresponding path is infeasible. In this case, we continue negating different sub-conditions until no more valid inputs are found. For example, inputs satisfying

$$(tasks_S - idlethreads_S) \leq (10 - threads_S)$$
$$\wedge (maxthreads - threads_S) > 0$$

will avoid the first **then**-branch, resulting in a different execution path.

The strategy how to select sub-conditions to negate determines the kind of coverage metric obtained. Note that the fraction of the program that can be covered depends on the program, the used coverage metric, and the symbolic values used. For example, the presence of unreachable code obviously makes full statement coverage impossible. The concrete test values from symbolic input vectors can be found by, e.g., using a constraint solver.

3   The Modeling Language Creol

Creol is a high-level executable modeling language targeting distributed systems in which concurrent objects communicate asynchronously [10]. The language decouples communication from synchronization. Furthermore, it allows local scheduling to be left underspecified but controlled through explicitly declared process release points. The language has a formal semantics defined in rewriting logic [15] and executes on the Maude platform [4]. In the remainder of this section, we present Creol and point out its essential features for DSE.

A concurrent object in Creol executes a number of processes that have access to its local state. Each process corresponds to the activation of one of the object's methods; a special method run is automatically activated at object creation time, if present, and captures the object's active behavior. Objects execute concurrently: each object has a processor dedicated to executing the processes of that object, so processes in different objects execute in parallel. In contrast to, e.g., Java, each Creol object strictly encapsulates its state; i.e., external manipulation of the object state happens via calls to the object's methods only.

Only one process can be active in an object at a time; the other processes in the object are *suspended*. We distinguish between *blocking* a process and *releasing* a process. Blocking causes the execution of the process to stop, but does not let a suspended process resume. Releasing a process suspends the execution of that process and lets another (suspended) process resume. Thus, if a process is blocked there is no execution in the object, whereas if a process is released another process in the object may execute. The execution of several processes within an object can be combined using *release points* within method bodies. At a release point, the active process may be released and *some* suspended process resumes. This way, (non-terminating) active and reactive behavior are easily combined within a concurrent object in Creol.

Communication in Creol is based on method calls. These are a priori asynchronous; method replies are assigned to labels (also called *future variables*, see [5]). There is no synchronization associated with *calling* a method. *Reading a reply* from a label, however, is a blocking operation and allows the calling object to synchronize with the callee. A method call that is directly followed by a read operation models a synchronous call. Thus, the calling process may decide at runtime whether to call a method synchronously or asynchronously. The local scheduling of processes inside an object is given by conditions associated with release points. These conditions may depend on the value of the local state, allowing cooperative scheduling between the processes within an object, but may also depend on the object's communication with other objects in the environment. Guards on release points include synchronization operations on labels, so the local scheduling can depend on both the object's state and the arrival of replies to asynchronous method calls.

To sum up: only one process is executing on each object's local state at a time, and interleaving of processes is flexibly controlled via (guarded) release points. Together with the fact that objects communicate exclusively via messages (strict

$T ::= C \mid \textbf{Bool} \mid \textbf{Void}$ $\qquad L ::= \textbf{class } C(\overline{v}) \textbf{ begin } \overline{\textbf{var } f : T}; \overline{M} \textbf{ end}$

$\quad \mid \textbf{Int} \mid \textbf{String} \mid \ldots$ $\quad M ::= \textbf{op } m(\textbf{in } \overline{x : T} \textbf{ out } \overline{x : T}) == \overline{\textbf{var } x : T}; \overline{s} \textbf{ end}$

$v ::= f \mid x$ $\qquad\qquad e ::= v \mid \textbf{new } C(\overline{v}) \mid \textbf{null} \mid \textbf{this} \mid v + v \mid \ldots$

$b ::= \textbf{true} \mid \textbf{false} \mid v$ $\quad s ::= l!e.m(\overline{e}) \mid !e.m(\overline{e}) \mid l?(v) \mid e.m(\overline{e}; \overline{v}) \mid \textbf{await } g$

$g ::= b \mid v? \mid g \wedge g$ $\qquad\quad \mid v := e \mid \textbf{skip} \mid \textbf{release} \mid \textbf{await } e.m(\overline{e}; \overline{v})$

$\qquad\qquad\qquad\qquad\qquad\qquad \mid \textbf{while } g \textbf{ do } \overline{s} \textbf{ end} \mid \textbf{if } g \textbf{ then } \overline{s} \textbf{ end}$

Fig. 1. Language syntax of a subset of Creol

encapsulation), this gives us the concurrency control necessary for extending DSE to the distributed paradigm.

Syntax. The language syntax of the subset of Creol used in this paper is presented in a Java-like style in Figure 1. In this overview, we omit some features of Creol, including interfaces, inheritance, non-deterministic choice and many built-in data types and their operations. For a full overview of Creol, see for example [10]. In the language subset used in the examples of this paper, classes L are of type C with a set of methods $\overline{M}$. *Expressions* e over variables v (either fields f or local variables x) are standard. *Statements* s are standard apart from the asynchronous method call $l!e.m(\overline{e})$ where the label l points to a reference to the reply, the (blocking) read operation $l?(\overline{v})$, and release points **await** g and **release**. *Guards* g are conjunctions of Boolean expressions b and synchronization operations $l?$ on labels l. When the guard in an **await** statement evaluates to *false*, the statement is *disabled* and becomes a **release**, otherwise it is *enabled* and becomes a **skip**. A **release** statement suspends the active process and another suspended process may be rescheduled. The *guarded call* **await** $e.m(\overline{e}; \overline{v})$ is a typical pattern which suspends the active process until the reply to the call has arrived and abbreviates $l!e.m(\overline{e}); \textbf{await } l?; l?(\overline{v})$.

3.1   Representation of a Run

A run of a Creol system captures the parallel execution of processes in different concurrent objects. Such a run may be perceived as a sequence of execution steps where each step contains a set of local transitions on a subset of the system's objects. However, only one process may be active at a time in each object and different objects operate on disjoint data. Therefore, the transitions in each execution step may be performed in a truly concurrent manner or in any sequential order, so long as all transitions in one step are completed before the next execution step commences. For the purposes of dynamic symbolic execution the run is represented as a sequence of statements which manipulate the state variables, together with the conditions which determine the control flow, as follows.

The representation of an assignment $\overline{v} := \overline{e}$ is straightforward: Because fields and local variables in different processes can have the same name and statements from different objects are interleaved, the variable names are expanded to a unique identifier by adding the object id for fields and the call label for local variables. This expansion is done transparently for all variables and we will omit the variable scope in the following.

An asynchronous method call in the run is reflected in four execution steps (the label value l uniquely identifies the steps that belong to the same method call): $o_1 \xrightarrow{l} o_2.m(\bar{e})$ represents the *call* of method m in object o_2 from object o_1 with arguments $\bar{e}$; $o_1 \overset{l}{\dashrightarrow} o_2.m(\bar{v})$ represents when the called objects starts execution, where $\bar{v}$ are the local names of the parameters for m; $o_1 \xleftarrow{l} o_2.m(\bar{e})$ represents the emission of the return values from the method execution; and $o_1 \xleftarrow{l} o_2.m(\bar{v})$ represents the corresponding reception of the values. These four events fully describe method calling in Creol. In this execution model the events reflecting a specific method call always appear in the same order, but they can be interleaved with other statements.

Object creation, **new** $C(\bar{v})$, is similar to a method call. The actual object creation is reduced to generating a new identifier for the object and a call to the object's **init** and **run** methods, which create the sequences as described above.

Conditional statements in Creol do not change the values of the variables and therefore can be treated as **skip** in DSE. For the sake of computing the input values, however, the condition of the taken branch is recorded as $\langle g \rangle$ (E.g., if the concrete execution selects the *then* branch of an statement **if** g, the condition $\langle g \rangle$ is recorded. If the *else* branch is selected, then the *negated* condition $\langle \neg g \rangle$ is recorded). Remark that statements **await** g requires careful treatment: if it evaluates to *false*, no code is executed. To reflect the information that the interpreter failed to execute a process because the condition g of the **await** statement evaluated to *false*, the negated condition $\langle \neg g \rangle$ is recorded and the interpreter proceeds by selecting another process.

4   Dynamic Symbolic Execution of Distributed Objects

This section presents the rules to actually compute the symbolic values for a given run. The formulas given in this section very closely resemble the rewrite rules of Creol's simulation environment [10], defined in rewriting logic [15] and implemented in Maude [4]. A rewrite rule $t \implies t'$ may be interpreted as a *local transition rule* allowing an instance of the pattern t in the configuration of the rewrite system to evolve into the corresponding instance of the pattern t' (where t and t' denote *states* of the model). When auxiliary functions that do not change the state are needed in the semantics, these are defined in equational logic, and are evaluated in between the state transitions [15]. The rules are presented here in a slightly simplified manner to improve readability.

Denote by $\bar{s}$ the representation of program statements. Let $\sigma = \langle v_1 \rhd e_1, v_2 \rhd e_2, \ldots v_n \rhd e_n \rangle = \langle \bar{v} \rhd \bar{e} \rangle$ be a map which records *key–value* entries $v \rhd e$, where a variable v is bound to a symbolic value e. The value assigned to key v is accessed by $v\sigma$. For an expression e and a map σ, define a parallel substitution operator $e\sigma$ which replaces all occurrences of every variable v in e with the expression $v\sigma$ (if v is in the domain of σ). For simplicity, let $\bar{e}\sigma$ denote the application of the

$$\bar{v} := \bar{e}; \bar{s}[\Theta, \sigma, \mathcal{C}] \Longrightarrow \bar{s}[\Theta, \sigma \uplus \langle \bar{v} \triangleright (\bar{e}\sigma) \rangle, \mathcal{C}] \qquad (\text{ASSIGN})$$

$$o_1 \xrightarrow{l} o_2.m(\bar{e}); \bar{s}[\Theta, \sigma, \mathcal{C}] \Longrightarrow \bar{s}[\Theta \uplus \langle l \triangleright \bar{e}\sigma \rangle, \sigma, \mathcal{C}] \qquad (\text{CALL})$$

$$o_1 \xrightarrow{l} o_2.m(\bar{v}); \bar{s}[\Theta, \sigma, \mathcal{C}] \Longrightarrow \bar{s}[\Theta, \sigma \uplus \langle \bar{v} \triangleright l\Theta \rangle, \mathcal{C}] \qquad (\text{BIND})$$

$$\langle g \rangle; \bar{s}[\Theta, \sigma, \mathcal{C}] \Longrightarrow \bar{s}[\Theta, \sigma, \mathcal{C}^\smallfrown \langle g\sigma \rangle] \qquad (\text{COND})$$

Fig. 2. Rewrite rules for symbolic execution of Creol statements

parallel substitution to every expression in the list $\bar{e}$. Furthermore, let the operator $\sigma_1 \uplus \sigma_2$ combine two maps σ_1 and σ_2 such that, when entries with the same key exist in both maps, the entry in σ_2 is taken. These operators are defined as equations in rewriting logic and are evaluated in between the rewrite steps. In the symbolic state σ, all expanded variable names are bound to symbolic expressions. However, operations for method calls do not change the value of the symbolic state, but generate or receive *messages* that are used to communicate actual parameter values between the calling and receiving objects. Similar to the expressions bound to variables in the symbolic state σ, the symbolic representations of these actual parameters are bound in a map Θ to the actual and unique label value l provided for each method call by Creol's operational semantics. Finally, the conditions of control statements along an execution path are collected in a list $\mathcal{C}$; the concatenation of a condition c to $\mathcal{C}$ is denoted by $\mathcal{C}^\smallfrown c$.

The *configurations* of the rewrite system for dynamic symbolic execution are given by $\bar{s}[\Theta, \sigma, \mathcal{C}]$, where $\bar{s}$ is a run represented as a sequence of statements that still have to be executed, Θ and σ are the maps for messages and symbolic variable assignments as described above, and $\mathcal{C}$ is the list of conditions. Recall that the run $\bar{s}$ (as described in Section 3.1) is in fact generated on the fly by the concrete rewrite system for Creol executed in parallel with the dynamic symbolic execution. Thus, the *rules* of the rewrite system have the form

$$\bar{s}[\Theta, \sigma, \mathcal{C}] \Longrightarrow \bar{s}'[\Theta', \sigma', \mathcal{C}']$$

The primed versions are updated results from the execution rule. The rules are given in Figure 2 and explained below.

Rule ASSIGN defines the variable updates that are performed for an assignment. All variables in the right hand side are replaced by their current values in σ, which is then updated by the new expressions. Note that we do not handle variable declarations, but work in the runtime-environment. We expect that a type check already happened during compile time and insert variables into σ the first time they appear. A method call as defined by Rule CALL emits a message that records the expressions that are passed to the method. Because of the asynchronous behavior of Creol, the call might be received at a later point in the run (or not at all if the execution terminates before the method was selected for execution) by Rule BIND, which handles the binding of a call to a new process and assigns the symbolic representation of the actual parameter values to the local variables in the new process. The emission and reception of return values are handled similarly to call statements and call reception.

Object creation is represented as a call to the constructor method `init` of the newly created object. In this case there is no explicit label for the call statement, so the object identifier is used to identify the messages to call the `init` and `run` methods, which are associated to the `new` statement. For conditionals, the local variables in the condition are replaced by their symbolic values (Rule COND). This process is analogous for the different kinds of conditional statements (**if**, **while**, **await**). The statement itself acts as a **skip** statement; it changes no variables and does not produce or consume messages. The resulting expression $g\sigma$ directly characterizes the equivalence class of input values that reach and fulfill the condition. The conjunction of all conditions found during symbolic evaluation give the set of input values that can perform that run. The tool records the condition that evaluated to *true* during runtime. Therefore, if the **else** branch of an **if** statement is entered or a disabled **await** statement with g approached, the recorded condition will be $\neg g$.

5   Testing Distributed Systems

Approaches to test case generation for structural coverage intend to find test a set that performs runs in the system for a specific coverage criterion. Two runs that cover the same parts of a system are considered equivalent. A good test set should maximize the coverage, while minimizing the number of equivalent runs in order to avoid superfluous efforts in executing the tests.

The execution of a distributed system is not fully controllable through its interface. One and the same test case can lead to arbitrarily different runs on the system under test (SUT). In practice, tools like ConTest [6] are used to execute single test cases multiple times on the SUT with different schedulings. For the model, on the other hand, it is straightforward to introduce additional variables to resolve the nondeterminism for the sake of examining all possible paths to build the optimal set of test cases. These techniques are complementary to the computation shown in this paper and should be applied additionally.

It is the responsibility of a testing engineer to write test objects (analogous to unit tests) that set up the system and perform interactions that will drive an interesting execution of the system. Presupposing this test scenario, we enhance the coverage by introducing symbolic values t_S in the test object and compute new values such that new, non-equivalent runs are performed.

Constructing the Test Set. Dynamic symbolic execution on a run gives the set of conditions that are combined to the path condition $C = \bigwedge_{1 \leq i \leq n} c_i$ (for n conditions), characterizing exactly the equivalence class of t_S that can repeat the same execution path. Only one test case that fulfills C is selected. A new test case is then chosen to specifically avoid that a particular branch is taken by violating the respective c_i. To maximize decision coverage (DC), for instance, test cases have to be created such that for each of the conditions c_i, there is also a test case that violates this condition. The process of generating new test cases ends after all combinations required for the coverage criteria are explored.

In the case of concurrent distributed systems, however, we frequently deal with scenarios in which the naive approach does not terminate. Most importantly, distributed systems usually contain active objects that do not terminate and thus creates an infinite run. In this case, execution on the model has to be stopped after exceeding some threshold (ideally after detecting a loop). The computation of the condition can be performed as before and will prohibit the same partial run in future computations. Creol also supports infinite datatypes. Therefore, for a code sample like **while** (i > 0) **do** i := i - 1 **end**, there is a finite run for each i, but there are infinitely many of them. To make sure that the approach terminates, an artificial limiting condition has to be introduced, e.g., by creating an equivalence class for all i greater than a constant k.

Running a Test Case. A test case as generated in this paper is used to test implementations of distributed systems by checking if the implementation under test complies to the model as described in previous work [1]. The test execution approach of that paper handles the difficulties of testing a distributed system by defining a set of actions and events that are used to control the implementation as well as the model, and to monitor the behavior of the implementation. So far the execution has not been monitored online, rather a log is generated that has been verified by using the model. A run of the implementation is considered successful if the model is able to reproduce the run.

The model is a direct specification of the implementation, and both systems share their internal control structure. Test cases optimized for structural coverage in the model will therefore also improve the structural coverage in the implementation.

6   Examples

This section shows the feasibility of the approach by means of two examples: The *peer to peer* example presents the exploration of existing test cases with respect to coverage, during which an important special case was discovered. The second example demonstrates how to derive new test cases on example of the *ASK system*, an industrial case study.

The dynamic symbolic interpreter allows to identify variables that are treated as normal variables for the concrete run, and as a symbolic value for the dynamic symbolic execution. These variables are identified by a special naming scheme, here denoted by the subscript s. This enables the flexible monitoring of symbolic values of variables at any arbitrary level in the code.

6.1   Peer to Peer

A peer to peer system connects several coequal components (peers) with the aim to share data between them. Each peer works both as client and as server holding local files. A client can search the network to find the location of a file, connect to the respective server and download the document. Communication between the components is established via channels. We use a sophisticated model describing such a system, which stems from the CREDO project to demonstrate various

```
1 class Test(cl :Client,b :Peer)          1 class TestDSE(cl :Client,b :Peer)
2 begin                                   2 begin
3   var reply :Data                       3   var reply :Data
4   op run ==                             4   op run ==
5     await                               5     var reqkeyS :Data;
6       cl.search("f1";reply)             6     reqkeyS := "f1" ;
7                                         7     await
8                                         8       cl.search(reqkeyS;reply)
9 end                                     9 end
```

Fig. 3. Predefined test case   **Fig. 4.** Test case for DSE

techniques for modeling distributed systems. It consists of 23 classes (not shown in this paper due to lack of space) and already comes with a small set of test cases that model a net consisting of three nodes with some files each. One of this test cases is given in Figure 3. Class Test models a user that communicates with one of the Peers through the user interface and searches for a file document named "f1"; the result is stored in the variable reply.

In order to examine the paths generated by this test case, we adapt the class by replacing the constant "f1" with the symbolic variable $reqkey_S$ (Figure 4). Recall that DSE performs a concrete and a symbolic run in parallel. The DSE interpreter of Creol therefore treats $reqkey_S$ as normal variable for the concrete run, but as symbolic value in the symbolic execution. The assign of the original value in Line 6 is only executed to generate the concrete run, the symbolic execution passes the symbolic value $reqkey_S$ to the method cl.search. Running the DSE interpreter on this program gives us two decisions in **if** statements within the peers that depend on $reqkey_S$:

```
{"ifthenelse" : not( in(reqkeyS, ["f2"])) }
{"ifthenelse" : in( reqkeyS, ["f1"]) }
```

The conditions represent checks if $reqkey_S$ is in the list of files that are stored at a server. The first server (Condition 1) has the file list ["f2"], which does not contain "f1". The concrete run therefore proceeds to the branch of the conditional where not(in($reqkey_S$, ["f2"])) is true (the else branch). The check at the second server is successful (Condition 2). Manual examination of all predefined test cases quickly shows that this pattern repeats for each test case. For proper coverage, we are interested in concrete values of $reqkey_S$ not satisfying the already taken decisions. In our example this means that we need a value executing a path that does not end in finding a file. Hence, a new concrete value (e.g. "f0") that is not contained in any of the three servers is assigned to $reqkey_S$, what leads to the following path condition:

```
{"ifthenelse" : not(in(reqkeyS,["f2"])) }
{"ifthenelse" : not(in(reqkeyS,["f1"])) }
{"ifthenelse" : not(in(reqkeyS,["f1", "f2", "f3"])) }
```

This new test case represents the important case that ensures that all servers are contacted and the client performs properly even if no file was found.

6.2   The ASK System

ASK is an industrial software system for connecting and organizing people, developed by the research company Almende and marketed by ASK Community Systems. The ASK system provides mechanisms for matching users requiring information or services with potential suppliers and is used by various organizations for applications like workforce planning and emergency response. The number of people connected varies from several hundred to several thousands.

A Creol reference model for ASK systems has been developed by Almende [1]. The ASK system consists of a number of components to receive and process requests. Each of these components is itself multi-threaded. The threads inside a component act as workers in a thread pool, the executing tasks are put into a component-wide shared task queue. A *balancer* is used to create and destroy worker threads depending on a given maximal number of threads, the currently existing number of threads and on the number of remaining tasks. Figure 5 shows one central part of this balancing task: the tail-recursive method `createThreads`. This method and its opponent in the model, `killThreads`, are responsible for creating and killing threads when appropriate. The balancer is initialized with the symbolic value $maxthreads_S$, the maximum number of threads that are allowed in the thread pool. Inside the balancer, the local variable `maxthreads` is then set to $maxthreads_S + 1$ to account for the balancer thread itself, which also runs inside the thread pool. The balancer has access to the number of threads that are active (`threads`), the number of threads that are processing some task (`busythreads`), and the number of tasks that are waiting to be assigned to a worker thread (`tasks`).

The **await** statement in Line 4 suspends the process if it is not necessary to create further worker threads, i.e. if the maximal number of threads is already reached or half of the threads are without a task (they are neither processing a task, nor is there a task open for processing). The **if** statement in Line 7 makes sure there are not more tasks created than allowed by `maxthreads`. Finally, the thread pool is ordered to create the required numbers of threads in Line 11.

We instantiate the model with a fixed number of tasks (10 in our example) and with a variable maximum of threads $maxthreads_S$, with the goal of finding different values for $maxthreads_S$ to optimize the coverage of the code in Figure 5. In the following, we show only the relevant parts of the calculated path conditions, leaving out conditions pertaining to other parts of the model (`killThreads`, the thread creation code inside `threadpool`, etc.).

For a first run we choose $maxthreads_S==0$. Dynamic symbolic execution with this starting value results in the path condition:

```
{"disabled_await" : not( 1< (maxthreadss +1) & true) }
```

After a little simplification it becomes clear that the path was taken because 0 $>=$ $maxthreads_S$. Any other start value will lead to a different run. We select a start value $maxthreads_S==15$ and get

```
1   op createThreads ==
2     var amountToCreate : Int;
3     var idlethreads : Int:= threads − busythreads;
4     await ((threads < maxthreads)
5           ∧ ((idlethreads − tasks) < (threads / 2)));
6     amountToCreate:= tasks − idlethreads + (threads / 2);
7     if (amountToCreate > (maxthreads − threads)) then
8       amountToCreate:= maxthreads − threads;
9     end;
10    if (amountToCreate > 0) then
11      await threadpool.createThreads(amountToCreate);
12    end;
13    createThreads();
```

Fig. 5. Model of thread pool balancing code in the ASK system. The fields threads, idlethreads and tasks are updated by outside method calls, so the conditions in the **await** statements can become true.

```
{"enabled_await" : (1 < (maxthreadsₛ +1) & true) }
{"ifthenelse" : not(10 > maxthreadsₛ ) }
```

The number 10 reflects the number of tasks we created. The path condition reflects that all inputs with $maxthreads_s$ >= 10 lead to the same path because in each case only the number of threads is created, which is 10 due to the 10 tasks with which the model was initialized. There is no condition for the **if** in Line 10 because the amount to create does not exceed $maxthreads_s$ and therefore is not dependent on it. A third run, created with $maxthreads_s$==5, results in

```
{"disabled_await" : (1 < (maxthreadsₛ +1) & true) }
{"ifthenelse" : 10 > maxthreadsₛ }
{"ifthenelse" : maxthreadsₛ > 0 }
```

In this test case the amount of tasks to create exceeded the maximal allowed number of tasks and therefore was recomputed in Line 8. The new value depends on $maxthreads_s$, which causes the **if** statement in Line 10 to contribute to the path condition. The new path condition does not further divide the input space, so the maximal possible coverage according to the chosen coverage criterion is reached.

7   Conclusions

The main contribution of this work is the novel extension of dynamic symbolic execution to non-trivial distributed and concurrent object models. This has been achieved by exploiting the properties of the Creol modeling language; in particular local scheduling control of the processes and strict encapsulation of the object state. This paper demonstrates how dynamic symbolic execution, combined with the executable architectural models of Creol, can be used to systematically derive interesting test cases, while avoiding the combinatorial explosion inherent in distributed concurrent systems. Our approach has been formalized in rewriting logic and implemented in Maude. A peer to peer example and an industrial case study of an agent system serve to illustrate the technique.

The current version of the tool reports the equivalence classes to the user, but does not automatically select and execute new test runs. Immediate future work will be an automation of this process by means of constraint solving techniques. Others have shown that this is feasible in practice, e.g. in [19].

Dynamic symbolic execution, as presented in this paper, should be applicable to other object-oriented languages with concurrency by enforcing serialization of processes in the object as well as strict encapsulation. In a multi-threaded concurrency model as found in Java, dynamic symbolic execution could in principle be achieved by declaring all methods as synchronized and all fields as private. However, such severe restrictions seem undesirable. It would be interesting if lighter restrictions for such languages could be identified that still enable dynamic symbolic execution.

References

1. Aichernig, B., Griesmayer, A., Schlatte, R., Stam, A.: Modeling and testing multi-threaded asynchronous systems with Creol. In: Proceedings of the 2nd International Workshop on Harnessing Theories for Tool Support in Software (TTSS 2008). ENTCS. Elsevier, Amsterdam (2009) (to appear)
2. Boyer, R.S., Elspas, B., Levitt, K.N.: Select-A formal system for testing and debugging programs by symbolic execution. SIGPLAN Not. 10(6), 234–245 (1975)
3. Chen, F., Hills, M., Roşu, G.: A Rewrite Logic Approach to Semantic Definition, Design and Analysis of Object-Oriented Languages. Technical Report UIUCDCS-R-2006-2702, Department of Computer Science, University of Illinois at Urbana-Champaign (2006)
4. Clavel, M., Durán, F., Eker, S., Lincoln, P., Martí-Oliet, N., Meseguer, J., Quesada, J.F.: Maude: Specification and programming in rewriting logic. Theoretical Computer Science 285, 187–243 (2002)
5. de Boer, F.S., Clarke, D., Johnsen, E.B.: A complete guide to the future. In: De Nicola, R. (ed.) ESOP 2007. LNCS, vol. 4421, pp. 316–330. Springer, Heidelberg (2007)
6. Edelstein, O., Farchi, E., Goldin, E., Nir, Y., Ratsaby, G., Ur, S.: Framework for testing multi-threaded Java programs. Concurrency and Computation: Practice & Experience 15(3), 485–499 (2003)
7. Gargantini, A., Heitmeyer, C.: Using model checking to generate tests from requirements specifications. In: Nierstrasz, O., Lemoine, M. (eds.) ESEC 1999 and ESEC-FSE 1999. LNCS, vol. 1687, pp. 146–162. Springer, Heidelberg (1999)
8. Godefroid, P., Klarlund, N., Sen, K.: DART: directed automated random testing. In: PLDI 2005: Proceedings of the 2005 ACM SIGPLAN conference on Programming language design and implementation, pp. 213–223. ACM, New York (2005)
9. Hong, H., Lee, I., Sokolsky, O., Ural, H.: A temporal logic based theory of test coverage and generation. In: Katoen, J.-P., Stevens, P. (eds.) TACAS 2002. LNCS, vol. 2280, pp. 327–341. Springer, Heidelberg (2002)

10. Johnsen, E.B., Owe, O.: An asynchronous communication model for distributed concurrent objects. Software and Systems Modeling 6(1), 35–58 (2007)
11. Khurshid, S., Pasareanu, C., Visser, W.: Generalized Symbolic Execution for Model Checking and Testing. In: Garavel, H., Hatcliff, J. (eds.) TACAS 2003. LNCS, vol. 2619, pp. 553–568. Springer, Heidelberg (2003)
12. King, J.: Symbolic execution and program testing. Communications of the ACM 19(7), 385–394 (1976)
13. Kirner, R.: Towards preserving model coverage and structural code coverage. EURASIP Journal on Embedded Systems (2009)
14. Long, B., Hoffman, D., Strooper, P.A.: Tool Support for Testing Concurrent Java Components. IEEE Trans. on Software Engineering, 555–566 (2003)
15. Meseguer, J.: Conditional rewriting logic as a unified model of concurrency. Theoretical Computer Science 96, 73–155 (1992)
16. Musuvathi, M., Qadeer, S., Ball, T., Basler, G.: Finding and reproducing heisenbugs in concurrent programs. In: Proceedings of the 8th USENIX Symposium on Operating Systems Design and Implementation, OSDI 2008 (2008)
17. Pretschner, A., Prenninger, W., Wagner, S., Kühnel, C., Baumgartner, M., Sostawa, B., Zölch, R., Stauner, T.: One evaluation of model-based testing and its automation. In: ICSE 2005: Proceedings of the 27th international conference on Software engineering, pp. 392–401. ACM, New York (2005)
18. Sen, K., Agha, G.: CUTE and jCUTE: Concolic unit testing and explicit path model-checking tools. In: Ball, T., Jones, R.B. (eds.) CAV 2006. LNCS, vol. 4144, pp. 419–423. Springer, Heidelberg (2006)
19. Tillmann, N., de Halleux, J.: Pex - white box test generation for .NET. In: Beckert, B., Hähnle, R. (eds.) TAP 2008. LNCS, vol. 4966, pp. 134–153. Springer, Heidelberg (2008)
20. Tretmans, J., Brinksma, H.: Torx: Automated model based testing. In: Proceedings of the 1st European Conference on Model-Driven Engineering (2003)
21. Visser, W., Havelund, K., Brat, G., Park, S.: Java PathFinder - second generation of a Java model checker. In: Proc. of Post-CAV Workshop on Advances in Verification, Chicago (July 2000)
22. Visser, W., Pasareanu, C., Khurshid, S.: Test input generation with Java PathFinder. In: Proceedings of the 2004 ACM SIGSOFT international symposium on Software testing and analysis, pp. 97–107. ACM, New York (2004)
23. Xie, T., Marinov, D., Schulte, W., Notkin, D.: Symstra: A framework for generating object-oriented unit tests using symbolic execution. In: Halbwachs, N., Zuck, L.D. (eds.) TACAS 2005. LNCS, vol. 3440, pp. 365–381. Springer, Heidelberg (2005)
24. Xie, Y., Chou, A., Engler, D.: Archer: using symbolic, path-sensitive analysis to detect memory access errors. In: ESEC/FSE-11: Proceedings of the 9th European software engineering conference held jointly with 11th ACM SIGSOFT international symposium on Foundations of software engineering, pp. 327–336. ACM, New York (2003)

Combining Model Checking and Testing in a Continuous HW/SW Co-verification Process

Paula Herber, Florian Friedemann, and Sabine Glesner

Berlin Institute of Technology, Berlin, Germany
pherber@cs.tu-berlin.de
http://www.pes.cs.tu-berlin.de

Abstract. SystemC is widely used for modeling and simulation in hardware/software co-design. However, the co-verification techniques used for SystemC designs are mostly ad-hoc and non-systematic. In this paper, we present an approach to overcome this problem by a systematic, formally founded quality assurance process. Based on a combination of model checking and conformance testing, we obtain a HW/SW co-verification flow that supports HW/SW co-development throughout the whole design process. In addition, we present a novel test algorithm that generates conformance tests for SystemC designs *offline* and that can cope with *non-deterministic* systems. To this end, we use a timed automata model of the SystemC design to compute expected simulation or test results. We have implemented the model checking and conformance testing framework and give experimental results to show the applicability of our approach.

1 Introduction

Embedded systems are usually composed of deeply integrated hardware and software components, and they are developed under severe resource limitations and high quality requirements. SystemC [15] is a language that supports design space exploration and performance evaluation efficiently throughout the whole design process even for large and heterogeneous HW/SW systems. In SystemC, simulation is used for both evaluation and validation. For quality assurance, however, simulation is necessary but not sufficient. This has two reasons. First, simulation is incomplete. It can neither be applied for all possible input scenarios (in particular for real-time systems), nor can it be assured that all possible executions are covered if the system behaves non-deterministically. Second, simulation alone is not sufficient for a systematic and comprehensive quality assurance approach because the degree of automation is limited. The evaluation of simulation results has to be done manually by the designer, e.g. by inserting assertions about the expected behavior all over the design.

The contribution of this paper is twofold: First, we define a continuous, comprehensive, and formally founded quality assurance process for SystemC designs. Second, we present a novel test algorithm that generates conformance tests for SystemC designs *offline* and that can cope with *non-deterministic* specifications.

C. Dubois (Ed.): TAP 2009, LNCS 5668, pp. 121–136, 2009.

We require our quality assurance process to fulfill the following criteria: a) The proposed verification and validation techniques must be suitable for both hardware and software parts of a given system. b) The quality assurance process should be *continuous*, i. e., it should support the complete system design flow from abstract design down to the final implementation. In particular, we want to ensure consistency between different abstraction levels in a refinement process. c) We want the verification and validation techniques used in the proposed process to be automatically applicable. d) The verification and validation results from high abstraction levels should be reusable on lower abstraction levels.

We obtain such a quality assurance process by a combination of model checking and conformance testing. The SystemC development process starts with an abstract design, which is stepwise refined down to the final implementation. We propose to use model checking to verify that the abstract SystemC design meets its requirements. Then, we generate conformance tests to verify that refined models or the final implementation conform to the abstract model. This approach yields a formally founded, comprehensive, and mainly automatic quality assurance process that continuously supports the HW/SW co-design flow throughout the whole design process.

In [12], we presented an approach to obtain a formal semantics for SystemC by a mapping into the well-defined semantics of UPPAAL timed automata [3]. The transformation from SystemC designs into UPPAAL timed automata models allows for the application of the UPPAAL model checker, and thus for the verification of safety, liveness and timing properties of a given SystemC design. However, model checking SystemC designs is very expensive for two major reasons: First, SystemC designs are inherently non-deterministic, as described above. Second, the aim of model checking is to yield absolute guarantees for every possible environment. Thus, the environment is usually modeled in a way that it yields every possible input trace. As a consequence, model checking can only be applied to small or abstract designs. Thus, we propose to generate conformance tests from the UPPAAL model of the abstract SystemC design to allow for the validation of refined designs or implementations. This allows for quality assurance throughout the whole design process and ensures consistency between designs on different abstraction levels.

The main challenge in the generation of conformance tests for SystemC designs is that they are inherently non-deterministic due to the semantics of the SystemC scheduler defined in [15], and in particular due to the principle of *delta-cycles*. Delta-cycles impose a partial order on parallel processes, which are chosen for execution non-deterministically. Furthermore, SystemC designs are usually developed in several refinement steps. Thus it is desirable to have test cases that can be applied repeatedly in each refinement step. As a consequence, we want our conformance test generation approach to meet two important requirements: First, it should be applicable to non-deterministic systems, and second, expected simulation or test results should be computed *offline*, such that they can be easily reused in later development stages.

To generate conformance tests under these requirements, we first use our mapping from SystemC to UPPAAL to translate an abstract SystemC design into a semantically equivalent UPPAAL model. Then, we use the UPPAAL model to statically compute all possible output traces for a given test suite consisting of a set of input traces. When the test suite is executed on a refined design or on the final implementation, we can compare the output traces produced by the refined design with the output traces computed from the UPPAAL model of the abstract design. To decide whether the refined design conforms to the abstract design, we use the *relativized timed input/output conformance (rtioco) relation* presented in [19]. Based on that we can use the output traces from the UPPAAL model as a *test oracle* to test the conformance of the refined to the abstract designs fully automatically.

This paper is organized as follows: In Section 2, we briefly introduce SystemC and UPPAAL. In Section 3, we present our overall quality assurance approach based on model checking and testing. In Section 4, we review our transformation from SystemC to UPPAAL, which allows for the application of the UPPAAL model checker. In Section 5, we present our approach to generate conformance tests from the generated UPPAAL model. In Section 6, we show experimental results. We discuss related work in Section 7 and conclude in Section 8.

2   Preliminaries

2.1   SystemC

SystemC [15] is a system level design language and a framework for HW/SW co-simulation. It allows for the modeling and execution of system level designs on various levels of abstraction, including classical register transfer level hardware modeling and transaction-level models. The design flow usually starts with approximately timed transaction-level models that are refined to time-accurate models of hardware and software components. SystemC is implemented as a C++ class library, which provides the language elements and an event-driven simulation kernel. A SystemC design is a set of communicating processes, triggered by events and interacting through channels. Modules and ports are used to represent structural information. SystemC also introduces an integer-valued time model with arbitrary time resolution. The execution of a SystemC design is controlled by the SystemC scheduler. It controls the simulation time and the execution of processes, handles event notifications, and updates primitive channels. Like typical hardware description languages, SystemC supports the notion of delta-cycles.

2.2   Uppaal Timed Automata

Timed Automata [1] are a timed extension of the classical finite state automata. A notion of time is introduced by a set of $\mathbb{R}_{\geq 0}$ valued clock variables C, which are used in clock constraints to model time-dependent behavior. A clock constraint is a conjunctive formula of atomic constraints of the form $x \sim n$ or $x - y \sim n$ for $x, y \in C, \sim \in \{\leq, <, =, >, \geq\}, n \in \mathbb{N}$. $B(C)$ denotes the set of clock constraints.

Definition 1. *A* timed automaton *is a tuple* (L, l_0, C, A, E, I), *where*

- *L is a set of locations, $l_0 \in L$ the initial location,*
- *C is a set of clocks, A a set of actions,*
- *$I : L \to B(C)$ assigns invariants to locations, and*
- *$E \subseteq L \times A \times B(C) \times \mathbb{P}^C \times L$ is a set of edges*

Definition 2. *A* network of timed automata (NTA) *consists of n timed automata* $\mathcal{A}_i = (L_i, l_i^0, C, A, E_i, I_i)$. *The semantics of NTA is defined by a transition system* $(S, s_0, \to)$. *Each state $s \in S$ is a tuple $(\bar{l}, u)$, where $\bar{l}$ is a location vector and u a clock valuation. $S = (L_1 \times \ldots \times L_n) \times \mathbb{R}^C$ denotes the set of states, $s_0 = (\bar{l}_0, u_0)$ the initial state, and $\to \subseteq S \times S$ the transition relation. Furthermore, τ denotes an internal action, c!, c? sending resp. receiving an event, g a clock guard, and $u' = [r \mapsto 0]u$ denotes a clock valuation where all clocks from r are reset to zero. A semantic step can be either a time step (1), an independent step of a single automaton (2), or a synchronization between two automata (3):*

(1) $(\bar{l}, u) \to (\bar{l}, u + d)$ *iff* $\forall d' : 0 \leq d' \leq d \Rightarrow u + d' \in I(\bar{l})$

(2) $(\bar{l}, u) \to (\bar{l}[l_i'/l_i], u')$ *iff* $\exists l_i \xrightarrow{\tau \, g \, r} l_i'$ *such that* $u \in g \wedge u' = [r \mapsto 0]u \wedge u' \in I(\bar{l})$

(3) $(\bar{l}, u) \to (\bar{l}[l_j'/l_j, l_i'/l_i], u')$ *iff* $\exists l_i \xrightarrow{c?g_i, r_i} l_i' \wedge l_j \xrightarrow{c!g_j, r_j} l_j'$
$\quad$ *such that* $u \in (g_i \wedge g_j) \wedge u' = [r_i \cup r_j \mapsto 0]u \wedge u' \in I(\bar{l})$

While the semantic state space of timed automata is infinite due to the real-valued clock variables, the *symbolic semantics* abstracts from certain points of time and uses clock zones instead. As a consequence, a state is then a tuple $(\bar{l}, D)$ where D is a difference bound matrix representing a clock zone. The resulting abstract model has a finite state space and can be model checked.

UPPAAL [3,4,2] is a tool set for the modeling, simulation, animation and verification of networks of timed automata. The UPPAAL model checker enables the verification of temporal properties, including safety and liveness properties. The simulator can be used to visualize counter-examples produced by the model checker. The UPPAAL modeling language extends timed automata by introducing bounded integer variables, binary and broadcast channels, and urgent and committed locations. A UPPAAL model comprises three parts: global declarations, parameterized timed automata (TA templates), and a system declaration. In the global declarations section, global variables, constants, channels and clocks are declared. In the system declaration, TA templates are instantiated and the system to be composed is given as a list of timed automata.

3 Quality Assurance Process

We obtain a continuous quality assurance process for HW/SW co-designs by a combination of model checking and testing, as shown in Fig. 1. We assume a HW/SW co-development process that starts with an abstract SystemC model and refines this model down to the implementation. In each refinement step, a refined SystemC design can be regarded as the implementation I of an abstract

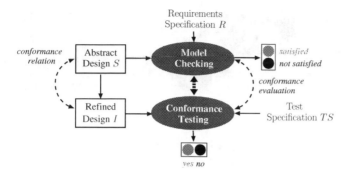

Fig. 1. Combining Model Checking and Testing

design that serves as specification S. We propose to use model checking to verify that the abstract model S meets its requirements R, as shown in [12]. Then, we generate conformance tests to verify that the refined model or implementation I conforms to the abstract model S.

A prerequisite for both model checking and conformance test generation is a formal semantics for SystemC. We build a formal model by our mapping from SystemC into the well-defined semantics of UPPAAL timed automata. This mapping instantly allows for the application of the UPPAAL model checker to verify that the abstract design or specification S satisfies the requirements R. Furthermore, we can use the UPPAAL model to generate conformance tests. To this end, we statically compute all possible output traces for a given test suite consisting of a set of input traces. Then, the refined design is executed several times for all the input traces from the test suite, and the observed behavior is compared to the previously computed execution traces, which are expected as simulation results. It is important to note that with our test approach, we are able to generate conformance tests for *non-deterministic* systems *offline*. That is vital because SystemC designs are inherently non-deterministic due to the semantics of the SystemC Scheduler as defined in [15]. In addition, the refinement process in which SystemC designs are developed generally comprises several steps. Only *offline* test generation allows for repeated execution of the test cases in each refinement step without re-computing all the expected results. In the following, we review our approach to translate SystemC into UPPAAL models, which allows for the application of the UPPAAL model checker. Then, we present our approach to generate conformance tests from UPPAAL models.

4   Model Checking SystemC Designs Using Uppaal

In [12], we presented an approach to model check SystemC designs using UPPAAL timed automata. In particular, we mapped the informally defined semantics of SystemC to the formally well-defined semantics of UPPAAL. The mapping from SystemC to UPPAAL allows for the application of the UPPAAL model checker and

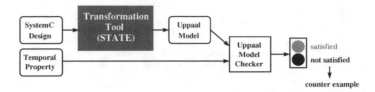

Fig. 2. Verification flow with STATE

thereby enables us to prove safety, liveness and timing properties on a given SystemC design. The main advantage of our approach is that once we have defined the mapping from SystemC to UPPAAL, the transformation of a given SystemC design can be performed automatically. We implemented this in our STATE (**S**ystemC to **T**imed **A**utomata **T**ransformation **E**ngine) tool. This transformation tool makes it possible to verify temporal properties of SystemC designs fully automatically. The automated verification flow is shown in Fig. 2. The STATE tool takes as input a SystemC design and a temporal property formulated in the UPPAAL requirement language (which is basically a subset of CTL). The SystemC design is translated into a UPPAAL model by our STATE tool and can then directly be passed to the UPPAAL model checker. The model checker tries to verify the property and generates a counter-example if it is not satisfied.[1]

Fig. 3 shows how we represent SystemC designs in UPPAAL. Each method is mapped to a single timed automata template. Process automata are used to encapsulate these methods and care for the interactions with events and the scheduler. The scheduler is explicitly modeled, and we use a predefined template for events and other SystemC constructs such as primitive channels. The interactions between the processes and the scheduler are modeled by two synchronization channels, *activate* and *deactivate*. The interactions between processes and event objects are modeled by *wait* and *notify*. The interactions between the event objects and the scheduler are used to synchronize their timing. The scheduler informs the event objects when a delta-cycle is completed to release delta-delay notifications, and conversely, the event objects inform the scheduler when time is advanced due to a timed notification.

To allow for compositional transformation, that is to make it possible that each SystemC module can be translated separately, we perform the mapping from SystemC to UPPAAL in three steps: first, we define a (general) timed automata representation for each SystemC language construct, such as methods, processes, and events. Using these general representations, we can then translate each given SystemC module into a set of parameterized timed automata. With the help of the template parameters, we can instantiate the module an arbitrary number of times without having to perform a new translation. When we compose a design, we instantiate the modules including their events and

---

[1] Note that the counter-example is given as a trace in UPPAAL semantics. However, the transformation from SystemC to UPPAAL preserves the structure by prefixing, such that it is transparent to the SystemC designer where the problem arises from. In addition, UPPAAL can be used to animate the counter-example graphically.

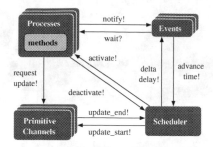

Fig. 3. Representation of SystemC designs in UPPAAL

processes and connect them using synchronization channels. Using this compositional approach, we are able to translate large designs in reasonable time and the generated models are structure-preserving and thus easily comprehensible to the designer. We can handle all relevant SystemC language elements, including process execution, interactions, dynamic sensitivity and timing behavior. If we want to model check the translated design, this requires two restrictions. First, UPPAAL can not handle dynamic process or object creation. Second, UPPAAL supports only bounded integer variables. Both are minor restrictions because dynamic object and process creation are rarely used in SystemC designs and most data types can be converted to bounded integers. Overall, the transformation gives us access to the complete UPPAAL tool suite, including the UPPAAL model checker. The applicability of the approach was shown in [12] by two case studies: a producer/consumer example, and a packet switch example from the SystemC reference implementation. Furthermore, we can use the UPPAAL models generated from abstract SystemC designs to derive conformance tests for later design phases.

5   Conformance Test Generation

As the model checking approach suffers from the state space explosion problem, we only use it early in the development process on abstract (and thus relatively small) models. To check the consistency of a refined design with a verified abstract design, and thus to yield continuous quality assurance throughout the whole design process, we generate conformance tests. The verification flow extended by conformance testing is shown in Fig. 4. The abstract SystemC design is translated into a UPPAAL model. This is used both for model checking and to generate conformance tests for refined SystemC designs.

The generated test benches contain both timed input traces as well as sets of expected timed output traces. Thus, they can be used to execute and evaluate conformance tests fully automatically. In future work, we want to extend the framework by the possibility to feed the test generator with coverage criteria to automatically select input traces. The generated test benches are executed on the refined SystemC design or the implementation and yield the result whether

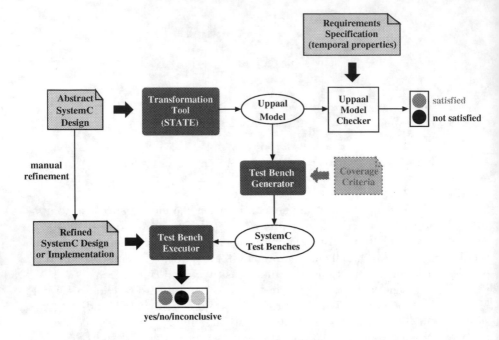

Fig. 4. Framework for Model Checking and Testing SystemC designs

or not the refined design conforms to the abstract design. As we consider non-deterministic specifications and want to generate test cases *offline*, the main task is to compute all possible output traces of a given UPPAAL model for a given input trace. In the following, we present the setting for test case generation, i. e.,the test specification, the conformance relation we use, and finally the test generation algorithm.

5.1   Test Specification

Embedded systems closely interact with a technical environment. Because of that, both SystemC designs and UPPAAL models comprise an explicit model of the environment beyond the system model. The environment model provides the inputs to the system model and consumes its outputs. A test case can be regarded as a specialized environment, providing a single input trace. It is specified as a timed automaton that provides a single input trace. It sends input events and data at certain times and waits for system reactions for a given amount of time. A particular location annotated with the label *tc_end* indicates the end of the input trace and can be used by the test algorithm for terminating the state space exploration. We call the automaton that provides the input trace a *test automaton*. If a test bench written in SystemC is available, it can be automatically transformed into such a test automaton. On the output side, we want to observe all possible behavior the specification could produce. Thus,

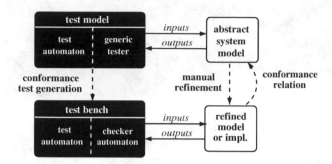

Fig. 5. Conformance test generation

we need an environment that accepts all possible outputs at arbitrary times. To provide the UPPAAL model with the necessary degree of freedom, we use a *generic tester* component accepting all possible responses as proposed in [24]. Like the test automaton, the generic tester can also be generated automatically from a corresponding SystemC test bench. Together, the test automaton and the generic tester constitute a test model that replaces the environment model in the UPPAAL model used for the test generation process, as shown in Fig. 5. From the test model together with the system model, conformance tests are generated. The resulting test benches still contain the test automaton, but the generic tester is replaced by an automaton accepting exactly those traces produced by the abstract system model or specification for the given input trace. We call this automaton a *checker automaton*. If the checker automaton reaches its final node during test execution, it received a complete and correct output trace and the test verdict is *pass*. If it does not reach its final node, the test verdict is *fail*. We are confident that the generated test benches, in particular the checker automata, can be easily translated into SystemC test benches, although we did not evaluate this until now.

5.2   Conformance Relation

If the model checking was successful, the result is that an abstract design or specification S satisfies a requirements specification R. If we have a manually refined SystemC design I in the next development phase, we want to know if it is consistent with the previously designed abstract model S. To check that, we generate conformance tests. As conformance relation, we use the *relativized timed input/output conformance (rtioco)* relation defined in [19,13].

Definition 3. *I conforms to S if for all timed input traces σ in a given testsuite or environment $\mathcal{E}$ the sequence of observations on the timed output trace of I is contained in the set of sequences of observations on the timed output traces of S for the same input trace.*

$$I \; rtioco \; S \quad \text{iff} \quad \forall \sigma \in TTr(\mathcal{E}) : obs((I, \mathcal{E}), \sigma) \subseteq obs((S, \mathcal{E}), \sigma)$$

The *rtioco* relation is derived from the *input/output conformance (ioco)* relation of Tretmans and de Vries [6] by taking time and environment constraints into account. Under the assumptions of weak input enabledness, *rtioco* coincides with timed trace inclusion. A *timed output trace* can be defined as follows:

Definition 4. *A timed output trace is a sequence of observations, where each observation is a tuple (e, D, v) consisting of an event e, a difference bound matrix D representing the clock zone in which the event occurs, and a vector v containing the valuations of externally visible data variables at this time.*

With that, we can define trace inclusion $\subseteq$ on timed output traces:

Definition 5. *We define the trace inclusion $\subseteq$ on sequences of observations such that an implementation may follow tighter time restrictions, but has to produce outputs expected by the specification in time zones where the specification prescribes it:*

$$obs((I, \mathcal{E}), \sigma) \subseteq obs((S, \mathcal{E}), \sigma) \quad \text{iff}$$
$$\forall o_S \in obs((S, \mathcal{E}), o_I \in obs((I, \mathcal{E}), \sigma) : o_I.e = o_S.e \wedge o_I.D \subseteq o_S.D \wedge o_I.v = oS.v$$

5.3   Test Generation Algorithm

To compute all possible timed output traces for a given input trace, we start with the initial symbolic state $(\bar{l}, D, V)$ consisting of a location vector $\bar{l}$, a difference bound matrix D representing a clock zone and a set of global variable valuations V. From that, we compute all possible successors. Then, we compute all possible successor states for each of the successors and so forth, until we reach the end of the test case defined in the test specification (cf. Algorithm 1.1). The computation of the successor states is done following the symbolic UPPAAL semantics as described in [4]. The result is a tree of all possible computation paths for a given timed input trace. To get the observable behavior, we just have to extract the outputs from the computation tree, including the corresponding difference bound matrices and externally visible data valuations.

As the system may be non-deterministic, the result of Algorithm 1.1 is a tree, where each path represents a possible timed output trace. By joining all its paths into a final node *pass*, as shown in Fig. 6, the tree can be transformed into a checker automaton as described in Section 5.1.

Note that we limit the number of internal computation steps between two output events to ensure termination of the algorithm in case of infinite internal loops. If the limit is exceeded, the corresponding node in the checker automaton is marked with the label *inconclusive*. If the checker automaton reaches this node, the verdict is *inconclusive*. That means that the test generation algorithm was not able to predict the correct behavior for the given input trace together with the previous observations.

Listing 1.1. Test Generation Algorithm

```
NTA:=(L, Ī₀, C, A, V, E, I);
WAIT:={⟨Ī₀, D₀, V₀⟩};
KNOWN:=∅;
STATESPACE:=∅;
while WAIT ≠ ∅ do
   select s = ⟨l̄ₛ, Dₛ, Vₛ⟩ from WAIT;
   if !isEnd(s) and !isDeadlock(s) and !limitExceeded(s)
      successors := getSuccessors(s);
      for each successor ∈ successors
         if successor ∉ KNOWN and successor ∉ WAIT then
            add successor to WAIT;
         end if
      end for
   end if
   add ⟨s, successors⟩ to STATESPACE;
   add s to KNOWN;
end while
return getObs(STATESPACE);
```

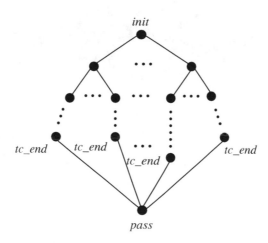

Fig. 6. Checker automaton

6   Experimental Results

We implemented the transformation from SystemC to UPPAAL, the symbolic semantics of UPPAAL, and the test generation algorithm. We used the Karlsruhe
SystemC Parser KaSCPar [7] as a front-end for SystemC designs and ANTLR
to generate a UPPAAL parser. The UPPAAL model is read from an XML file and

Table 1. Computational effort of model checking

	Computation time (in seconds)			
	1m1s	2m1s	1m2s	2m2s
translation	1.46	1.59	1.52	1.70
property (1)	20.82	54.90	42.21	209.56
property (2)	127.70	45.04	296.89	543.18

Table 2. Computational effort of onformance test generation

	Computation time (in seconds)			
	1m1s	2m1s	1m2s	2m2s
translation	7.82	9.91	9.38	10.93
compilation	8.54	10.04	9.05	9.7
test generation	8.75	14.32	23.95	34.14

translated into an executable representation in Java. The automatically generated Java code is executed by the test generation algorithm. The experiments were run on a machine with an Intel Pentium 3.4 GHz CPU running a Linux operating system.

As a case study, we used a slight modification of the packet switch example from the SystemC reference implementation (ca. 500 LOC). As in [12], we translated the SystemC design into a UPPAAL model (30 automata are generated) and used the model checker to verify (1) deadlock freedom and (2) that packets are forwarded within a given time limit. Then, we generated conformance tests. In all experiments, we varied the numbers of masters and slaves (1m1s, 1m2s, 2m1s, 2m2s). Table 1 presents the computation times needed for the transformation from SystemC to UPPAAL and the verification of properties (1) and (2), both averaged over 10 runs.

For conformance test generation, the UPPAAL model was first translated into an executable java representation, then compiled and finally executed to compute all possible output traces for a given input trace. We have not implemented the generation of SystemC test benches from these output traces yet, thus no test execution results are given at the time. Table 2 shows the computation times of the test generation process, again averaged over 10 runs. The run-time performance of the test generation is not as good as one could have expected. But, as the test cases are generated *offline*, this has to be done only once in the whole development process. Thus, the computational effort is more than acceptable. However, we see a lot of optimization potential in our initial implementation, which was mainly developed as a proof of concept. We are currently working on some optimizations, e.g. memory efficient representations of DBMs and the computation tree, and depth-first search as an alternative.

Overall, the experimental results show that both the model checking and the conformance testing approach can be applied to practical examples with acceptable computational effort. In particular, the experiments show that the proposed verification flow is feasible and can be fully automated.

7 Related Work

There have been several approaches to give SystemC a formal semantics, and some of them have also been used for model checking [16] or conformance testing [11,10]. However, most of them are restricted to a synchronous subset of SystemC [21,25,26,8,9], or they cannot cope with time and dynamic sensitivity [11,10,20]. In [28], a mapping from SystemC to PROMELA is proposed, but they only handle SystemC designs at transaction level, do not model the non-deterministic scheduler and cannot cope with primitive channels. Furthermore, the transformation is manual. In [16], SystemC designs are verified using a petri-net based representation. The approach covers most of the important SystemC language constructs, but introduces a huge overhead because interactions between subnets can only be modeled by introducing additional subnets.

With our approach to give SystemC a formal semantics, we can handle all relevant SystemC language elements, including process execution, interactions between processes, dynamic sensitivity and timing behavior. The informally defined behavior and the structure of SystemC designs are completely preserved. The mapping from SystemC designs into UPPAAL timed automata is fully automated, introduces a negligible overhead, produces compact and comparably small models and enables the use of the UPPAAL model checker and tool suite.

In [23] and in [17], automated test generation approaches for SystemC are presented. In [23], a model-driven validation approach for SystemC is proposed. There, directed tests are generated from ASM models. In contrast to our work, the designer has to define the specification manually. Furthermore, the focus is on directed input generation for a certain test purpose, automatic conformance evaluation is not considered. In [17], automatic test generation for SystemC design based on manually specified use cases is proposed. They do not make any use of existing abstract SystemC designs, nor does their approach include an automatic verification of the specification itself, as we do with UPPAAL.

There have been several approaches to generate conformance tests for real-time systems from timed automata models, and in particular to generate such tests from UPPAAL. However, most of them either consider only a restricted subclass of the timed automata model, or they do not allow for static (*offline*) test generation. The authors of [27] present an approach to generate minimal test suites with complete path coverage from timed automata models. They prove that exhaustive testing is possible for real-time systems by reducing the dense-time model to a discrete model using equivalence classes. However, the authors only consider a deterministic subclass of the timed automata model. Furthermore, the size of a complete test suites is highly exponential. In [5], a similar approach is used, extended by a technique called *hiding*. This technique allows for an abstraction of the timed automata model in order to hide parts of the system that are not relevant with respect to the test purpose. This reduces the size of a complete test suite, but the approach still cannot cope with non-deterministic specifications. In [22], a technique for the automatic generation of real-time black-box conformance tests for non-deterministic systems is presented, but only for a determinizable subclass of timed automata specifications with restricted use of clocks, guards or clock resets. In [18], an algorithm for real-time test case generation for non-deterministic systems is proposed, but it is based on an on-the-fly determinization of the specification.

There also exists some work on test generation from UPPAAL models. In Uppsala, the CoVer tool was developed [14,13]. CoVer allows for coverage-driven conformance test generation for UPPAAL models. The test cases are generated statically and a *relativized timed input output conformance (rtioco)* relation is used to evaluate test results. However, the approach is again restricted to deterministic timed automata models. In contrast to that, the TRON (*Testing Real-time systems ONline*) tool developed in Aalborg [19,13] can also be applied to non-deterministic systems. However, it uses an *online* test generation algorithm and thus can not be used to generate repeatable test cases. The *rtioco* relation is used again to evaluate test results.

For conformance testing in HW/SW co-verification processes, it is vital to generate conformance tests *offline*. Particularly in the context of HW/SW co-design processes based on SystemC, it is indispensable to repeatedly execute test cases on each refinement stage, and thus to ensure consistency between different abstraction levels. Furthermore, SystemC designs are inherently non-deterministic. Thus, the approaches described above are not sufficient, as they either generate test cases *online*, or they do not support non-deterministic specifications. With our approach, we can generate conformance tests *offline* and for *non-deterministic* systems.

8   Conclusion

In this paper, we presented a quality assurance process that assists the HW/SW co-design flow efficiently and continuously throughout the whole design process. The combination of model checking and conformance testing is very promising, as it can be applied fully automatically. In particular, even the formalization of a given design is derived automatically. That means that the designer does not have to perform the time-consuming and error-prone task of formal specification any more. We just take the simulation model, which the designer builds anyway, and extract our formal model automatically. The only task that has to be done manually is the formalization of the requirements specification. Furthermore, our approach can be applied to both the hardware and the software parts of a given HW/SW co-design, to synchronous and asynchronous designs, and on different levels of abstraction. The verification and test generation effort is acceptable, in particular as it has to be done only once in the whole development process. The conformance test generation algorithm presented here is novel since we are able to generate tests from *non-deterministic* specifications *offline*.

To complete our framework, we are currently working on the automatic translation of the checker automata into SystemC test benches, and on a larger case study (an automotive control application). With that, we will be able to evaluate the approach in more detail, and in particular also its error detecting capability. Furthermore, we plan to extend our framework with the ability to select input traces based on dedicated SystemC coverage criteria.

References

1. Alur, R., Dill, D.L.: A Theory of Timed Automata. Theoretical Computer Science 126, 183–235 (1994)
2. Behrmann, G., David, A., Larsen, K.G.: A Tutorial on UPPAAL. In: Bernardo, M., Corradini, F. (eds.) SFM-RT 2004. LNCS, vol. 3185, pp. 200–236. Springer, Heidelberg (2004)
3. Bengtsson, J., Larsen, K.G., Larsson, F., Pettersson, P., Yi, W.: UPPAAL — a Tool Suite for Automatic Verification of Real–Time Systems. In: HS 1995. LNCS, vol. 1066, pp. 232–243. Springer, Heidelberg (1995)
4. Bengtsson, J., Yi, W.: Timed automata: Semantics, algorithms and tools. In: Desel, J., Reisig, W., Rozenberg, G. (eds.) Lectures on Concurrency and Petri Nets. LNCS, vol. 3098, pp. 87–124. Springer, Heidelberg (2004)
5. Cardell-Oliver, R.: Conformance tests for real-time systems with timed automata specifications. Formal Aspects of Computing 12(5), 350–371 (2000)
6. de Vries, R., Tretmans, J.: On-the-fly conformance testing using spin. Software Tools for Technology Transfer 2(4), 382–393 (2000)
7. FZI Research Center for Information Technology. KaSCPar - Karlsruhe SystemC Parser Suite
8. Grosse, D., Drechsler, R.: Checkers for SystemC designs. In: Formal Methods and Models for Codesign, pp. 171–178. IEEE Computer Society, Los Alamitos (2004)
9. Grosse, D., Kuhne, U., Drechsler, R.: HW/SW Co-Verification of Embedded Systems using Bounded Model Checking. In: Great Lakes Symposium on VLSI, pp. 43–48. ACM Press, New York (2006)
10. Habibi, A., Moinudeen, H., Tahar, S.: Generating Finite State Machines from SystemC. In: Design, Automation and Test in Europe, pp. 76–81. IEEE Press, Los Alamitos (2006)
11. Habibi, A., Tahar, S.: An Approach for the Verification of SystemC Designs Using AsmL. In: Peled, D.A., Tsay, Y.-K. (eds.) ATVA 2005. LNCS, vol. 3707, pp. 69–83. Springer, Heidelberg (2005)
12. Herber, P., Fellmuth, J., Glesner, S.: Model Checking SystemC Designs Using Timed Automata. In: International Conference on Hardware/Software Codesign and System Synthesis (CODES+ISSS), pp. 131–136. ACM Press, New York (2008)
13. Hessel, A., Larsen, K.G., Mikucionis, M., Nielsen, B., Pettersson, P., Skou, A.: Testing Real-Time Systems Using UPPAAL. In: Hierons, R.M., Bowen, J.P., Harman, M. (eds.) FORTEST. LNCS, vol. 4949, pp. 77–117. Springer, Heidelberg (2008)
14. Hessel, A., Larsen, K.G., Nielsen, B., Petterson, P., Skou, A.: Time-optimal test cases for real-time systems. In: Petrenko, A., Ulrich, A. (eds.) FATES 2003. LNCS, vol. 2931, pp. 114–130. Springer, Heidelberg (2004)
15. IEEE Standards Association. IEEE Std. 1666–2005, Open SystemC Language Reference Manual (2005)
16. Karlsson, D., Eles, P., Peng, Z.: Formal verification of SystemC Designs using a Petri-Net based Representation. In: Design, Automation and Test in Europe, pp. 1228–1233. IEEE Press, Los Alamitos (2006)
17. Kirchsteiger, C.M., Trummer, C., Steger, C., Weiss, R., Pistauer, M.: Specification-based Verification of Embedded Systems by Automated Test Case Generation. In: Distributed Embedded Systems: Design, Middleware and Resources, pp. 35–44. Springer, Heidelberg (2008)
18. Krichen, M., Tripakis, S.: Real-time testing with timed automata testers and coverage criteria. In: Lakhnech, Y., Yovine, S. (eds.) FORMATS 2004 and FTRTFT 2004. LNCS, vol. 3253, pp. 134–151. Springer, Heidelberg (2004)

19. Larsen, K.G., Mikucionis, M., Nielsen, B.: Online Testing of Real-time Systems Using Uppaal. In: Grabowski, J., Nielsen, B. (eds.) FATES 2004. LNCS, vol. 3395, pp. 79–94. Springer, Heidelberg (2005)
20. Man, K.: An Overview of SystemCFL. Research in Microelectronics and Electronics 1, 145–148 (2005)
21. Müller, W., Ruf, J., Rosenstiel, W.: An ASM based SystemC Simulation Semantics. In: SystemC: Methodologies and Applications, pp. 97–126. Kluwer, Dordrecht (2003)
22. Nielsen, B., Skou, A.: Automated test generation from timed automata. In: Margaria, T., Yi, W. (eds.) TACAS 2001. LNCS, vol. 2031, pp. 343–357. Springer, Heidelberg (2001)
23. Patel, H.D., Shukla, S.K.: Model-driven validation of systemc designs. EURASIP J. Embedded Syst. 2008(3), 1–14 (2008)
24. Robinson-Mallett, C., Hierons, R.M., Liggesmeyer, P.: Achieving communication coverage in testing. ACM SIGSOFT Software Engineering Notes 31(6), 1–10 (2006)
25. Ruf, J., Hoffmann, D., Gerlach, J., Kropf, T., Rosenstiehl, W., Müller, W.: The Simulation Semantics of SystemC. In: Design, Automation and Test in Europe, pp. 64–70. IEEE Press, Los Alamitos (2001)
26. Salem, A.: Formal Semantics of Synchronous SystemC. In: Design, Automation and Test in Europe, pp. 10376–10381. IEEE Computer Society, Los Alamitos (2003)
27. Springintveld, J., Vaandrager, F., D'Argenio, P.R.: Testing timed automata. Theoretical Computer Science 254(1–2), 225–257 (2001)
28. Traulsen, C., Cornet, J., Moy, M., Maraninchi, F.: A SystemC/TLM semantics in Promela and its possible applications. In: Bošnački, D., Edelkamp, S. (eds.) SPIN 2007. LNCS, vol. 4595, pp. 204–222. Springer, Heidelberg (2007)

Symbolic Execution Based Model Checking of Open Systems with Unbounded Variables

Nicolas Rapin

CEA LIST
Laboratory of Model Driven Engineering for Embedded Systems
Boîte Courrier 65, Gif sur Yvette, F-91191 France
nicolas.rapin@cea.fr

Abstract. We describe fundamental aspects of a method we have developed in order to check linear temporal logic formulas over Input Output Symbolic Transition Systems (IOSTSs). IOSTSs are used to describe reactive systems with communication channels and variables of different types ; in particular variables can take unbounded values. Thus the method can be applied to open systems, communicating with their environment, or with other modules that are not precisely specified. The method consists in a semi-decision algorithm based on symbolic execution techniques, usually used for tests generation purposes. We provide an adaptation of this technique in order to evaluate a LTL formula along a symbolic path ; moreover we have developed a termination criterion of the semi-decision algorithm for IOSTSs whose data part is specified by a decidable first order theory.

Keywords: Symbolic Execution, Verification, Linear Temporal Logic, Input Output Symbolic Transition Systems.

1 Introduction

Developing reliable reactive systems is of utmost importance in the case of safety critical systems. Therefore the design cycle of those systems must include formal methods in order to increase their reliability. To facilitate the use of formal methods it is important to provide formal languages to engineers that are close to the way they describe their systems and suited for automated validation and verification techniques. Previous works have shown that the formalism of Input Output Transition Systems (IOSTSs) is well adapted for automatic test cases generation [19,10,11]. In recent works a methodology is presented which improves the reliability of incremental refinement of IOSTSs by using test cases generation and conformance relations between IOSTSs [16]. But it is useless to test an implementation against a model if this latter doesn't satisfy the requirements. In this paper we present fundamental aspects of a model checking algorithm whose purpose is to check if an IOSTS model satisfies a requirement expressed in a temporal logic inspired from Linear Temporal Logic (LTL). We call this logic ioLTL. The prefix *io* means that some atomic propositions of this logic allows

C. Dubois (Ed.): TAP 2009, LNCS 5668, pp. 137–152, 2009.

to specify properties over inputs or outputs of the model. The main difficulty of checking IOSTSs is due to the fact that the state space of an IOSTS can be infinite, so the verification of the temporal property is an undecidable problem in general [12]. Then we can only develop a semi-decision algorithm, *i.e.* which does not terminate for every IOSTS and temporal logic formula. Our semi-decision algorithm combines seminal techniques of LTL model checking [17,20] with the so-called symbolic execution technique [15]. Let us suppose that g is the ioLTL requirement, then the algorithm tries to establish the existence of executions of the IOSTS model being in contradiction with g. The main idea is to use tableau calculus over the negation of g in order to generate the constraints that any execution being in contradiction with g should satisfy and to use simultaneously the symbolic execution technique in order to check if such executions actually exist. In some sense the tableau calculus is used to generate some tests from the negation of the ioLTL requirement and the symbolic execution is used to check wether or not there are some executions passing those tests. The algorithm also relies on a result presented in Sec. 5.5 which establishes that we can prove the existence of infinite executions satisfying a property from the existence of finite symbolic paths when a relation over symbolic states is verified. Related works include model checking of infinite systems. Usually, the properties that can be checked are limited to the reachability of states, as in the tools LASH [21], Trex [3], or Fast [4]. Regular model checking [7] has been extended to prove formulas of an extension of LTL [2] but over particular models (with a finite number of configurations). Action language verifier [8,9] can be used to prove computation tree logic (CTL) formulas over Action Language specifications. Nevertheless these approaches are not dedicated to systems communicating with sub-specified environments (dealing with unbounded inputs). The paper is organized as follows. IOSTS formalism is described in Section 2 and the execution of an IOSTS in Section 2.2. In Section 3 the temporal logic ioLTL is defined. Section 4 presents symbolic execution applied to IOSTSs. In Section 5 we present a set of inference rules defining how the symbolic execution technique is combined with the tableau calculus for ioLTL. Then in Section 5.5 we present two theorems grounding our model-checking approach. They state that, given a temporal formula and an IOSTS, a finite application of the rules either proves that there exists a run of the IOSTS satisfying the temporal formula or certifies that no runs satify the formula. In Section 6 we describe how the inference rules and the termination criteria are coordinated to form the verification algorithm. Section 7, the last before the Conclusion, is dedicated to implement issues and experimental results.

2   Input Output Symbolic Transition Systems

Input Output Symbolic Transition Systems. IOSTSs represent IOLTS [18] in a concise manner by using *variables*. An IOSTS is composed of a graph part and a data part. The data part is specified by a decidable first-order theory T of a first order language L both with a structure M being a model of this theory. In the sequel *variables* refers to the variables V of L. $\mathcal{T}_A$ (resp. $\mathcal{F}_A$) denotes the set of terms (resp. formulas) of L containing only variables of $A \subseteq V$. A map $\nu \in M^A$ (resp. $\sigma \in \mathcal{T}^A$) where $A \subseteq V$ is called an interpretation (resp. a substitution) of variables of A. Interpretations and substitutions are canonically extended to terms and formulas. Thus we may use this abusive notation $\nu \circ \sigma$ which denotes the map of M^A being such that $\forall x \in A, (\nu \circ \sigma)(x)$ is the interpretation of the term $\sigma(x)$ with respect to ν. If μ and δ are two interpretations with disjoint ranges, we will note (μ, δ) the interpretation being their union.

2.1   Input Output Symbolic Transition Systems

To define an IOSTS, we need to specify its variables and communication channels: this is done by defining an IOSTS-signature.

Definition 1 (IOSTS-signature). *An IOSTS-signature Σ is defined as a couple (A, Ch) where A is a finite set of variable names and Ch is a set of communication channel* names.

An IOSTS communicates with its environment through communication actions.

Definition 2 (Actions). *The* set of communication actions *is denoted by $Act(\Sigma) = Input(\Sigma) \cup Output(\Sigma) \cup \{\tau\}$, where*

$$Input(\Sigma) = \{c?y \mid c \in Ch, y \in A\} \quad and \quad Output(\Sigma) = \{c!t \mid c \in Ch, t \in \mathcal{T}_A\}$$

Elements of $Input(\Sigma)$ are stimulations of the system from the environment: $c?x$ represents the reception of a value through channel c which is assigned to x. $Output(\Sigma)$ are responses of the system to the environment: $c!t$ is the emission of the evaluation of t through the channel c. The symbol $\overset{*}{\tau}$ is used to characterize internal transitions (invisible from the environment).

Definition 3 (IOSTS). *An IOSTS over Σ is a triple $G = (Q, q_0, Trans)$ where Q is a finite set of locations, $q_0 \in Q$ is the initial location and $Trans \subseteq Q \times \mathcal{F}_A \times Act(\Sigma) \times \mathcal{T}_A{}^A \times Q$. A transition $tr := (q, \varphi, act, \rho, q')$ of $Trans$ is composed of a source location q, denoted by $src(tr)$, a guard φ denoted by $grd(tr)$, an action act denoted by $act(tr)$, a substitution of variables ρ and a target location q' denoted by $tgt(tr)$. For each location $q \in Q$, there is a finite number of transitions of source location q. We consider IOSTS having no sink states i.e. for all $q \in Q$ we have* $\bigvee\limits_{tr \in T, src(tr)=q} grd(tr)$ *is a tautology.*

A transition $tr = (q, \varphi, act, \rho, q')$ may also be noted $q \xrightarrow{\varphi[act]\rho} q'$.

Example 1. Figure 1 represents an IOSTS modeling an ATM system which checks the bank balance B of a customer wanting to withdraw an amount M on account C, and that sends through channel $disp$ the result of the request. If the withdrawal is accepted, the customer balance is updated by the substitution $B \mapsto B - M$.

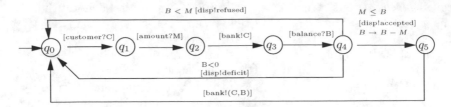

Fig. 1. Account request

2.2 Paths and Runs of an IOSTS

A path of an IOSTS $(Q, q_0, Trans)$ is any map p of $\mathbb{N} \rightarrow Trans$ such that $src(p(0)) = q_0$ and for all $i \in \mathbb{N}$, $tgt(p(i)) = src(p(i+1))$. A run of an IOSTS will be defined as an interpretation of one of its paths. In order to provide this definition we need some preliminary definitions. All are given with respect to an IOSTS $G = (Q, q_0, Trans)$ of signature (A, Ch).

$Act(M) = (Ch \times \{?, !\} \times M) \cup \{\tau\}$ is the set of *concrete communications*. An interpretation $\nu \in M^A$ of variables is called a *concrete assignment*, or *concrete state* of G. A *concrete transition* is a triple $(\nu, act_M, \nu') \in M^A \times Act(M) \times M^A$. A *concrete path* r is a map of $\mathbb{N} \rightarrow (M^A \times Act(M) \times M^A)$ of concrete transitions, such that for all i, if $r(i) = (\nu_i, a_i, \nu'_i)$ and $r(i+1) = (\nu_{i+1}, a_{i+1}, \nu'_{i+1})$ then $\nu'_i = \nu_{i+1}$.

First we define a transition run, that is the interpretation of one transition, say tr, of G. Its source state has to satisfy the guard of tr ; the label is a concrete communication according to the communication action of tr. Variables are updated according to the substitution defined in tr.

Definition 4 (Transition run). *Let* $tr = q \xrightarrow{\varphi[act]\rho} q' \in Trans$ *(i.e. tr is a transition of G). The set $Truns(tr) \subseteq M^A \times Act(M) \times M^A$ of transition runs of tr is such that $(\nu, act_M, \nu') \in Truns(tr)$ iff $\langle M, \nu \rangle \models \varphi$ and :*

if act = c!t (resp. act = τ) then $\nu' = \nu \circ \rho$ and $act_M = (c, !, \nu(t))$ (resp. $act_M = \tau$) or
if act is of the form c?y then there exists ν'' such that $\nu''(z) = \nu(z)$ for all $z \neq y$, $\nu' = \nu'' \circ \rho$ and $act_M = (c, ?, \nu''(y))$.

For a transition run $r = (\nu, act_M, \nu')$, also denoted by $\nu \xrightarrow{act_M} \nu'$, $src(r)$, $act(r)$ and $tgt(r)$ denote respectively ν, act_M and ν'.

Definition 5 (Runs of an IOSTS). *A concrete path r of an IOSTS G is a run of G if there exists a path p of G, such that $r(i) \in Truns(p(i))$ for all $i \in \mathbb{N}$. $Runs(G)$ is the set of runs of G.*

Example 2.

$$\nu_0 \xrightarrow{customer?42007} \nu_1 \xrightarrow{amount?50} \nu_2 \xrightarrow{bank!42007} \nu_2 \xrightarrow{balance?-500} \nu_3 \xrightarrow{disp!deficit} \nu_3$$

is a run of the IOSTS of Fig. 1, with $\nu_3(C) = 42007$, $\nu_3(M) = 50$, $\nu_3(B) = -500$.

3 Temporal Logic for IOSTS

The described temporal logic is used to specify temporal properties of runs of an IOSTS.

3.1 Syntax of ioLTL

Let $\Sigma = (A, Ch)$ be an IOSTS signature. The set of atomic formulas is $AF = \mathcal{F}_A \cup OF$ where $OF = \{\mathbf{O}[c@y]f \ / \ c \in Ch, @ \in \{?, !\}, y \notin A, f \in \mathcal{F}_{(A \cup \{y\})}\}$. Formulas in OF are called *Observation formulas*. $\mathbf{O}[c@y]f$ means informally that a value y satisfying the constraint f is observed through channel c (as an input or an output depending on @ which can be ! or ?). For example, $\mathbf{O}[c!y](y < x+5)$ is an atomic formula which denotes the reception, through channel c, of a value less than $x + 5$ (where x is supposed to be the name of a state variable). In the sequel, the symbol @ denotes input (?) or output (!) symbols.

Definition 6 (ioLTL). *The temporal logic ioLTL is defined by:*

> *if $f \in AF$ then $f \in ioLTL$*
> *if $f \in ioLTL$ then $\neg f \in ioLTL$*
> *if $f \in ioLTL$ and $g \in ioLTL$ then $f \wedge g$ and $f \vee g$ are in ioLTL*
> *if $f \in ioLTL$ and $g \in ioLTL$ then $\mathbf{X}f$, $f\mathbf{U}g$ and $f\mathbf{R}g$ are in ioLTL*

Thanks to de Morgan's laws and duality of operators any *ioLTL* formula can be transformed into a semantically equivalent formula where negation occurs only in front of atoms. In the sequel we always consider that formulas are in this form.

3.2 Semantics of ioLTL

If r is a run of an IOSTS and i a positive integer, then r_i denotes a concrete path being such that $r_i(k) = r(i + k)$ for all $k \in \mathbb{N}$, *i.e* r_i is the suffix of r beginning at the ith transition.

Definition 7 ($r \vDash f$). *The satisfaction relation $\vDash \subseteq Runs(G) \times ioLTL$ is inductively defined as follows[1]:*

> $r \vDash p$ $(p \in \mathcal{F}_A)$ *iff* $\langle M, source(r(0)) \rangle \vDash p$
> $r \vDash a$ $(a \in OF, a = \mathbf{O}[c@y]f)$ *iff there exists an interpretation ν of y such that $act(r(0)) = (c, @, \nu(y))$ and $\langle M, source(r(0)), \nu \rangle \vDash f$*
> $r \vDash \neg a$ $(a \in OF)$ *iff* $r \nvDash a$
> $r \vDash f \wedge g$ *iff* $r \vDash f$ *and* $r \vDash g$
> $r \vDash f \vee g$ *iff* $r \vDash f$ *or* $r \vDash g$
> $r \vDash \mathbf{X}f$ *iff* $r_1 \vDash f$
> $r \vDash f\mathbf{U}g$ *iff* $r_i \vDash g$ *for some* $i \geq 0$ *and for all* $0 \leq j < i$, $r_j \vDash f$
> $r \vDash f\mathbf{R}g$ *iff for all* $i \geq 0$, *if for every* $0 \leq j < i, r_j \nvDash f$ *then* $r_i \vDash g$

---

[1] We use the classical notation $r \vDash f$ instead of $(r, f) \in \vDash$.

Definition 8. *Let G be an IOSTS and f an ioLTL formula. We say that G satisfies f and we note* $G \vDash f$ *if for all* $r \in Runs(G)$, $r \vDash f$.

Example 3. For example IOSTS of Fig. 1 does not satisfy the formula *false R g* (equivalent to Globally *g*) with $g = (\mathbf{O}[balance@y](y < 0) \Rightarrow \mathbf{X}(\mathbf{O}[disp!y](y = $ "deficit"))) which means that when a negative balance is received, "deficit" must be displayed next. Indeed there is another possibility (due to non determinism of this IOSTS model) which is the display of the message "refused".

4   Symbolic Execution

Symbolic execution, which was first defined for programs [15], allows to explore executions of a program without enumerating all possible values of all variables. Symbolic execution produces a concise representation of executions like, in set theory, comprehensive definitions are concise for defining huge sets. The main idea of this technique is to use a new fresh symbol of variable instead of a value, each time that a reception (including initialization) occurs. The role of this new fresh variable is to represent any value of the input. This technique can naturally be adapted to the framework of IOSTS. In the sequel, the set of *symbolic inputs* will be the countable set F of new fresh variables ($F \cap A = \emptyset$). Consequently state variables are assigned by terms and the guard of a transition specifies a condition on those terms for the transition to be executable. Along a path, the conjunction of those conditions is the necessary condition (over symbolic inputs) under which a symbolic state can be reached from the initial state: it is called a *path-condition*. Accordingly a symbolic state is a triplet containing a location, a path-condition and a symbolic assignment of the variables (which associates to each variable of the IOSTS a term over symbolic inputs).

Definition 9 (Symbolic state). *A symbolic state over* F *of* G *is a triple* $\eta = (q, \pi, \sigma)$ *where* $q \in Q$, $\pi \in \mathcal{F}_F$ *is called a* path-condition *and* $\sigma \in T_F^A$ *is called a* symbolic assignment. $\eta = (q, \pi, \sigma)$ *is said to be consistent if* π *is satisfiable.*[2]

The following definition shows the construction of one step of a symbolic execution, that is the symbolic transition, or transition between symbolic states, associated with a transition of G. Note that if the communication action of the transition is an input message affecting a variable, then a new fresh symbol is introduced.

Definition 10 (Symbolic transition). *A symbolic transition over* F *is a triple* (η, sa, η'), *where* η, η' *are symbolic states, and sa is an action over* (F, Ch). *Let* $tr = q \xrightarrow{\varphi[act]\rho} q'$ *be a transition of* G. *Let* $\eta = (q, \pi, \sigma)$ *be a symbolic state over* F *of* G. *Let* z *be a variable in* F *such that* z *is used neither in* π *nor in* $\sigma(v)$ *for all variable* $v \in A$ *(z is a fresh variable not used in* η). *Then the symbolic transition associated with tr and* η *is* (η, sa, η'), *where* η' *and sa are defined by:*

---

[2] Let us recall that here, π is *satisfiable* if and only if there exists $\mu \in M^F$ such that $\langle M, \mu \rangle \models \pi$ since variables of π are in F by construction.

if act $= c!t$, *then* $sa = c!\sigma(t)$ *and* $\eta' = (q', \pi \wedge \sigma(\varphi), \sigma \circ \rho)$,
if act $= c?x$ *with* x *in* A *then* $sa = c?z$, *and* $\eta' = (q', \pi \wedge \sigma(\varphi), \sigma \circ [z/x] \circ \rho)$,
if act $= \tau$ *then* $sa = \tau$, *and* $\eta' = (q', \pi \wedge \sigma(\varphi), \sigma \circ \rho)$.

A symbolic transition $sp = (\eta, sa, \eta')$ is denoted by $\eta \xrightarrow{sa} \eta'$; $source(sp) = \eta$ and $target(sp) = \eta'$.

Definition 11 (Symbolic path). *A symbolic path is a countable infinite sequence of symbolic transitions* $[st_0, \ldots, st_n, \ldots]$ *associated with an IOSTS such that for all* $i \in \mathbb{N}$, $target(st_i) = source(st_{i+1})$. *It is said* consistent *if all of its symbolic states are consistent.*

A symbolic path $[\eta_0 \xrightarrow{sa_0} \ldots \eta_{n-1} \xrightarrow{sa_{n-1}} \ldots]$ is called a *symbolic execution path* of G iff $\eta_0 = (q_0, true, \sigma_0)$, where q_0 is the initial location and σ_0 is an injective substitution in F^A, and each symbolic transition is associated with a transition of G. The following definition shows how a symbolic path can be interpreted as concrete paths of the IOSTS.

Definition 12 (Interpretation of a symbolic path). *Let* $sp = [(q_0, \pi_0, \sigma_0)$ $\xrightarrow{sa_0} \ldots (q_n, \pi_n, \sigma_n) \xrightarrow{sa_n} \ldots]$ *be a symbolic path. If* $\mu \in M^F$ *is an interpretation of variables of* F *such that* $\langle M, \mu \rangle \vDash \pi_i$ *for all* $i \in \mathbb{N}$, *then the interpretation of* sp *by* μ *is* $r = [\nu_0 \xrightarrow{act_0} \ldots \nu_n \xrightarrow{act_n} \ldots]$ *such that for all* $i \in \mathbb{N}$:

$$\nu_i(x) = \mu(\sigma_i(x))$$
$$act_i = c@\mu(t) \text{ if } sa_i = c@t \text{ else } act_i = \tau.$$

Symbolic execution is correct and complete i.e. the union of all interpretations of all symbolic paths of an IOSTS G is exactly $Runs(G)$.

5 Unfolding Rules

Our model-checking algorithm, as usual, unfolds the model in order to prove that there exists at least one run satisfying the negation ($\neg g$) of the expected property g to be checked. In this section we describe some unfolding rules applying to an IOSTS and an ioLTL formula (supposed to be the negation of the expected property). The purpose of those rules is to compute symbolic paths of the IOSTS being such that any of their numerical interpretations satisfies the formula. Those rules are inspired from tableau unfolding of LTL formulas whose principle consists in the decomposition of a formula into two main sets of formulas: the set of atomic formulas that have to be satisfied in the current state and the set of formulas that have to be satisfied in the next state. For example $p\mathbf{U}q$ holds in a state either if q holds in this state or p holds in this state and $p\mathbf{U}q$ holds in the next state. Our rules perform a synchronization between the unfolding of the formula and the symbolic execution of the IOSTS: atoms generated by the decomposition of the formula are added to the path conditions in order to keep only symbolic paths semantically compatible with the formula. This is reflected by the fact that a rule transforms a *context* which is a couple whose first component is a symbolic state η and whose second component is a quadruple of four sets of ioLTL formulas $(\Phi, \Gamma, \Theta, \Upsilon)$. The application of the rules builds paths of contexts which are sequences of transitions linking contexts. The set Φ, called *Until Set*, contains *until* formulas of the form $\varphi \mathbf{U} \psi$, such that ψ has to be checked in the future; Γ, called *Current Set*, is the set of formulas to be checked in the current state; Θ, called *Observation Set*, is the set of observation formulas to be checked in the outgoing transition; Υ, called *Next Set* is the set of formulas to be checked in the next state.

Let G be an IOSTS whose initial location is q_0 and whose set of state variables is A. The *initial symbolic state* is $init = (q_0, true, \sigma_0)$ where σ_0 is an injective substitution in F^A (where F is the set of fresh variables, see section 4). If f is the temporal formula given as an input to our set of rules, the first context is $[init, (\Phi_{init}, \{f\}, \emptyset, \emptyset)]$ where Φ_{init} is the set containing all *until* sub-formulas of f (*i.e* of the form $\varphi \mathbf{U} \psi$).

5.1   Transition Rule: Symbolic Transitions Extended to Contexts

Let $\eta \xrightarrow{sa} \eta'$ be a symbolic transition associated with G (see definition 10), such that η and η' are consistent. Then the Transition Rule is the following: if the last context of the path is $[\eta, (\Phi, \emptyset, \Theta, \Upsilon)]$ and $\Phi \neq \emptyset$ then build

$$\eta, (\Phi, \emptyset, \Theta, \Upsilon) \xrightarrow{sa} \eta', (\Phi, \emptyset, \Theta, \Upsilon), \bullet$$

When Until set is empty (*i.e* all *until* formulas have been checked), the new Until Set is Φ_{init}, the set of all *until* sub-formulas; the Next Set Rule $[NSR]$ will remove unnecessary formulas. So the rule is:

$$\eta, (\emptyset, \emptyset, \Theta, \Upsilon) \xrightarrow{sa} \eta', (\Phi_{Init}, \emptyset, \Theta, \Upsilon), \bullet$$

$[(\eta, C) \xrightarrow{sa} (\eta', C'), \bullet]$ is a symbolic transition extended to contexts. The symbol $\bullet$ is used to trigger the application of rules dedicated to observation formulas after the construction of a transition (since the observation sa is defined only after the execution of a transition). Note that this rule is only applied when the *Current Set* is empty (*i.e* when there is no remaining formula to be checked in the current state). After the application of the Transition rule, the context at the source of the transition will remain unchanged by the following rules.

5.2   Observation Rules and Next Set Rule

A fraction style rule denotes a substitution: the upper context vanishes and is replaced by the lower context of the fraction bar. The rules $[OR_1]$ to $[OR_3]$ can not be applied to the first context, so rules related to Current Set (given in Section 5.3) are directly applied before the construction of a symbolic transition (transition rule).

The following rules are applied after the construction of the symbolic transition $[\eta, (\Phi, \emptyset, \Theta, \Upsilon) \xrightarrow{sa} \eta', (\Phi, \emptyset, \Theta, \Upsilon), \bullet]$ where $\eta = (q, \pi, \sigma)$ and $\eta' = (q', \pi', \sigma')$, and are related to the observation formulas over communication actions. For example rule $[OR_1]$ is applied when the Observation Set contains a formula $\mathbf{O}[c@y]h$, and the the symbolic action of the symbolic transition is of the form $c@z$ for a term z. $[z/y](h)$ is obtained by substituting y in the formula h by the term z; $\sigma \circ [z/y](h)$ is then obtained by substituting each remaining variable x by its image $\sigma(x)$ (σ is the symbolic assignment in η). This resulting property must hold in η; so it is added by conjunction with the path condition of η': its consistency will be checked when the Transition Rule is applied again.

$[OR_1]$ If $sa = c@z$

$$\frac{(q', \pi', \sigma'), (\Phi, \emptyset, \{\mathbf{O}[c@y]h\} \cup \Theta, \Upsilon), \bullet}{(q', \pi' \wedge (\sigma \circ [z/y](h)), \sigma'), (\Phi, \emptyset, \Theta, \Upsilon), \bullet}$$

$[OR_2]$ If for all term t, $sa \neq c@t$

$$\frac{\eta', (\Phi, \emptyset, \{\neg\mathbf{O}[c@y]h\} \cup \Theta, \Upsilon), \bullet}{\eta', (\Phi, \emptyset, \Theta, \Upsilon), \bullet}$$

$[OR_3]$ If $sa = c@z$

$$\frac{(q', \pi', \sigma'), (\Phi, \emptyset, \{\neg\mathbf{O}[c@y]h\} \cup \Theta, \Upsilon), \bullet}{(q', \pi' \wedge \neg(\sigma \circ [z/y](h)), \sigma'), (\Phi, \emptyset, \Theta, \Upsilon), \bullet}$$

When the Observation Set Θ is empty, *Next Set Rule*$[NSR]$ can be applied: the formulas in Next Set Υ have to be checked in the new state, so they are put in Current Set Γ. Moreover the new Until Set is the intersection of the previous Until Set with this new Current Set: so Until Set will contain until formulas that still have to be checked. The symbol $\bullet$ is removed, so the other rules (related to Current Set) can be applied.

$$[NSR] \quad \frac{\eta', (\Phi, \emptyset, \emptyset, \Upsilon), \bullet}{\eta', (\Phi \cap \Upsilon, \Upsilon, \emptyset, \emptyset)}$$

5.3 Rules Related to Current Set

After the application of the Next Set Rule, the rules related to Current Set Γ are applied until $\Gamma = \emptyset$ (and then a symbolic transition can be constructed by the Transition rule). If the rule $[Disjunct_1]$ can be applied, so can the rule $[Disjunct_2]$: then the algorithm forks in two avatars; on each avatar is applied one of the two rules. The same happens with rules *Until* and *Release*.

$[Atom]$ $p \in \mathcal{F}_A$

$$\frac{(q, \pi, \sigma), (\Phi, \{p\} \cup \Gamma, \Theta, \Upsilon)}{(q, \pi \wedge \sigma(p), \sigma), (\Phi, \Gamma, \Theta, \Upsilon)}$$

$[Observation]$ $a \in OF$ or $a = \neg b, b \in OF$

$$\frac{\eta, (\Phi, \{a\} \cup \Gamma, \Theta, \Upsilon)}{\eta, (\Phi, \Gamma, \Theta \cup \{a\}, \Upsilon)}$$

$[Conjunct]$

$$\frac{\eta, (\Phi, \{f \wedge g\} \cup \Gamma, \Theta, \Upsilon)}{\eta, (\Phi, \{f, g\} \cup \Gamma, \Theta, \Upsilon)}$$

$[Disjunct_1]$

$$\frac{\eta, (\Phi, \{f \vee g\} \cup \Gamma, \Theta, \Upsilon)}{\eta, (\Phi, \{f\} \cup \Gamma, \Theta, \Upsilon)}$$

$[Disjunct_2]$

$$\frac{\eta, (\Phi, \{f \vee g\} \cup \Gamma, \Theta, \Upsilon)}{\eta, (\Phi, \{g\} \cup \Gamma, \Theta, \Upsilon)}$$

$[Until_1]$

$$\frac{\eta, (\Phi, \{f\mathbf{U}g\} \cup \Gamma, \Theta, \Upsilon)}{\eta, (\Phi, \{g\} \cup \Gamma, \Theta, \Upsilon)}$$

$[Until_2]$

$$\frac{\eta, (\Phi, \{f\mathbf{U}g\} \cup \Gamma, \Theta, \Upsilon)}{\eta, (\Phi, \{f\} \cup \Gamma, \Theta, \Upsilon \cup \{f\mathbf{U}g\})}$$

$[Release_2]$

$$\frac{\eta, (\Phi, \{f\mathbf{R}g\} \cup \Gamma, \Theta, \Upsilon)}{\eta, (\Phi, \{g\} \cup \Gamma, \Theta, \Upsilon \cup \{f\mathbf{R}g\})}$$

$[Release_1]$

$$\frac{\eta, (\Phi, \{f\mathbf{R}g\} \cup \Gamma, \Theta, \Upsilon)}{\eta, (\Phi, \{f, g\} \cup \Gamma, \Theta, \Upsilon)}$$

$[Next]$

$$\frac{\eta, (\Phi, \{\mathbf{X}f\} \cup \Gamma, \Theta, \Upsilon)}{\eta, (\Phi, \Gamma, \Theta, \Upsilon \cup \{f\})}$$

By applying these rules, the formulas in the Current Set are decomposed in atomic formulas or *next* formulas, *i.e* formulas of the form Xg. When an atomic formula in $\mathcal{F}_A$ is reached, it is added to the path condition after substitution of variables by the terms defined by the symbolic assignment (rule $[Atom]$): its consistency will be checked when the Transition Rule is applied. When an *observation* formula is reached, it is inserted in the Observation Set (rule $[Observation]$). When Xg is reached, g is inserted in the Next Set (rule $[Next]$). Rules $[Until]$ are explained by the equivalence between $f\mathbf{U}g$ and $g \vee (f \wedge \mathbf{X}(f\mathbf{U}g))$. Rules $[Release]$ are explained by the equivalence between $f\mathbf{R}g$ and $(g \wedge f) \vee (g \wedge \mathbf{X}(f\mathbf{R}g))$.

5.4   Correctness and Completeness of the Rules

Definition 13. *We call an f-unfolding of an IOSTS G a finite or infinite sequence of transitions $[(\eta_0, C_0) \xrightarrow{sa_0} (\eta_1, C_1) \xrightarrow{sa_1} (\eta_2, C_2) \ldots]$ resulting from the application of rules defined above (i.e for all i, $(\eta_i, C_i) \xrightarrow{sa_i} (\eta_{i+1}, C_{i+1})$ can be obtained by unfolding rules), starting at $[init, (\Phi_{init}, \{f\}, \emptyset, \emptyset)]$. The symbolic projection of an unfolding is the sequence $[\eta_0 \xrightarrow{sa_0} \eta_1 \xrightarrow{sa_1} \eta_2 \ldots]$ obtained by ignoring the second coordinate of contexts.*

The correctness lemma states that if we consider an infinite unfolding for a formula f, such that the Until Set is empty infinitely often, then any instance of the symbolic projection satisfies f.

Lemma 1 (Correctness). *Let $[(\eta_0, C_0) \xrightarrow{sa_0} (\eta_1, C_1) \xrightarrow{sa_1} (\eta_2, C_2) \ldots]$ be an infinite f-unfolding and suppose that for any integer i there exists a context $[\eta_n, (\Phi_n, \Gamma_n, \Theta_n, \Upsilon_n)]$ in this unfolding, with $n > i$, such that $\Phi_n = \emptyset$. Then any run r being an interpretation of the symbolic projection $[\eta_0 \xrightarrow{sa_0} \eta_1 \xrightarrow{sa_1} \eta_2 \ldots]$ is such that $r \vDash f$.*

The completeness lemma states that any run of G satisfying a formula is the instance of the projection of an f-unfolding of G.

Lemma 2 (Completeness). *Let $r \in Runs(G)$, f a ioTL formula, and let us suppose that $r \vDash f$. Then there exists an f-unfolding u of G whose symbolic projection path admits r as an interpretation, such that if $u = [(\eta_0, C_0) \xrightarrow{sa_0} (\eta_1, C_1) \ldots]$ then for any any integer i there exists a context $[\eta_n, (\Phi_n, \Gamma_n, \Theta_n, \Upsilon_n)]$ in u, with $n > i$, such that $\Phi_n = \emptyset$.*

The proofs of these two lemmas are similar to the usual ones in LTL model checking. The main point is that an interpretation of an infinite f-unfolding verifies f, unless an *until* property $\varphi \mathbf{U} \psi$ has to be satisfied at a certain state, but ψ is never verified by its successors. Under hypotheses of Lemma 1 this case is impossible, because $\varphi \mathbf{U} \psi$ would be present in all Current Sets after a given context; then, even if an Until Set of a successor can be empty, it is only possible once and not infinitely often. In the case of Lemma 2, if there is a run satisfying f, it is possible to construct an unfolding such that no *until* sub-formulas of f remains present forever in the current sets after a given context: so each sub-formula disappears from the Until Set until it is empty, and this empty set appears infinitely often.

5.5   Termination Criteria

In this section we describe a sufficient condition to find a run of an IOSTS satisfying the temporal formula f, and a sufficient condition to be sure that no run of an IOSTS satisfies f. The first condition (used in Theorem 1) shows the existence of a sequence of inputs leading to a recurring state and therefore the existence of an infinite execution satisfying f. The second condition (used in Theorem 2) indicates when an unfolding can be stopped because any prolongation will prove nothing more. Those conditions depend on the intersection or inclusion of particular sets of interpretations of variables in A (state variables of the IOSTS) but also of subsets of F (symbolic inputs of the symbolic execution). Those sets are called omega sets of a symbolic state. Intuitively the omega set of a symbolic state η characterizes the relation existing between concrete assignations of the system variables and interpretations of the symbolic inputs they depend on. For example with $M = (\mathbb{Z}, +, <)$, $A = \{x\}$ and $\eta = (q, a > 0, x \mapsto a + 1)$ the omega set of η relatively to $\{a\}$, noted $\Omega_\eta^{\{a\}}$, is $\{(x \mapsto 2, a \mapsto 1), (x \mapsto 3, a \mapsto 2), (x \mapsto 4, a \mapsto 3) \dots\}$. The couple $(x \mapsto 2, a \mapsto 1)$ expresses the fact that x is assigned by 2 when the interpretation of a is 1. By considering intersection of omega sets of symbolic states belonging to the same symbolic path one can characterize the existence of numerical lassos (numerical executions constituted of a preamble and a loop). For this purpose we consider omega sets with respect to symbols shared by the two considered symbolic states. For example, consider $eta' = (q, a > 0 \wedge b < 3, x \mapsto a + 3 - b)$ being a state situated after η in a symbolic path. Those two states share the set $\{a\}$ of symbolic inputs. Then let us consider the omega sets of η and η' with respect to $\{a\}$. In η, since x only depends on $\{a\}$, the value of x is a function of a. This function is indeed characterized by the omega set of η with respect to $\{a\}$. The non emptiness of the intersection of omega sets of η and η' with respect $\{a\}$ means: there exists a value for b such that x and a are in the same functional relation in both η and η' i.e. there exists an interpretation of b such that x remains unchanged. Finally we deduce the existence of a numerical loop. For example the intersection of omega sets of η and η' with respect to $\{a\}$ is non empty since it contains the couple $(x \mapsto 2, a \mapsto 1)$ by choosing in η' $b = 2$ (which satisfies $b < 3$). We deduce that for $b = 2$ there exists a loop on the state $(q, x \mapsto 2)$. In the following definition $SI(\pi)$ denotes the set (included in F) of symbolic inputs having at least an occurrence in the path-condition π. The set

$SI(Ran(\sigma))$, where σ is a symbolic assignment, denotes the union of the sets of symbols of symbolic inputs having at least one occurrence in the term $\sigma(x)$ for $x \in A$.

Definition 14 (Omega set of a symbolic state). *Let $\eta = (q, \pi, \sigma)$ be a symbolic state over F. Let us note δ a finite subset of symbols of variables of F and $\gamma = [SI(\pi) \cup SI(Ran(\sigma))] \setminus \delta$. The omega set of η relatively to δ, noted Ω_η^δ is*

$$\{(\nu, \mu) \in M^A \times M^\delta / \exists \beta \in M^\gamma, \langle M, \nu, \mu, \beta \rangle \vDash (\pi \wedge \bigwedge_{x \in A} (x = \sigma(x)))\}$$

Note that $\Omega_\eta^\emptyset$ is the set of numerical states denoted by the symbolic state η. So, intuitively, when we have $\Omega_{\eta'}^\emptyset \subseteq \Omega_\eta^\emptyset$, this means that all numerical states (and paths starting from them) of η' are already represented by η. Those intuitions guide the following definitions. Let $ct = [\eta, (\Phi, \emptyset, \Theta, \Upsilon)]$ and $ct' = [\eta', (\Phi, \emptyset, \Theta, \Upsilon)]$ be two contexts associated to the same IOSTS, such that $\eta = (q, \pi, \sigma)$ and $\eta' = (q, \pi', \sigma')$ (note that the formulas sets $(\Phi, \emptyset, \Theta, \Upsilon)$ are the same in the two contexts, and that η and η' have the same location q ; moreover Current set is empty because the following criteria are only checked on persistent contexts, *i.e* contexts on which the transition rule is applied). Then ct' is said to be *strongly related* to ct if $\Omega_\eta^{SI(Ran(\sigma))} \cap \Omega_{\eta'}^{SI(Ran(\sigma))} \neq \emptyset$. ct' is said to be *included in* ct if $\Omega_{\eta'}^\emptyset \subseteq \Omega_\eta^\emptyset$. Note that the binary relation *is strongly related to* is asymmetric since it depends on the symbolic inputs of ct. Now let G be an IOSTS and $P = [ct_0 \xrightarrow{sa_0} ct_1 \xrightarrow{sa_1} \cdots ct_n]$ a f-unfolding of G.

1. If for some $i \in \{0, \ldots, n-1\}$, ct_n is strongly related to ct_i, then P is said to satisfy the *lasso criterion*.
2. If for some $i \in \{0, \ldots, n-1\}$, ct_n is included in ct_i, then P is said to satisfy the *inclusion criterion*.
3. If P satisfies (1) or (2) and is such that there is an empty Until set among $\Phi_i, \ldots, \Phi_n$ of the contexts $ct_i, \ldots, ct_n$, then P is said to satisfy the *Until criterion*.

With respect to those definitions we can state the two theorems mentioned above.

Theorem 1. *If a f-unfolding of G satisfies the lasso criterion and the Until criterion, then there is a run in the semantics of G satisfying f.*

Proof. To simplify, without lost of generality, suppose $A = \{x\}$. Let us consider P a f-unfolding satisfying the lasso criterion and the Until criterion. So P is of the form $[ct_0 \cdots ct_n]$ where ct_n is strongly related to a context ct_i of P. Let η_i (resp. η_n), be the symbolic state associated to ct_i (resp. ct_n). Suppose in η_i the symbolic assignation σ_i is $x \mapsto t_i(a_1, \ldots, a_n)$. We have $SI(Ran(\sigma_i)) = \{a_1, \ldots, a_n\}$. So, given μ an interpretation of $a_1 \ldots a_n$, we have $\nu = \mu(t_i(a_1, \ldots, a_n))$. Let us consider $(\nu_i, \mu_i) \in \Omega_{\eta_i}^{\{a_1, \ldots, a_n\}} \cap \Omega_{\eta_n}^{\{a_1, \ldots, a_n\}}$. So ν_i is completely defined: $\nu_i = \mu_i(t_i(a_1, \ldots, a_n))$. Now the sequence s of transitions fired between η_i and η_n may have introduce new symbolic inputs $b_1 \ldots b_k$. Therefore in η_n, σ_n is

$x \mapsto t_n(c_1, \ldots, c_j, b_1, \ldots, b_k)$ where $\{c_1, \ldots, c_j\} \subseteq \{a_1, \ldots, a_n\}$. Note that we have $\{b_1, \ldots, b_k\} = (SI(\pi_\eta \cup SI(\sigma_n)) \setminus \{a_1, \ldots, a_n\}$. By hypothesis $(\nu_i, \mu_i) \in \Omega_{\eta_n}^{\{a_1, \ldots, a_n\}}$ so there exists an assignment β of $b_1 \ldots b_k$ such that $\nu_i = (\mu_i, \beta)(t_n(c_1, \ldots, c_j, b_1, \ldots, b_k))$. This proves that there exists an interpretation of $b_1 \ldots b_k$ such that, starting from the numerical state ν_i the execution of the sequence s returns to the state ν_i. Therefore the interpretation of P with respect to μ_i and β is a numerical lasso (a path constituted of a prefix followed by a loop), the loop always returning to the numerical state ν_i. Suppose that u is the sequence of transition fired between ct_0 and ct_i. Then the path $u.s^*$ is a non empty infinite path. Clearly it satisfies hypothesis of Lemma 1. Thus P proves that f is satisfied by at least one numerical run.

Theorem 2. *If all f-unfoldings of G are finite or satisfy the inclusion criterion but not the until criterion, then there is no run in $Runs(G)$ satisfying f.*

Proof. A finite f-unfoldings is said maximal iff any extension is non consistent (see the Transition Rule). A finite maximal (any extension is non consistent) f-unfolding is then obviously in contradiction with f. Now the case of a f-unfolding satisfying the inclusion criterion. Consider the context $ct_i = (\eta_i, C_i)$ and a posterior one $ct_n = (\eta_n, C_n)$ of a f-unfolding P, and suppose that ct_n is included in ct_i. So $C_i = C_n$ and $\Omega_{\eta_n}^\emptyset \subseteq \Omega_{\eta_i}^\emptyset$. $C_i = C_n$ states that the same formulas have to be proved by those two contexts. So let us prove that C_n cannot prove those formulas. For tr a transition let us note $tr(\eta_i)$ (resp. $tr(\eta_n)$) the symbolic state resulting from the symbolic execution of tr from η_i (resp. η_n). We clearly have: $\Omega_{\eta_n}^\emptyset \subseteq \Omega_{\eta_i}^\emptyset \Rightarrow \Omega_{tr(\eta_n)}^\emptyset \subseteq \Omega_{tr(\eta_i)}^\emptyset$. So if ct_i contains formulas not proved between ct_i and ct_n, they cannot be proved after ct_n since all its successors are attached to symbolic states denoting states already denoted by the symbolic states of $ct_i \ldots ct_n$.

6   Model Checking Process

Like in [5] for efficiency reasons, firstly we compute the negation f of the property g to be checked then we try to find a witness of f in the semantics of the model G by achieving a f-unfolding of the model G, following the rules of Section 5. This requires that the negation operator occurs only in front of atoms. As mentioned in Section 3 it is always possible to obtain such a form. The construction of a particular f-unfolding terminates in three cases:

1. the path condition of the last context becomes non satisfiable after the application of a rule. This unfolding cannot provide us an example for f (i.e a counterexample for g),
2. the last context is of the form $(\eta, (\Phi, \emptyset, \emptyset, \emptyset))$: it means that all formulas have been satisfied and hence that any run admitting as a prefix an instance of the symbolic path computed so far satisfies f. The whole process is over. A numerical counter-example can be generated by solving the path condition,

3. the unfolding satisfies a criterion of section 5.5, *i.e* the unfolding verifies the lasso criterion and Until criterion, or it satisfies the inclusion criterion and not the Until criterion.

The third case can be described as follows. Let $P = [ct_0 \xrightarrow{sa_0} ct_1 \xrightarrow{sa_1} \cdots ct_n]$ be the unfolding, and $\Phi_0, \ldots, \Phi_n$ the Until Sets of the contexts. Let ct_i be the last context before ct_n such that $\Phi_i = \emptyset$ (i is supposed to be -1 if there is no such empty Until set). If $0 \leq i < n$ then the lasso criterion is checked for contexts ct_k with $k \leq i$, *i.e* we check if ct_n is strongly related to ct_k. If the lasso criterion is fulfilled, then the process is over: as the Until criterion is also fulfilled, according to Theorem 1, we conclude that the model can exhibit a counter-exemple. If the lasso criterion is not found and if $i < n$ then the inclusion criterion is checked for contexts between $i + 1$ and $n - 1$, *i.e* we check if ct_n is included in ct_k for $k \in \{i+1, \ldots, n-1\}$. If the inclusion criterion is not found, the process continues on this unfolding ; but if the inclusion criterion is found, the process terminates on this unfolding ; the whole process goes on with the other unfoldings. Finally, if all unfoldings are discarded or satisfy the inclusion criterion then, by Theorem 2, we can conclude that the IOSTS can not exhibit a run satisfying f. In practice, checking satisfiability of path conditions, intersection or inclusion of omega sets are particular cases of verifying satisfiability of first order formulas. It is in particular possible for decidable theories: for example Presburger arithmetic, the theory of integers without multiplication, is a decidable theory, as first order theory of reals. It means that data types that can be used include $(\mathbb{Z}, <, +)$ and $(\mathbb{R}, <, +, \times)$. These verifications can then be done thanks to dedicated tools: our prototype uses the Omega library [14] to deal with Presburger arithmetic.

Example 4. The negation f of the formula of example 3 can be written *true U g* with $g = (\mathbf{O}[balance?z](z \overset{\scriptstyle <}{} 0) \wedge \mathbf{X}(\neg\mathbf{O}[disp!y](y = \text{deficit})))$. An f-unfolding of IOSTS of Fig. 1 is: $[ct_0 \xrightarrow{account?C_1} \ldots ct_4 \xrightarrow{disp!refused} ct_5]$ where $ct_4 = [(q_4, true, \sigma_4), (\emptyset, \emptyset, \{\neg\mathbf{O}[disp!y](y = \text{deficit})\}, \emptyset)]$, $\sigma_4(B) = B_1$, $\sigma_4(M) = M_1$, $\sigma_4(C) = C_1$ and $ct_5 = [(q_0, B_1 \leq M_1 \wedge (\text{refused} \neq \text{deficit}), \sigma_4), (\emptyset, \emptyset, \emptyset, \emptyset)]$. Therefore $[ct_0 \xrightarrow{account?C_1} \ldots ct_4 \xrightarrow{disp!refused} ct_5]$, where OR_3 is the last rule applied, provides a counter-example to formula of Example 3.

7   Experimental Results and Implementation Issues

The verification algorithm described in the previous sections is implemented as an extension of the AGATHA tool [6,18] which provides a symbolic execution engine for the IOSTS formalism and supports Presburger arithmetics for the data part (thanks to the Omega Library [1]). A first significant experimentation of this algorithm has been conducted in the context of diagnosability checking. Diagnosability can be defined as the problem of determining whether a faulty mode in a given system can be distinguished from a normal mode through a finite number of observations. Using the so-called *twin-plant* approach inspired from [13], we had to check formulas of the form $F(G(Amb))$ (where F f stands for *true U f*, *G f* for $\neg F \neg f$ and *Amb* is an atomic formula which is true when the fault occurred only in one instance of the twin-plant) over the synchronized product $G \otimes G$ ($\otimes$ synchronize executions having the same observable traces) of an IOSTS model G representing a real industrial embedded system. This quite complex system is intended to be embedded in vehicles, it combines a speed regulation function with an anti-collision function. The experiment has proved the non-diagnosability of some faults. Moreover path conditions associated with witnesses brought some good intuitions to understand and explain the highlighted cases of non-diagnosability. This qualitative aspect was particularly appreciated by the end user. To illustrate, returning 0 for a broken sensor is a non diagnosable fault if there exists a scenario where the same operational sensor always measures 0 from its environment. For this particular fault and relatively to a sensor measuring a relative speed we obtained a witness reflecting this analysis since the path condition of this witness was clearly referring to the scenario where the vehicle equipped with the system keeps running at exactly the same speed than the vehicle running in front.

8   Conclusion

We have presented fundamentals elements of an approach for the verification of temporal logic formulas over IOSTSs. This latter formalism is used to describe open reactive systems, communicating with an unspecified environment, and allows to use unbounded variables. The temporal logic is an extension of linear temporal logic, called ioLTL, that can specify properties of variables along an execution (as equalities or inequalities of variables), and also properties over input or output messages. This approach is based on symbolic execution which is used to check if there exists some executions satisfying the constraints generated from the negation of the ioLTL requirement by means of tableau calculus. It was successfully experimented on an industrial case study in the context of diagnosability checking. With some adaptations, starting from an ioLTL formula, the technique could be transformed in order to select finite symbolic execution paths of an IOSTS. This could be useful to automatically generate test purposes in the sense exposed in [11]. This would lead to a kind of refinement of test purposes. This perspective will be studied in a close future.

References

1. Omega 1.2. The Omega Project: Algorithms and Frameworks for Analyzing and Transforming Scientific Programs (1994)
2. Abdulla, P.A., Jonsson, B., Nilsson, M., d'Orso, J., Saksena, M.: Regular model checking for ltl(mso). In: Alur, R., Peled, D.A. (eds.) CAV 2004. LNCS, vol. 3114, pp. 348–360. Springer, Heidelberg (2004)
3. Annichini, A., Bouajjani, A., Sighireanu, M.: Trex: A tool for reachability analysis of complex systems. In: Berry, G., Comon, H., Finkel, A. (eds.) CAV 2001. LNCS, vol. 2102, pp. 368–372. Springer, Heidelberg (2001)

4. Bardin, S., Leroux, J., Point, G.: Fast extended release. In: Ball, T., Jones, R.B. (eds.) CAV 2006. LNCS, vol. 4144, pp. 63–66. Springer, Heidelberg (2006)
5. Biere, A., Cimatti, A., Clarke, E.M., Strichman, O., Zhu, Y.: Bounded model checking. Advances in Computers 58, 118–149 (2003)
6. Bigot, C., Faivre, A., Gallois, J.-P., Lapitre, A., Lugato, D., Pierron, J.-Y., Rapin, N.: Automatic test generation with AGATHA. In: Garavel, H., Hatcliff, J. (eds.) TACAS 2003. LNCS, vol. 2619, pp. 591–596. Springer, Heidelberg (2003)
7. Bouajjani, A., Jonsson, B., Nilsson, M., Touili, T.: Regular model checking. In: Emerson, E.A., Sistla, A.P. (eds.) CAV 2000. LNCS, vol. 1855, pp. 403–418. Springer, Heidelberg (2000)
8. Bultan, T., Gerber, R., Pugh, W.: Symbolic model checking of infinite state systems using presburger arithmetic. In: Grumberg, O. (ed.) CAV 1997. LNCS, vol. 1254, pp. 400–411. Springer, Heidelberg (1997)
9. Bultan, T., Yavuz-Kahveci, T.: Action language verifier. In: ASE, pp. 382–386. IEEE Computer Society, Los Alamitos (2001)
10. Frantzen, L., Tretmans, J., Willemse, T.A.C.: Test generation based on symbolic specifications. In: Grabowski, J., Nielsen, B. (eds.) FATES 2004. LNCS, vol. 3395, pp. 1–15. Springer, Heidelberg (2005)
11. Gaston, C., LeGall, P., Rapin, N., Touil, A.: Symbolic execution techniques for test purpose definition. In: Uyar, M.Ü., Duale, A.Y., Fecko, M.A. (eds.) TestCom 2006. LNCS, vol. 3964, pp. 1–18. Springer, Heidelberg (2006)
12. Henzinger, T.A., Majumdar, R., Raskin, J.-F.: A classification of symbolic transition systems. ACM Trans. Comput. Logic 6(1), 1–32 (2005)
13. Jiang, S., Huang, Z., Chandra, V., Kumar, R.: A polynomial algorithm for testing diagnosability of discrete event systems. IEEE Transactions on Automatic Control 46, 1318–1321 (2000)
14. Kelly, W., Maslov, V., Pugh, W., Rosser, E., Shpeisman, T., Wonnacott, D.: The omega library interface guide. Technical report, College Park, MD, USA (1995)
15. King, J.C.: Symbolic execution and program testing. Commun. ACM 19(7), 385–394 (1976)
16. LeGall, P., Rapin, N., Touil, A.: Symbolic execution techniques for refinement testing. In: Gurevich, Y., Meyer, B. (eds.) TAP 2007. LNCS, vol. 4454, pp. 131–148. Springer, Heidelberg (2007)
17. Lichtenstein, O., Pnueli, A.: Checking that finite state concurrent programs satisfy their linear specification. In: POPL 1985, pp. 97–107. ACM Press, New York (1985)
18. Rapin, N., Gaston, C., Lapitre, A., Gallois, J.-P.: Behavioural unfolding of formal specifications based on communicating automata. In: Proceedings of the first Workshop on Automated technology for verification and analysis, Taiwan (2003)
19. Rusu, V., du Bousquet, L., Jéron, T.: An approach to symbolic test generation. In: Grieskamp, W., Santen, T., Stoddart, B. (eds.) IFM 2000. LNCS, vol. 1945, pp. 338–357. Springer, Heidelberg (2000)
20. Vardi, M.Y., Wolper, P.: An automata-theoretic approach to automatic program verification. In: Proceedings of the First Symposium on Logic in Computer Science, pp. 322–331 (1986)
21. Wolper, P., Boigelot, B.: Verifying systems with infinite but regular state spaces. In: Y. Vardi, M. (ed.) CAV 1998. LNCS, vol. 1427, pp. 88–97. Springer, Heidelberg (1998)

Finding Errors of Hybrid Systems by Optimising an Abstraction-Based Quality Estimate[*]

Stefan Ratschan[1,**] and Jan-Georg Smaus[2,***]

[1] Academy of Sciences of the Czech Republic
stefan.ratschan@cs.cas.cz
[2] University of Freiburg, Germany
smaus@informatik.uni-freiburg.de

Abstract. We present an algorithm for falsifying safety properties of hybrid systems, i.e., for finding a trajectory to an unsafe state. The approach is to approximate how close a point is to being an initial point of an error trajectory using a real-valued quality function, and then to use numerical optimisation to search for an optimum of this function. The function is computed by running simulations, where information coming from abstractions computed by a verification algorithm is exploited to determine whether a simulation looks promising and should be continued or cancelled. This information becomes more reliable as the abstraction becomes more refined. We thus interleave falsification and verification attempts.

1 Introduction

A hybrid system is a dynamical system with combined discrete and continuous state and evolution. An important problem is to ensure correctness, i.e., *verification*. However, during the design (debugging) process, hybrid systems are usually not correct yet, and hence *error detection* is equally important.

We address here the problem of automatically finding error trajectories that lead the system from an initial to an unsafe state. We distinguish ourselves from other recent works [3,18] by two main aspects:

- The above methods aim at systems with a high amount of non-determinism (e.g., in the form of inputs), and do a broad search in the statespace spanned by the non-deterministic choices. For systems with completely deterministic evolution however, it is important to distinguish and prefer those regions of the search space that are most promising, which is the aim of this work.

---

[*] An extended version of this paper has appeared as a technical report [20]. We acknowledge the help of Tomáš Dzetkulič with the implementation.
[**] The work of Stefan Ratschan has been supported by GAČR grant 201/08/J020 and by the institutional research plan AV0Z100300504.
[***] The work of Jan-Georg Smaus has been supported by the German Research Council (DFG) as part of the Transregional Collaborative Research Center "Automatic Verification and Analysis of Complex Systems" (SFB TR14/AVACS).

C. Dubois (Ed.): TAP 2009, LNCS 5668, pp. 153–168, 2009.
© Springer-Verlag Berlin Heidelberg 2009

- In a similar way as related work in program verification [11,17], we do not assume a-priori that our system is incorrect, but rather, we interleave verification, using abstractions of the system, and falsification attempts. The information contained in abstractions is valuable both for verification and falsification. More specifically, the abstraction allows for estimating whether a simulation approaches an unsafe state or not and is thus a promising candidate for an error trajectory.

The main idea of our algorithm is the following: We define a real-valued function (the *quality estimate*) onto the state space that approximates the notion of a given point being close to an initial point of an error trajectory. Then we use numerical optimisation techniques to search for an optimum of this quality estimate. The quality estimate is computed using information from the abstraction, and its accuracy improves as the abstraction is refined, hereby improving the chances of numerical search finding an actual error trajectory.

The rest of this paper is organised as follows: In the next section we define hybrid systems and abstractions thereof. In Sec. 3 we explain our search algorithm. In Sec. 4 we define the quality estimate. In Sec. 5 we discuss and analyse our method. Section 6 explains the implementation and reports on experiments. Section 7 is on related work, and Sec. 8 concludes.

2   Hybrid Systems and Abstractions

We briefly recall our formalism for modelling hybrid systems. It captures many relevant classes of hybrid systems, and many other formalisms for hybrid systems in the literature are special cases of it.

A hybrid system has a finite and nonempty set S of *modes*. $I_1, \ldots, I_n \subseteq \mathbb{R}$ are compact intervals over which the n continuous variables of a hybrid system range. The state space of a hybrid system is denoted by $\Phi = S \times I_1 \times \cdots \times I_n$.

Definition 1. *A hybrid system H is a tuple (Flow, Jump, Init, Unsafe), where Flow $\subseteq \Phi \times \mathbb{R}^n$, Jump $\subseteq \Phi \times \Phi$, Init $\subseteq \Phi$, and Unsafe $\subseteq \Phi$.*

The set *Init* specifies the initial states of a hybrid system and *Unsafe* the set of unsafe states. The relation *Flow* specifies the possible continuous flows of the system by relating each state to corresponding derivatives, and *Jump* specifies the possible discontinuous jumps by relating each state to a successor state. Formally, the behaviour of H is defined as follows:

Definition 2. *A flow of length $l \geq 0$ is a function $r : [0, l] \to I_1 \times \cdots \times I_n$, differentiable on $[0, l]$. A trajectory of H is a sequence of mode/flow pairs $(s_0, r_0), \ldots, (s_k, r_k)$ of lengths $l_0, \ldots, l_k$ such that for all $i \in \{0, \ldots, k\}$,*

1. *if $i > 0$ then $((s_{i-1}, r_{i-1}(l_{i-1})), (s_i, r_i(0))) \in Jump$, and*
2. *if $l_i > 0$ then $((s_i, r_i(t)), \dot{r}_i(t)) \in Flow$, for all $t \in [0, l_i]$, where $\dot{r}_i$ is the derivative of r_i.*

An error trajectory *of a hybrid system H is a trajectory* $(s_0, r_0), \ldots, (s_k, r_k)$ *H such that* $(s_0, r_0(0)) \in Init$ *and* $(s_k, r_k(l_k)) \in Unsafe$. *H is safe if it does not have an error trajectory.*

We use the following constraint language to specify hybrid systems: the variable s and the tuple of variables $\mathbf{x} = (x_1, \ldots, x_n)$ range over S and $I_1 \times \cdots \times I_n$, respectively. The tuple $\dot{\mathbf{x}} = (\dot{x}_1, \ldots, \dot{x}_n)$, ranging over $\mathbb{R}^n$, denotes the derivatives of $x_1, \ldots, x_n$. The variable s' and the tuple $\mathbf{x}' = (x'_1, \ldots, x'_n)$, ranging over S and $I_1 \times \cdots \times I_n$, respectively, denote the targets of jumps. Constraints are arbitrary Boolean combinations of equalities and inequalities over terms that may contain function symbols, like $+$, $\times$, exp, sin, and cos. Based on this, the flows, jumps, initial and unsafe states of a hybrid system are given by constraints $Flow(s, \mathbf{x}, \dot{\mathbf{x}})$, $Jump(s, \mathbf{x}, s', \mathbf{x}')$, $Init(s, \mathbf{x})$ and $Unsafe(s, \mathbf{x})$, respectively.

Usually [7], abstractions are defined so that for every concrete behaviour, there is a corresponding abstract behaviour The rationale is that if the abstract system is error-free, then so is the concrete system. However, for this very rationale, all that matters is that each *error* behaviour is mapped to some abstract error behaviour, while not all *correct* behaviours need to be captured.

Definition 3. *Given a hybrid system H, let A be a directed graph whose nodes (the* abstract states*) are subsets of the state-space Φ. Some nodes are marked as initial, and some as unsafe.*

For a mode/flow pair (s, r) of length l, an abstraction is a path $a_1, \ldots, a_{\bar{k}}$ in A such that there exist $0 = \ell_0 \leq \ell_1 \leq \ldots \leq \ell_{\bar{k}} = l$ such that for every $t \in [0, l]$ where $\ell_{j-1} \leq t \leq \ell_j$, it holds that $(s, r(t)) \in a_j$.

For an error trajectory $(s_0, r_0), \ldots, (s_k, r_k)$ with flow lengths $l_0, \ldots, l_k$, an abstract error trajectory is a path $a_{1,1}, \ldots, a_{1,\bar{k}_1}, \ldots, a_{k,1}, \ldots, a_{k,\bar{k}_k}$ in A such that $a_{1,1}$ is initial, $a_{k,\bar{k}_k}$ is unsafe, and for every $i \in \{0, \ldots, k\}$, we have that $a_{i,1}, \ldots, a_{i,\bar{k}_i}$ is an abstraction of (s_i, r_i).

We call the directed graph A an abstraction *of H iff, for each concrete error trajectory, there is an abstract error trajectory.*

Abstractions can be useful for falsification because the abstract error trajectories narrow down the search space for concrete error trajectories. There are several methods available for computing such abstractions [1,6]. We use a technique where each abstract state is a mode paired with a hyper-rectangle (*box*) $\subseteq I_1 \times \cdots \times I_n$, as implemented in the tool HSOLVER [19]. In HSOLVER, an abstraction that is not fine enough yet to verify the desired property is refined by *splitting* a box (usually the biggest) in half. It does not seem hard to adapt our method to other kinds of abstraction.

Note that we do *not* assume that abstractions cover the whole state space (or reach set) with abstract states, but they do cover the set of all points lying on an error trajectory. In fact, one of the main features of HSOLVER is that it removes points from the abstraction for which it can prove that they cannot lie on an error trajectory. We call this *pruning*. Another kind of pruning is to use the underlying constraint solver to remove points from abstract states that do not fulfil a given (e.g., initial) constraint.

A *simulation* is an explicitly constructed sequence of points in Φ corresponding to the points of a trajectory at discrete moments in time. The distance between these moments is called *step size* (Δ). We do not give a precise definition here, as our search algorithm is independent of the concrete method for doing simulations (see Sec. 6). In this paper, we neglect aspects of imprecision of simulation methods.

Unlike actual error trajectories, a simulation might a-priori leave the abstraction, due to the fact that our abstraction covers, in general, a set that is smaller than the reach set, and also because the simulation might even leave the statespace, in which case it a-fortiori leaves the abstraction.

3 The Search Algorithm

3.1 The Problem and a Naïve Solution

We have a hybrid system with possibly several modes, and for each mode, a bounded statespace ($[l_1, u_1] \times \ldots \times [l_n, u_n]$). We want to find an error trajectory, i.e., a trajectory leading from an initial state to an unsafe state.

We focus on systems that are deterministic in two senses: in the *continuous* sense (the flow is described by differential equations, not inequalities) and in the *discrete* sense (the jumps occur deterministically). Hence the problem reduces to determining the startpoint of an error trajectory among the initial states.

In practice, trajectories are *constructed* by running a *simulation*. Since our hybrid systems are deterministic, the only decision to take about a running simulation is when to cancel it.

To understand the problem, it is helpful to give a naïve solution, obtained by running simulations exhaustively. We use $grid(\Phi, w)$ to denote a set of grids of width w (one for each mode) consisting of points in the statespace, and $simulate(p, l)$ to denote a procedure which starts a simulation in p for l steps and returns *true* iff this simulation is an error trajectory, i.e., it starts in an initial state, reaches an unsafe state, and never leaves the statespace in between.

procedure *find_startpoint*
    $w := 1.0;\ l := 100$ /*ad-hoc*/
    while true
        foreach $p \in grid(\Phi, w)$
            if $simulate(p, l)$ **return** p
        $w := w/2;\ l := l * 2$

Fig. 1. Naïve solution

From this naïve solution, it is clear that we have a search problem whose search space consists of two components. On the one hand, we search in Φ for a startpoint, on the other hand, we search in $\mathbb{N}$ for determining a sufficient simulation length that will actually produce an error trajectory.

Unfortunately, running simulations is expensive, and hence we should try to avoid unnecessary simulation steps. The naïve procedure simulates unnecessarily on three different levels of granularity, leading to three aims of our work:

- If the system is safe, the procedure will run forever, although one might be able to prove safety quickly—our aim is thus to interleave verification with falsification attempts so that we can prove safety or unsafety, as applies.

- The procedure will run simulations evenly distributed on the whole states-pace, even if some parts look more promising than others—our aim is thus to give preference to the more promising simulations.
- Each individual simulation will run for a pre-determined amount of time, ignoring the information gained during the simulation run—our aim is thus to cancel simulations when they do not look promising enough anymore.

To address these three aims we view the falsification problem as the problem of searching for an error trajectory, where the search procedure tries to exploit the information available from verification. The search procedure uses a quality estimate for simulations in order to determine which startpoints are the most promising, and when to cancel a simulation. The main features of the quality estimate are the following:

1. The estimate should measure the *relative* closeness of a simulation to representing an error trajectory, i.e., if simulation A gets a better estimate than simulation B, then A should be closer to being an error trajectory than B.
2. The faithfulness of the estimate should improve as the abstraction is refined.
3. Computation of the quality estimate should be on-the-fly, i.e., for each simulation step, the quality estimate of the simulation up to that point should be available (this is important for deciding when to cancel a simulation).
4. The overhead of computing the quality estimate should be low.

Our approach can be understood without knowing the precise definition of the quality estimate, and thus we will have three subsections addressing the above aims in turn. The corresponding algorithm is summarised in Fig. 2.

3.2   Interaction with Verification

Recall from Def. 3 that an error trajectory can only start within an *initial* abstract state. Hence we only search for error trajectories in these abstract states.

Now we must decide when to start such a search and for how long to run it, i.e., we have to strike a balance between verification and falsification attempts. Secondly, we have to strike the balance between *exploitation* (searching in regions that looked promising so far) and *exploration* (searching everywhere) [22].

Our design decision for striking those balances is to call the falsification algorithm after a refinement whenever an initial abstract state has been split or pruned, i.e., to keep running the verification while this is not the case (line 6). For the first balance, the rationale is that refinements of the abstraction that affect an initial state are likely to actually affect, i.e., improve, the quality estimate for simulations starting in this initial state. For the second balance, the rationale is that every initial state will have its turn to be affected by an abstraction refinement, so that that part of the search space will be explored.

Note that as the boxes converge towards size 0, we ensure completeness of our search procedure just like using the naïve procedure of Sec. 3.1. Why a refined abstraction improves the quality estimate will be explained in Sec. 5.1.

Just like the verification procedure "decides" when to pass the baton to falsification, the falsification procedure reciprocates (see Sec. 3.3).

1: $A :=$ initial abstraction /*Initialisation*/
2: **foreach** $B \in A$
3:     $B.crossmid := mid(strongbox(B));\ B.crosstips := makecross(strongbox(B))$
4: **while true**
5:     $\mathcal{B} := \emptyset$ /*Verification part*/
6:     **while** $\mathcal{B} = \emptyset$
7:         refine and prune A; $\mathcal{B} :=$ set of changed initial boxes of A
8:         **if** $\not\exists$ errorpath in A **then output** SAFE; **exit**
9:     $moves := 0;\ shrinks := 0$ /*Falsification part*/
10:     **choose** $B \in \mathcal{B}$ **with** $qual(sim(B.crossmid, A))$ **maximal**
11:     **if** $B.crossmid \notin strongbox(B)$ **or**
12:         $qual(sim(mid(strongbox(B)), A)) > qual(sim(B.crossmid, A))$
13:         $B.crossmid := mid(strongbox(B));\ B.crosstips := makecross(strongbox(B))$
14:     **while** $moves \leq cros\_chg$ **and** $shrinks \leq cros\_chg$
15:         **choose** $p \in B.crosstips$ **with** $qual(sim(p, A))$ **maximal**
16:         **if** $qual(sim(p, A)) > qual(sim(B.crossmid, A))$
17:             $B.crossmid := p$
18:             $B.crosstips := shiftcross(B.crossmid, B.crosstips)$
19:             $moves := moves + 1$
20:         **else**
21:             $B.crosstips := halvecross(B.crosstips)$
22:             $shrinks := shrinks + 1$

Fig. 2. Overview of our algorithm

3.3   Doing the Right Simulations

We only start simulations in points in initial abstract states. But we can prune the candidate startpoints even more. For an initial abstract state (box), we compute a sub-box by pruning the parts for which we can show that they contain no initial points. We call this sub-box *strong* initial box. It can be much smaller than the entire initial box, leading to a vast reduction of the search space.

Merely relying on the strong initial boxes to become small enough to find a startpoint of an error trajectory is likely to be extremely inefficient—it is crucial to attempt to find a good simulation within such a box *quickly*.

Essentially, we understand the search problem of doing the right simulations as a numerical optimisation problem, where the objective function to be optimised is the quality estimate. We use so-called direct search methods [13], specifically the *compass method*.

The compass method guarantees that one finds a *local* optimum of continuously differentiable functions with Lipschitz continuous gradient [13, Theorem 3.11]. However, it also works well in practice for non-differentiable or even discontinuous functions [13, Section 6] which is the main reason for its usefulness in our context.

The method can be explained using the metaphor of searching a geographical landmark using maps that are initially coarse and then successively become finer.

We do this by taking a strong initial box B and considering an n-dimensional cross that fits exactly into B. That is, if the midpoint of B is $(s_1, \ldots, s_n)$ and the size of B is $(2d_1, \ldots, 2d_n)$, then we have $1 + 2n$ points $(s_1, \ldots, s_n), (s_1 - d_1, s_2, \ldots, s_n), \ldots, (s_1, \ldots, s_{n-1}, s_n + d_n)$. For each point, we start a simulation and compute a quality estimate f. If f has an optimum in some point p other than $(s_1, \ldots, s_n)$, we move the cross to p and continue. If the optimum is in $(s_1, \ldots, s_n)$, we halve the size of the cross and continue. Note that the number of simulation points of a given cross in the compass method is *linear* in the dimension n. The actual compass method is shown in lines 14-22.

However, we do not run the compass method for each modified initial box, but rather, we only consider the most promising box (line 10).

The compass method terminates when either the number of cross shrinkings or of cross moves has exceeded the threshold *cros_chg* (see Sec. 6). The current cross midpoint and cross size are remembered. When the falsification is later resumed, if the cross midpoint is still contained in the *modified* strong initial box B (see Sec. 3.2), and its quality is still higher than the quality of a simulation at the midpoint of B, then the search is continued using this cross. Otherwise, we assume that the quality estimate has changed considerably, and hence the search is restarted with a cross that fits exactly into B (lines 11-13). Note that it is assumed that the function *sim* will output an error trajectory if it finds one and exit the entire computation.

3.4   Doing Simulations Right

Since—apart from the set of initial states—our hybrid systems are completely deterministic, the only choice to be taken during a simulation is when to cancel it. Intuitively, we cancel simulations that are not improving sufficiently quickly. In detail, we cancel a simulation if one of the following situations occur:

- an unsafe state is hit, or
- the simulation has run outside of the abstraction for more than *sim_cnc* (a constant) steps, or
- the global quality estimate has not improved during the last *sim_cnc* steps, the local quality estimate has not improved in the very last step, and the simulation is currently within the abstraction. The notions "global" and "local" will become clearer in Sec. 4.

Note that any cancelling incurs the risk that a simulation might not run long enough to prove that it could actually be a good simulation. This risk is countered by the fact that our abstraction is refined over time, as explained in Sec. 5.1.

4   The Definition of the Quality Estimate

Slightly simplifying, the quality of a simulation consisting of points $p_0, \ldots, p_q$ is defined by

$$ini\_wgh * isInit(p_0) + \max_i \{-scaledDist(p_i) \cdot \frac{i}{i - distAbstr(p_0, \ldots, p_i)}\} \quad (1)$$

In the rest of this section we explain this formula.

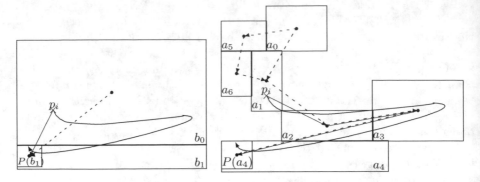

Fig. 3. Illustrating the distance estimate

The most basic aspect of a simulation being close to an error trajectory is whether it actually starts in an initial state. We reward a simulation that does so with a constant *ini_wgh*. One might argue that starting a simulation in a non-initial state is a waste since the simulation will definitely not be an error trajectory. However, such a simulation can be still be close to an error trajectory, since, of course, a non-initial point can be close to an initial point.

The second aspect is how close the simulation *eventually* gets to an unsafe state. We compute the closeness of all individual simulation points to an unsafe state, and take the optimum of these (see the max in (1)). Note that this optimum can be easily computed on-the-fly.

We now turn to the individual points, i.e., the expression inside of the maximisation, which we may refer to as *local* quality of point p_i, whereas the overall formula defines the *global* quality. The ideal measure for the local quality of p_i would be the negation of the length of the trajectory from p_i to some unsafe state, $-\infty$ if the trajectory from this point never reaches an unsafe state. This is illustrated in Fig. 3, r.h.s. The curve shows the trajectory starting from p_i, and we assume that it ends in an unsafe state. However, it is the very effort of computing this curve that we want to avoid. Therefore, we approximate this ideal measure by taking the length of a certain line segment sequence, based on information from the abstraction.

As explained in Sec. 2, an abstraction is a directed graph, and in our particular case the nodes of this graph are mode/box pairs (in the sequel, we speak of boxes and assume that the mode is clear from the context). Therefore, we shall use a geometrical rendering of this graph as an approximation of concrete trajectories, by taking the line segments between the midpoints of boxes within the same mode, for any abstract states that are connected in the graph. This is again illustrated in Fig. 3, r.h.s. Here a_0 is an initial abstract state and a_4 is an unsafe abstract state, and $P(a_4)$ is the *strong* unsafe box corresponding to a_4, defined in analogy to the strong initial boxes explained in Sec. 3.2. The dashed lines are the line segments between connected abstract states. For the point p_i, the estimated distance is the length of the solid line segment sequence, which partly coincides with the dashed line segments, namely from a_2 to $P(a_4)$. Note that the sequence resembles the actual trajectory, the curve. For a coarser abstraction, there will be no or little such resemblance, see l.h.s. figure and Sec. 5.1.

We will now explain this formally. For any box a, we denote by $M(a)$ the midpoint of a, and by J_a the maximal distance between any two points in a, i.e., $\sqrt{\sum_{i=1}^n d_i^2}$, where $d_1, \ldots, d_n$ are the sidelengths of a. For two points p, p', we denote by $|p - p'|$ the Euclidean distance between p and p'.

For a moment, let us leave aside the fact that we are looking at a particular point p_i, and just consider the abstraction. Using a graph algorithm, we compute the shortest abstract error trajectories using the edge weights $w(a, a') =$

$$\begin{cases} |M(a) - M(a')| & \text{if } a \text{ and } a' \text{ lie in the same mode and are connected} \\ & \text{by an abstract transition;} \\ J_{a'} & \text{if } a \text{ and } a' \text{ are connected by a jump;} \\ \infty & \text{otherwise.} \end{cases}$$

Stated briefly, the rationale for choosing $J_{a'}$ as edge weight above is that $J_{a'}$ estimates the length of a trajectory segment within a', making the "pessimistic" assumption that the trajectory goes from one corner to the opposite corner.

Above, we have said that we are interested in the distance of p_i to "some" unsafe state. In order to use an approximation of the set of unsafe states that is as tight as possible, we use the *strong* unsafe box of each unsafe state here. In analogy, for abstract states for which the next element in the shortest path has a different mode, the trajectory has to do a jump, and so we compute a subset containing all the points from which a jump might start. For any abstract state a as just said, we denote this (possibly non-proper) subset by $P(a)$. For other abstract states, P is simply the identity, to simplify the notation.

Now we reconsider the point p_i. We determine the abstract state a_1 that contains the point p_i, provided such an abstract state exists (the case that it does not exist will be considered later). Since our abstraction only contains states that lie on an abstract error trajectory (see Def. 3) there must be an abstract trajectory from a_1 to an unsafe abstract state. Letting $a_1, \ldots, a_{k'}$ be the shortest one, we define the distance $dist(p_i)$ as follows:

If $k' \geq 2$ and a_1, a_2 have the same mode, then we define $dist(p_i)$ as $|p_i - M(P(a_2))| + \sum_{j=2,\ldots,k'-1} w(P(a_j), P(a_{j+1}))$.

Otherwise, we either have $k' = 1$ (i.e., a_1 is an unsafe box), or a_1 is a jump source box. In this case, we would like to compute the distance of p_i to $P(a_1)$, call it δ. But what exactly do we mean by the distance from a point to a box? The answer is illustrated by the figure to the right: the boundary of $P(a_1)$ is drawn with thick lines; for the midpoint we have $\delta = 0$, and each rectangle (possibly with rounded corners) contains points with identical δ. Given that $P(a_1)$ has sidelengths $d_1, \ldots, d_n$, we formally define δ as follows: If p_i is inside of $P(a_1)$, then $\delta := \max\{|\frac{x_1}{d_1}|, \ldots, |\frac{x_n}{d_n}|\} \frac{d_1 + \cdots + d_n}{n}$,

Fig. 4. Level sets

where $x_1, \ldots, x_n$ is the distance of p_i to the individual components of $M(P(a_1))$. If p_i is outside of $P(a_1)$, then δ is defined as the Euclidean distance to the nearest point on the box boundary plus $\frac{d_1+\cdots+d_n}{2n}$ The latter expression is the distance assigned to a point lying on the box boundary. Finally, we define $dist(p_i)$ as $\delta + \sum_{j=1,\ldots,k'-1} w(P(a_j), P(a_{j+1}))$. Observe that the summation of $w(P(a_j), P(a_{j+1}))$ starts with $j = 1$, unlike in the previous paragraph, because δ only "covers" the distance to the jump source point within a_1, whereas the expression $|p_i - M(P(a_2))|$ "covers" some of the way within a_2.

In order to make the quality measure independent of the actual size of the state space, all distances are scaled to the interval $[0, 1]$ by dividing them by the length of the diagonal of the statespace in the corresponding mode. The result is denoted by $scaledDist(p_i)$, see (1).

We now consider the situation that a simulation contains points outside of the abstraction, which is possible, as explained in Sec. 2. A simulation that leaves the abstraction, or even the statespace, cannot be an error trajectory; but in analogy to simulations not starting in an initial state, it can still be *close* to an error trajectory. Therefore, we penalise such simulations but we do not reject them altogether. We do this by weighting the quality estimate for each simulation point according to the proportion of simulation points having lied outside of the abstraction up to that point (see the term $\frac{i}{i-distAbstr(p_0,\ldots,p_i)}$ in (1)). Simulation points that lie outside of the abstraction themselves receive distance ∞, so they do not have any influence on the overall quality of the simulation. The degree to which a simulation leaves the abstraction is thus a third aspect of a simulation being close to an error trajectory.

Why do we use the *shortest* abstract error path to estimate how far a point is from an error state? In fact, it might happen that some or *the* actual error trajectory follows some longer abstract error path. However, the probability that we are able to find an error trajectory in short time is highest in the case where this error trajectory is *short*. Hence we try to aim our search at areas likely to contain such a short error trajectory.

5   Analysis of Our Method

5.1   Discussion of the Quality Estimate

We now discuss the four features listed in Sec. 3.1. Concerning the first two, we also have some formal results, see Sec. 5.2.

Concerning the first feature, the evidence, besides the fact that the quality measure was designed with this feature as foremost feature in mind, is in the successful experiments in Sec. 6.

Now consider the second feature. As explained in Sec. 3.4, any cancelling incurs the risk that a simulation might not run long enough to prove that it could actually be a good simulation. In fact, if the flow is such that from a point p it first moves away from the unsafe states and then approaches them, then simply using Euclidean distance for quality measurement would wrongly suggest that the simulation starting in point p is deteriorating at the beginning. This is illustrated in Fig. 3, r.h.s.: if the simulation from point p_i stays very close to the solid line in its first steps, it actually moves away from $P(a_4)$. However, we also see that the abstraction shown is fine enough, so that the quality will increase during the first steps, i.e., the quality function is sufficiently faithful to recognise that the simulation is really improving. This is in contrast to the l.h.s. figure, where the abstraction is coarse. Note that the refinement has two effects:

1. The good simulations are more likely to run longer than the bad ones.
2. All good simulations will run longer than on previous tries.

The first effect will help the first component of the search (see Sec. 3.1): finding the right startpoint. The second effect will help the second component of the search: making simulations run long enough.

Concerning the third feature, the fact that the measure is computed on-the-fly is clear from the construction.

For the fourth feature, it turns out that although computing $dist(p)$ is costly (it involves a shortest path computation on the abstraction graph etc.), this cost is amortised because the abstraction remains constant at least throughout the current simulation. Thus, computing the quality estimate does not increase the complexity order of the simulation computation.

5.2 Formal Analysis

In this section, we will first formally prove that our definition of quality estimate fulfils a formalisation of the first two desired features of Section 5.1. Based on this, we will then prove that our algorithm finds all error trajectories that are robust in a certain, yet to be defined sense. All formal results in this section depend on the assumption that we do our simulations with enough precision concerning floating-point computation and time discretisation. The actual proofs can be found in the technical report [20].

We assume that we can compute arbitrarily precise abstractions:

Definition 4. *A sequence of abstractions* $A_1, A_2, \ldots$ *is* convergent *iff for every trajectory that is not an error trajectory there is a k such that for all $i \geq k$ there is no corresponding trajectory in A_i.*

Now we formalise what it means for a quality estimate to become arbitrarily precise:

Definition 5. *A sequence of functions* $f_1, f_2, \ldots$ *in $\Phi \to \mathbb{R}$ is* convergent *iff for two points p and q on the same error trajectory h such that p occurs earlier than q on h, there is a k such that for all $i \geq k$, $f_i(q) < f_i(p)$.*

We now prove Item 2 of our desired features. We denote by $dist_A$ the distance function (see Sec. 4) based on abstraction A.

Theorem 1. *Let $A_1, A_2, \ldots$ be a convergent sequence of abstractions. Then the sequence $dist_{A_1}, dist_{A_2} \ldots$, is convergent.*

Now call an error trajectory h *robust* iff there is an $\varepsilon > 0$ such all trajectories starting with a distance smaller than ε from h is also an error trajectory. We call a hybrid system that has a robust error trajectory *robustly unsafe*.

Theorem 2. *Our falsification algorithm finds an error trajectory for every robustly unsafe hybrid system H.*

Note that the above are theoretical completeness results: we will eventually find every error trajectory thanks to the fact that our abstractions will eventually be extremely precise. In practice, relying on this alone is extremely inefficient, just like the naïve algorithm, for which the same completeness result also holds. Hence, the theorems should be interpreted in the sense of: "Although our method cancels simulations whenever the abstraction suggests no further improvement, the method is still complete".

6   Implementation and Experiments

We implemented our method and tested it on some well-known benchmarks.

In our prototype we use a simple Euler method for solving ordinary differential equations (e.g. [21]) with only naïve handling of jumps. In practice, more sophisticated ODE-solvers and precise jump detection [16] could be used. Due to re-use of HSOLVER (i.e., verification) code, this prototypical implementation runs quite slowly (3 orders of magnitude slower than hard-coded C simulation) but serves as an experimentation platform.

We now discuss the choices of the implementation parameters. The optimal choice of Δ depends on the speed of the behaviour of each individual example. For simplicity, we took $\Delta = 0.01$ which worked well for most examples.

We set $cros\_chg = 2$, which is much smaller than what we intuitively expected to be reasonable, but we found that for bigger values, the compass method will get trapped in local minima of a poor quality estimate.

We set $sim\_cnc = 200$, which seems rather small to us, and yet, to demonstrate that simulations eventually "survive" thanks to the faithfulness of the quality estimate, rather than a generously chosen value of sim_cnc, we set sim_cnc much smaller for some experiments reported below.

We set $ini\_wgh = 0.5$, which roughly means that whether a simulation starts in an initial state is as important as the other aspects mentioned in Sec. 4.

For the experiments, we used a machine with two Intel Xeon processors running at 3.02 GHz with 6 GB RAM.

Our benchmarks were obtained by modifications of various well-known benchmarks from the literature, see `http://hsolver.sourceforge.net/benchmarks/falsification`. The modifications were necessary because the benchmarks were mostly safe, and so we injected an error into those systems by relaxing some constraints describing the initial or unsafe states or the jump guards.

We have also run some experiments on safe systems, to evaluate the cost of falsification attempts. HSOLVER ran between comparably fast and up to an order of magnitude slower when run in the mode where falsification and verification attempts are interleaved. For space reasons we do not give any figures [20].

Table 1 shows the results for the unsafe examples: the runtime in seconds, the number of abstraction refinements, simulations, the total number of single simulation steps, and the number of jumps of the trajectory that was found. We give figures for our algorithm and the naïve algorithm of Sec. 3.1 (as will be discussed in the next section, all related work assumes systems with inputs and behaves similar to the naïve algorithm in our case without inputs). We consider the main figure for evaluating efficiency to be the number of simulation steps, since this number is independent of the actual implementation of the method.

The naïve algorithm performs very well on some apparently easy examples, where the method we propose here also performs well, but on numerous examples it does not terminate within several hours, indicated by ∞. For hard examples, using a more sophisticated method such as ours is absolutely crucial, while for easy examples, one might easily hit an error trajectory by chance.

One observation when doing the modifications was that for some benchmarks, relaxing these constraints to some extent still resulted in a safe system. In fact, ideally what happens when one gradually relaxes a safe system is that it gradually transcends from "easy to prove safe" to "hard to prove safe" to "impossible to prove either way" to "hard to prove unsafe" to "easy to prove unsafe". This is the case e.g. for 2-tanks, and *partly* for real-eigen (see Table 1, where real-eigen5 is the hardest and real-eigen is the easiest). However, we found numerous exceptions from this ideal, where some of the changes are very abrupt or not monotonic: clock, convoi, real-eigen, van-der-pole2.

Note that we have several examples where an error trajectory containing one or two jumps is found. For eco, we verified that these jumps are necessary, i.e., when we remove the jumps, the system becomes safe. This indicates that our quality estimate works reasonably well even for simulations that contain a jump.

We did an experiment with focus showing that even for a too small value of sim_cnc, simulations will eventually "survive" long enough thanks to the refinement of the quality function. The example is extremely easy for HSOLVER, provided sim_cnc is not too small. For $sim\_cnc = 20$, an error trajectory is found but after 434 refinements. In this experiment, the startpoint found eventually is tried dozens of times before, but each time the simulation is cancelled prematurely. The same effect occurred for eco and eco2.

We have also created an example where we isolate the aspect just mentioned: parabola. In this example, the flow is $y = 20x^2$, and the initial and unsafe states are small boxes around the points $(-1, 20)$ and $(1, 20)$, respectively. That is, the error trajectory looked for is an extremely tight parabola. The search for the right startpoint is trivial; the problem is though that if sim_cnc is too small and the quality function is not faithful enough yet, then the simulations will be cancelled prematurely. This can be seen in the table where we tried values for sim_cnc ranging from 30 to 105.

For mutant, choosing $\Delta = 0.01$ is inappropriate, because 0.01 is minute relative to the state space size. We therefore chose $\Delta = 0.5$.

Table 1. Unsafe Systems

Example	our algorithm					naïve algorithm		
	time	ref.	sim.	sim. steps	jumps	time	sim.	sim. steps
2-tanks	11.5	7	130	23943	0	230.7	2372	554303
car	0.5	0	6	1033	1	0.6	3	272
clock	0.3	0	21	4387	0	4.3	175	59264
convoi	0.04	0	1	7	0	∞	∞	∞
eco $sim\_cnc{=}400$	0.1	0	1	328	2	0.1	1	327
eco	2.1	10	63	21154	2	0.1	1	313
eco2 $sim\_cnc{=}400$	0.1	0	1	328	2	0.1	1	327
eco2	45.3	152	422	118862	2	0.1	1	313
focus	0.1	0	10	2626	0	0.04	1	131
focus $sim\_cnc{=}20$	29.7	434	288	13218	0	0.04	1	131
mutant $\Delta{=}0.5$	196.7	6	150	1421803	0	∞	∞	∞
navigation	1.6	0	22	5454	1	2.9	3	241
navigation2	1937.7	14	506	138206	1	∞	∞	∞
parabola $sim\_cnc{=}105$	0.0	0	1	201	0	∞	∞	∞
parabola $sim\_cnc{=}100$	0.3	4	43	4443	0	∞	∞	∞
parabola $sim\_cnc{=}50$	1.0	35	71	4751	0	∞	∞	∞
parabola $sim\_cnc{=}30$	18.0	353	113	7495	0	∞	∞	∞
real-eigen	0.7	1	44	8523	0	∞	∞	∞
real-eigen2	2.5	4	126	24165	0	∞	∞	∞
real-eigen3	4.5	10	214	41853	0	∞	∞	∞
real-eigen4	58.1	87	816	166450	0	∞	∞	∞
real-eigen5	250.8	314	1521	312567	0	∞	∞	∞
van-der-pole	0.4	1	36	3725	1	0.2	1	35
van-der-pole2	1.7	3	88	14546	1	∞	∞	∞

7   Related Work

Our work has some resemblance with heuristic search in artificial intelligence (AI), namely with *pure optimisation* problems, where the aim is to find a node in a graph which is good or optimal according to some *objective function*. One may also introduce such an objective function just for providing guidance in search algorithms. This is similar to our approach. It is distinctive of our work that the objective *function* itself improves over time. Our search method, the compass method, is similar to *local search* methods in AI.

In contrast to heuristic search in AI, we do not decide *whether* to do a simulation depending on the cheaply pre-computed quality of that simulation, but rather, we compute the quality as we do the simulation, and depending on this quality we will do other simulations in the neighbourhood. This is similar to reinforcement learning [22].

Methods that directly try to falsify hybrid systems (in contrast to using simulation for verification, as discussed below) usually consider hybrid systems with inputs, searching for inputs that drive the system from an initial to an unsafe state. One major approach in this direction is to adapt techniques from robotic motion planning [3,18] to compute an under-approximation of the set of trajectories of a given hybrid system. Another approach studies how to avoid redundant simulations as much as possible by merging similar parts of simulations [14].

Although these methods were designed for systems with input, it is possible to apply them to systems without input (i.e., with deterministic evolution). However, their strategy is to try to fill the state space as much as possible with simulations. As a result, they would start a huge number of simulations in parallel (similar to our naïve algorithm from Sec. 3.1). In the case of highly non-deterministic systems, such a strategy is promising since the probability of hitting upon an error trajectory is high. However, for systems with little or no non-determinism, this creates many useless simulations. We avoid this by guiding our search using abstractions in order to quickly arrive at a simulation close to to an error trajectory.

In software model checking, the synergy between verification and falsification (i.e., testing, debugging) is the subject of a lot of recent research, see for example, Gulavani [11] and the references therein. Also, the idea to use abstraction to define a heuristic function for local search has been studied in software model checking (e.g., [17]). In contrast to that, hybrid systems have a partially continuous state space with corresponding geometrical properties which we exploited in our search algorithm and our definition of the quality estimate.

Recently a new paradigm of *verification by simulation* has received attention [10,9,5]. The main goal is verification of a correct input system. Error trajectories may be computed as a by-product.

An alternative approach to the verification/falsification paradigm is to use test coverages [4,12,15] , where—instead of trying to fully verify a property— one defines a function that measures how large a part of the hybrid system is covered by a given set of simulation runs. Then one tries to cover the state space with simulations in such way that this test coverage function is optimised which again contrasts our strategy of trying to find *one single error trajectory*.

8   Conclusion

We have presented a method for finding error trajectories of hybrid systems. We consider the main challenge for future work to be the exploitation of the *partially* continuous nature of hybrid systems and the fact that numerical analysis provides a myriad of optimisation algorithm for continuous functions.

References

1. Alur, R., Dang, T., Ivančić, F.: Predicate abstraction for reachability analysis of hybrid systems. Trans. on Embedded Computing Sys. 5(1), 152–199 (2006)
2. Bemporad, A., Bicchi, A., Buttazzo, G. (eds.): HSCC 2007. LNCS, vol. 4416. Springer, Heidelberg (2007)

3. Bhatia, A., Frazzoli, E.: Incremental search methods for reachability analysis of continuous and hybrid systems. In: Alur, R., Pappas, G.J. (eds.) HSCC 2004. LNCS, vol. 2993, pp. 142–156. Springer, Heidelberg (2004)
4. Bhatia, A., Frazzoli, E.: Sampling-based resolution-complete algorithms for safety falsification of linear systems. In: Egerstedt, M., Mishra, B. (eds.) HSCC 2008. LNCS, vol. 4981, pp. 606–609. Springer, Heidelberg (2008)
5. Cheng, P., Kuma, V.: Sampling-based falsification and verification of controllers for continuous dynamic systems. Int. J. of Robotics Research 27(11-12), 1232–1245 (2008)
6. Clarke, E., Fehnker, A., Han, Z., Krogh, B., Ouaknine, J., Stursberg, O., Theobald, M.: Abstraction and counterexample-guided refinement in model checking of hybrid systems. Int. J. of Foundations of Comp. Sci. 14(4), 583–604 (2003)
7. Clarke, E.M., Grumberg, O., Peled, D.A.: Model Checking. MIT Press, Cambridge (1999)
8. Damm, W., Hermanns, H. (eds.): CAV 2007: 19th Int. Conf. on Computer Aided Verification. LNCS, vol. 4590. Springer, Heidelberg (2007)
9. Donzé, A., Maler, O.: Systematic simulation using sensitivity analysis. In: Bemporad, et al. (eds.) [2], pp. 174–189
10. Girard, A., Pappas, G.: Verification using simulation. In: Hespanha, J.P., Tiwari, A. (eds.) HSCC 2006. LNCS, vol. 3927, pp. 272–286. Springer, Heidelberg (2006)
11. Gulavani, B.S., Henzinger, T.A., Kannan, Y., Nori, A.V., Rajamani, S.K.: SYNERGY: a new algorithm for property checking. In: Young, M., Devanbu, P.T. (eds.) SIGSOFT '06/FSE-14: Proc. of the 14th ACM SIGSOFT Int. Symp. on Foundations of Software Engineering, pp. 117–127. ACM, New York (2006)
12. Julius, A.A., Fainekos, G.E., Anand, M., Lee, I., Pappas, G.J.: Robust test generation and coverage for hybrid systems. In: Bemporad, et al. (eds.) [2], pp. 329–242
13. Kolda, T.G., Lewis, R.M., Torczon, V.: Optimization by direct search: New perspectives on some classical and modern methods. SIAM Review 45(3), 385–482 (2003)
14. Lerda, F., Kapinski, J., Maka, H., Clarke, E., Krogh, B.: Model checking in-the-loop: Finding counterexamples by systematic simulation. In: American Control Conf. (2008)
15. Nahhal, T., Dang, T.: Test coverage for continuous and hybrid systems. In: Damm, Hermanns (eds.) [8], pp. 449–462
16. Park, T., Barton, P.I.: State event location in differential-algebraic models. ACM Trans. Model. Comput. Simul. 6(2), 137–165 (1996)
17. Paula, F.M.D., Hu, A.J.: An effective guidance strategy for abstraction-guided simulation. In: DAC 2007: 44th Annual Conf. on Design Automation, pp. 63–68. ACM, New York (2007)
18. Plaku, E., Kavraki, L.E., Vardi, M.Y.: Hybrid systems: From verification to falsification. In: Damm, Hermanns (eds.) [8], pp. 463–476
19. Ratschan, S., She, Z.: Safety verification of hybrid systems by constraint propagation based abstraction refinement. ACM Trans. in Embedded Computing Systems 6(1) (2007)
20. Ratschan, S., Smaus, J.-G.: Finding errors of hybrid systems by optimising an abstraction-based quality estimate. Technical Report 51, AVACS (2009), http://www.avacs.org
21. Sewell, G.: The Numerical Solution of Ordinary and Partial Differential Equations. Academic Press, London (1988)
22. Sutton, R.S., Barto, A.G.: Reinforcement Learning. MIT Press, Cambridge (1998)

Author Index